BRESCIA UNIVERSITY COLLEGE LIBRARY

3 6277 00023555 8

MCS
2006

D1453854

UNIVERSITY COLLEGE
BBrescia

BERYL IVEY LIBRARY

PR
408
.G46
F53
2006

Materializing Gender in Early Modern English Literature and Culture

Through examining some of the everyday items that helped establish a person's masculinity or femininity, this book offers a new analysis of gender identity in early modern English literature and culture. Individual chapters focus on items such as codpieces, handkerchiefs, beards, and hair. Fisher argues that these seemingly peripheral parts were in fact constitutive, and consequently that early modern gender was materialized through a relatively wide range of parts or features, and that it was also often conceptualized as being malleable. The book deliberately brings together sexual characteristics (beard growth and hair length) and gendered accessories (codpieces and handkerchiefs) in order to explore the limitations of using the modern conceptual distinction between sex and gender to understand early modern ideas about masculinity and femininity. *Materializing Gender* engages with a range of historical materials including drama, poetry, portraiture, medical texts, and polemical tracts, and a range of theoretical issues.

WILL FISHER is an Associate Professor in the Department of English at Lehman College, The City University of New York. He works primarily on the history of gender and sexuality. His articles have appeared in *Renaissance Quarterly*, *ELH*, *Shakespeare Studies*, and *Textual Practice*.

Cambridge Studies in Renaissance Literature and Culture

General Editor
Stephen Orgel
Jackson Eli Reynolds Professor of Humanities, Stanford University

Editorial board
Anne Barton, *University of Cambridge*
Jonathan Dollimore, *University of York*
Marjorie Garber, *Harvard University*
Jonathan Goldberg, *Johns Hopkins University*
Peter Holland, *University of Notre Dame, Indiana*
Kate Mcluskie, *The Shakespeare Institute, University of Birmingham*
Nancy Vickers, *Bryn Mawr College*

Since the 1970s there has been a broad and vital reinterpretation of the nature of literary texts, a move away from formalism to a sense of literature as an aspect of social, economic, political, and cultural history. While the earliest New Historicist work was criticized for a narrow and anecdotal view of history, it also served as an important stimulus for post-structuralist, feminist, Marxist, and psychoanalytical work, which in turn has increasingly informed and redirected it. Recent writing on the nature of representation, the historical construction of gender and of the concept of identity itself, on theatre as a political and economic phenomenon and on the ideologies of art generally, reveals the breadth of the field. Cambridge Studies in Renaissance Literature and Culture is designed to offer historically oriented studies of Renaissance literature and theatre which make use of the insights afforded by theoretical perspectives. The view of history envisioned is above all a view of our history, a reading of the Renaissance for and from our own time.

Recent titles include
Elizabeth Spiller, *Science, Reading and Renaissance Literature: The Art of Making Knowledge, 1580–1670*
Deanne Williams, *The French Fetish from Chaucer to Shakespeare*
Douglas Trevor, *The Poetics of Melancholy in Early Modern England*
Christopher Warley, *Sonnet Sequences and Social Distinction in Renaissance England*
Garrett A. Sullivan, Jr., *Memory and Forgetting in English Renaissance Drama: Shakespeare, Marlowe, Webster*
Michael Wyatt, *The Italian Encounter with Tudor England: A Cultural Politics of Translation*

A complete list of books in the series is given at the end of the volume.

Materializing Gender in Early Modern English Literature and Culture

Will Fisher

Lehman College, CUNY

CAMBRIDGE
UNIVERSITY PRESS

BRESCIA UNIVERSITY
COLLEGE LIBRARY

CAMBRIDGE UNIVERSITY PRESS
Cambridge, New York, Melbourne, Madrid, Cape Town, Singapore, São Paulo

Cambridge University Press
The Edinburgh Building, Cambridge CB2 2RU, UK
Published in the United States of America by Cambridge University Press, New York

www.cambridge.org
Information on this title: www.cambridge.org/9780521858519

© Will Fisher 2006

This publication is in copyright. Subject to statutory exception
and to the provisions of relevant collective licensing agreements,
no reproduction of any part may take place without
the written permission of Cambridge University Press.
First published 2006

Printed in the United Kingdom at the University Press, Cambridge

A catalogue record for this publication is available from the British Library

ISBN-13 978-0-521-85851-9 hardback
ISBN-10 0-521-85851-8 hardback

Cambridge University Press has no responsibility for the persistence or accuracy of
URLs for external or third-party internet websites referred to in this publication, and
does not guarantee that any content on such websites is, or will remain, accurate or
appropriate.

For Valerie, Phyllis, and Peter

Contents

List of illustrations   *page* viii
Acknowledgements   x

Introduction: prosthetic gender in early modern England   1

1   That Shakespearean rag: handkerchiefs and femininity   36

2   "That codpiece ago": codpieces and masculinity   59

3   "His majesty the beard": beards and masculinity   83

4   "The ornament of their sex": hair and gender   129

5   Conclusion: detachable parts and the individual   159

Notes   171
Bibliography   204
Index   219

Illustrations

1. Jacob Ochtervelt, *A Woman Playing a Virginal, Another Singing and a Man Playing a Violin* (1675–80). By permission of the National Gallery, London.   *page* 21

2. Jacob Jordaens, *King Candaules of Lydia showing his Wife to Gyges* (1646). By permission of the Nationalmuseum, Stockholm.   21

3. Unknown Artist, *Robert Dudley, 1st Earl of Leicester with Dog* (*c.* 1564). By permission of a private collector.   37

4. Hans Eworth, *Thomas Howard, 4th Duke of Norfolk* (1563). By permission of a private collector.   39

5. Quentin Metsys the Younger, *Elizabeth I: 'The Sieve Portrait'* (*c.* 1583). By permission of the Pinacoteca Nazionale, Siena.   43

6. Albrecht Dürer, *The Standard Bearer* (1498). By permission of the Warburg Institute.   60

7. Agnolo Bronzino, *Portrait of Guidobaldo della Rovere* (1532). By permission of the Galleria Palatina, Florence.   61

8. Wood engraving from John Bulwer, *Anthropometamorphosis* (1654). By permission of the Huntington Library.   63

9. Two views of Henry VIII's codpiece from the Tower of London. By permission of the Royal Armouries.   71

10. Unknown Artist, *The Somerset House Conference* (1604). By permission of the National Portrait Gallery.   95

11. Daniel Mytens, *King Charles I* (1631). By permission of the National Portrait Gallery.   96

12. Wood engraving of John Knox (1580). By permission of the National Portrait Gallery.   97

13. John Bettes the Elder, *An Unknown Man in a Black Cap* (1545). By permission of Art Resource.   98

14. Title page of John Foxe's *Book of Martyrs* (1563). By permission
    of the Huntington Library.   101

15. José de Ribera, *Magdalena Ventura* (1631). By permission
    of the Museo Nacional del Prado.   114

16. Title page of Hobbes, *Leviathan* (1651). By permission
    of the Huntington Library.   163

Acknowledgements

I have been very fortunate on my travels in academia, and it therefore makes me very happy to be able to acknowledge some of the people who have been so generous with me over the years.

There is only one place to begin and that is with Valerie Traub. Valerie was my undergraduate teacher and advisor, and without her guidance and training, I'm sure I wouldn't be where I am. She continues to this day to support me and read my work, and I can't even begin to explain how much this – and her friendship – mean to me.

Phyllis Rackin took me under her wing before I arrived at the University of Pennsylvania and I haven't forgotten that. I'm very glad she did because she turned out to be a wonderful mentor and role model. Her passionate, life-long commitment to feminism and progressive politics is an inspiration to me (as it has been to so many others). If, at the end of my career, I can look back and say that I was half as dedicated as she has been during hers, I'll consider myself a success.

The word that I always use to describe Peter Stallybrass is "amazing" and I think it suits him like one of his silk shirts. For me, it is the only word that begins to capture the creativity and range of Peter's intellect, not to mention his boundless enthusiasm. The debt that I owe Peter and his work will, I suspect, be immediately apparent to anyone who reads this book or even hears about its subject matter, but I have nevertheless tried to acknowledge it in my notes (as is the custom). In the end, however, these are really only signposts to something far more pervasive.

In addition to finding a wonderful set of advisors, I have also had the good fortune to be part of several vibrant scholarly communities. First, at the University of Pennsylvania, I benefited from the innovative teaching and scholarship of people like Rebecca Bushnell, Margreta de Grazia, Lynda Hart, and Maureen Quilligan. Margreta read my entire dissertation, and the project still bears the imprint of her comments and critique. I benefited, as well, from the intelligence, wit, and camaraderie of fellow students like Rebecca Bach, Stephen Best, Jeannine DeLombard, Lynn Festa, Rayna Kalas, Cynthia Port, Suzie Verderber, and Antonio Viego. The Furness Library was a terrific place to work, and many people there gave me invaluable help with my research: especially Michael Ryan, Dan Traister, Lynn Farrington, John Pollack, David Azolina, Sarah Cohen, and Owen Williams. While I was still at Penn, I met a group of scholars who I now think of as the core of my academic community: Jeff Masten, Nick Radel, Rick Rambuss, Pat Parker, Gail Paster, Stephen Guy-Bray, Gil Harris, Madhavi Menon, Henry Turner, and Wendy Wall. Finally, I want to thank the friends who made my time in Philly as enjoyable as it was productive: Stephen Best, Myrna Gabbe, Rachel Greene, Russ Gage, Kendall Johnson, David Roman, and Sarah Werner. Virgil Marti deserves special mention for being so fabulous and for always being able to make me laugh.

London has been my home away from home for some time now. I first discovered the city with Sophie Carter and Dan White, and even now, its streets and locales conjure good memories of those times. At the British Library, Antje Bank, James Daybell, Frans DeBruyn, Jerome de Groot, Sharon Ruston, Chris Mouns, Markman Ellis, and Sue Wiseman all shared tea and good company. And finally, Eliane Glaser followed me home from the BL one day, and turned out to be a great sidekick and partner in crime. She helped me work through many of the ideas in this book, and also distracted me enough from the project to keep me going. I thank her for being brave.

I am very pleased to be able to call New York City my home. Scott Westrem deserves much of the credit for helping bring me here, and I am also grateful to him for his generosity in showing me the ropes once I arrived. I was already friends with Mario DiGangi before we became colleagues, but in the intervening years I've come to appreciate him even more. I can't count the number of times I've barged into his office with some question about teaching or research (or just to chat), and he always has the perfect response. Many of my other colleagues at Lehman have also provided encouragement and/or assistance along the way, especially Gerhard Joseph, Anne Humphreys, Jack Kligerman, and Walter Blanco.

Joe Wittreich and Stuart Curran are like family. They have done their best to try to give me a little NY polish and culture, and while I am grateful for this, I think that the thing that I cherish most about them is simply their irrepressible joie de vivre – it always brings a smile to my face. One of my primary sources of scholarly engagement (and good food!) here in the city is the Renaissance Group: Natasha Korda, Mary Bly, Bonnie Gordon, Fiona McNeill, and Bianca Calabresi (as well as honorary members Fran Dolan and Scott Shershow). They not only helped to shape this book through their comments, but they also consistently stimulated me with their own research and conversation.

Finally, I want to thank my friends here and further afield, especially Ana Eire, Dave Laski, James and Jean Lin, Karen Moulding, and Cara Murray.

I've been lucky to have Robert Kaplan as a neighbor since I arrived in the city. Commiserating with him has, more than anything, helped me get by in the current political climate. Alan Stewart's wit and conviviality are a constant treat and I'm very glad that he landed here. I also thank him for generously opening his home to me on several occasions. To Kerry Moore, I am grateful for all of the stories, and for knowing just how to tell them. I am also grateful to her for being so adept at retying the knot of our friendship (I can almost feel her tugging my sleeve as I write this). Last, but certainly not least, I want to thank Julie Crawford and Liza Yukins, for simply being their warm and wonderful selves.

My parents' love and support is the rock on which this book was built. I know that things haven't always been easy for them, but we've managed to find a way through. My brother, Scott, and sister, Jean, hold down the fort at home and help me with all my ridiculous projects. My auntie Karen is my soul sister (not to mention a confidante and a co-conspirator in the family). And finally, my grandparents, Henry and Mabel Schmidt, are a blessing that I am very grateful for. My grandmother's generous heart and strength of character are just two of the many things I treasure about her. Unfortunately my grandfather didn't make it to see this book's publication, but he is certainly not forgotten, and I take some comfort in knowing that he and his signature baby-blue blazer lurk in these pages.

Introduction: prosthetic gender in early modern England

With every tool, man is perfecting his own organs . . . by means of spectacles he corrects defects in the lens of his own eye; by means of the telescope he sees into the far distance . . .With the telephone he can hear at distances which would be unattainable even in a fairy tale. . . Man has, as it were, become a kind of prosthetic God. When he puts on all his auxiliary organs, he is truly magnificent; but those organs have not grown on to him and they still give him much trouble at times.

> Freud, *Civilization and its Discontents*[1]

DIL   . . . a girl has her feelings.
FERGUS   Thing is, Dil, you're not a girl.
DIL   Details, baby, details.

> Neil Jordan, *The Crying Game*[2]

In 1573, the French physician Ambroise Paré published *Monsters and Marvels*. Along with its descriptions of monstrous births and other portentous signs of nature, this book contains a section on "hermaphrodites" where Paré gives advice to his fellow medical practitioners about how to examine people and "discerne" whether they ought to be classified as the "male or female sexe." One thing that Paré recommends is that his colleagues inspect the individual's genitalia, and specifically "whether the female sex organ is of proper dimensions to receive the male rod and whether the menses flow through it," and "whether the male rod is well-proportioned in thickness and length, and whether it can [become] erect, and whether seed issues from it." In addition, Paré urges physicians to observe

the face and . . . the hair, whether it is fine or coarse; whether the speech is virile or shrill; whether the teats are like those of men or of women; similarly whether the whole disposition of the body is robust and effeminate; whether they are bold or fearful, and other actions like those of males and females.

Finally, he suggests looking "to see whether there is a good deal of body hair on the groin and around the seat, for commonly and almost always woman have none on their seat."[3]

Paré's advice about how to "discerne" the "sexe" of a "hermaphrodite" was included in the 1632 English translation of his *Works*. Interestingly, the

1

features mentioned in the translation differ slightly from those in the original French version. The English text stipulates that the "signs" of gender are "most apparent in the privities and face." It also recommends that physicians ascertain whether "the haire of the head bee long, slender, and soft," whether the individual has "a timide and weake condition of the minde," and finally, whether the individual has "the *Perinaeum* and fundament full of haires" because "women are commonly without any."[4]

Paré's comments are discussed by Ruth Gilbert in *Early Modern Hermaphrodites* and by Lorraine Daston and Katharine Park in "The Hermaphrodite and the Orders of Nature." These scholars contend that Paré's advice marks an important shift in the juridical procedures that were used to deal with intersexed individuals. During the middle ages, they argue, the sex of these individuals was usually determined by a midwife or by the parents, though sometimes individuals were allowed to choose their own sex provided that they scrupulously maintained their chosen identity afterwards. During the sixteenth and seventeenth centuries, however, these practices slowly began to change, and more and more frequently, physicians like Paré were called upon to make a "professional" or "objective" assessment.[5]

This history is of interest to me because it suggests that through the course of the early modern period, sexual difference was increasingly viewed as a fact of nature. But Paré's advice is also of interest because it tells us something about how an individual's gender identity was constituted in the early modern period – or about the range of parts and features that might have helped establish masculinity or femininity. When seen from this perspective, it is significant that Paré does not advise his colleagues to focus solely on the genitalia. Instead, he recommends examining a wide range of corporeal features including the tone of the person's voice, the length and texture of the hair, the shape of the breasts, and the presence or absence of hair on the "seat." Even more striking is the fact that Paré recommends considering other, non-corporeal, characteristics such as whether the persons are "bold or fearful" or whether they display "other actions like those of males and females."

The modern medical protocols for determining the sex of a "hermaphrodite" are very different from those outlined by Paré in his text. According to Alice Dreger's *Hermaphrodites and the Medical Invention of Sex*, doctors now begin by ascertaining the chromosome pattern of the person in question. While this plays an important part in their deliberations, they also place a lot of emphasis on the shape and size of the genitalia. If the individual has an XX chromosomal pattern, that individual is invariably classified as a female, but in the other cases, the individual is assigned a gender identity based entirely on genital morphology. This is true not only for individuals with an XY pattern, but also for those with an XXY pattern, or with some cells exhibiting

XX and others exhibiting XY. In practice, this means that whatever the chromosomal makeup, only infants who have penises that are at least two and a half centimeters long when stretched (this is about an inch) are categorized as male. If this criterion is not met, then the infant is usually declared a female and a vagina is surgically constructed. Dreger explains that the medical thinking is that people "must have acceptable penises if they are to be assigned the male gender."[6] Analogous thinking also lies behind the decision to classify all people with an XX chromosome pattern as female. That decision is not simply a testament to the underlying importance of genetic makeup of the individual, it also reflects the doctors' belief that it is easier surgically to construct a vagina than a penis. In this regard, it is worth pointing out that if a child is categorized as female, its genitalia are also "normalized." In practice, this means that if the clitoris exceeds one centimeter in length, it is surgically reduced so that the individual will not look or act "masculine" (183).

I begin by contrasting the early modern procedures used to determine the sex of a "hermaphrodite" with the modern ones because I think this contrast suggests that masculinity and femininity may have been materialized in a slightly different way in the earlier periods. In broadest terms, this is a book about the discourses and practices of gender in England in the sixteenth and early seventeenth centuries. I approach this topic by focusing on a series of gendered features or "parts" – handkerchiefs, codpieces, beards, and hair. It is my contention that all of these items played fundamental roles in forming masculine and feminine identity.[7]

Some might say that this continues to be true in our own time. In the 1960s, for example, the hair of the head became an important source of generational conflict and gender identity. The tonsorial norms of the nineteen fifties were challenged by long-haired men wearing styles such as the "mop top" popularized by the Beatles, and by short-haired women wearing styles such as the bob and the "boyish cut." It is therefore hardly surprising to find that one of the defining cultural productions of the era was the musical *Hair*. Similarly, in the 1970s, the moustache became a crucial component of the exaggerated, class-inflected masculinity that was dominant at the time.[8] While codpieces and handkerchiefs have not been part of the physical portrait for some time, there are certainly other articles of clothing that continue to have profound gendered significance. Recent studies of the "power suit" and stiletto heels, to take just two examples, argue that these items are crucial elements in the formation of masculinity and femininity.[9]

Nevertheless, I would argue that the details of dress and bearing were even more fundamental in English culture during the sixteenth and early seventeenth centuries. Indeed, Paré's advice to his fellow physicians begins to suggest this. As further evidence of this historical shift, I would point to the fact that none of the parts under scrutiny here is now classified as "primary" – facial hair is considered a "secondary sexual characteristic" and the rest are generally considered elements of gender, and are sometimes labeled "tertiary characteristics."[10] This hierarchized classificatory schema does not seem to have been fully in place during the Renaissance. The features that Paré says will help physicians determine the "sexe" of a "hermaphrodite" are certainly not organized according to such a schema. For Paré, the "primary" features are the genitals and the face, though the term "primary" is not entirely appropriate since he simply says that they are the sites where gender is "most evident." Furthermore, Paré does not distinguish at all between "secondary" and "tertiary" features: he mentions "secondary" characteristics such as the form of the individual's "teats" alongside "tertiary" characteristics such as the length and texture of their hair or the way in which they behave.

If Paré's advice thus suggests that the modern taxonomy of primary, secondary, and tertiary characteristics was not fully in effect in the earlier period, this is not to say that there was an alternative hierarchy in place at that time. In other words, I don't mean to say that beards, hair, codpieces and handkerchiefs were themselves *the* primary characteristics. The parts at the center of this study are not extraordinary, but are instead meant to be exemplary: they are simply some of the items that actively worked to constitute gender identity during this period. A more complete list would have to include all of the things mentioned by Paré, as well as things like swords, thighs, daggers, wigs, hands, cosmetics, and farthingales.[11]

My rationale for focusing on these four particular "parts" is largely theoretical. I wanted to combine some items that are natural parts of the body (beards and hair) with others that are culturally constructed elements of gender (handkerchiefs and codpieces) because the conceptual division of "nature" and "culture" – and by extension "sex" and "gender" – lies at the heart of our modern theorizations of masculinity and femininity. Today, gender formation is typically imagined as a developmental process in which a person begins with a set of natural biological characteristics (sex) that are then modified, or "constructed," by society and experience through the course of a lifetime (gender). Accordingly, any particular characteristic or feature tends to be seen as either primarily natural or cultural, essential or constructed.[12]

Feminists have begun the process of revising or rethinking this schema, but it still tends to dominate our understanding of gender formation. This was not the case during the Renaissance. Lorraine Daston and Katharine Park maintain that while the theoretical "opposition of nature versus culture" has proved to be quite "illuminating for us in our attempts to sort out the humanly universal from the culturally local," it is "deeply misleading when imposed upon earlier periods." As they explain, "Renaissance conceptions of 'nature' could embrace considerations as familiar to modern ears as anatomy and as unfamiliar as 'complexion', 'character', or 'conduct'." Likewise, "the social constructs of gender seemed to early modern medical writers as fully 'natural' as the anatomical signs of sex."[13] Daston and Park's point here is that the modern distinction between "nature" and "culture" (or "sex" and "gender") was a consequence of the Enlightenment and scientific revolution and that before that time, the terms themselves had a different range of meanings.

Paré's advice to his fellow physicians illustrates this point quite nicely. Although he claims to be advising his colleagues about how to determine the "sexe" of the individual in question, many of the things that he mentions would not today be considered part of the apparatus of sex. This is perhaps clearest in the original French version where Paré recommends examining whether the person is "bold or fearful," and whether that person displays other "*actions* like those of males or females." These would today be considered gendered characteristics rather than sexual ones. So in the end, Paré expands the category of "sexe" along precisely the lines that Daston and Park indicate by including things like "character" or "conduct" in his discussion.

If the sex/gender conceptual model was not firmly in place in the earlier period, then this also helps to explain why physical features like beards, hair, codpieces, and handkerchiefs would have been less peripheral. In order to understand this connection, we first need to recognize that the sex/gender schema not only encourages us to distinguish between sex and gender, nature and culture, it also encourages us to privilege sex/nature over gender/culture. Hence, we tend to view natural sexual characteristics such as genital morphology or genetic makeup as somehow more constitutive or essential than culturally constructed gender characteristics such as behavior or clothing. The privileging of sex over gender, and nature over culture, is encoded in the hierarchized taxonomy of primary, secondary, and tertiary characteristics that I mentioned earlier: natural sexual characteristics are given precedence by being classified as either primary or secondary, whereas gendered characteristics are diminished by being classified as tertiary. If these conceptual rubrics were not entirely operative before the Enlightenment, then parts like the ones under scrutiny here would not have been relegated to "secondary" or "tertiary" status.

Stephen J. Gould goes so far as to question the usefulness of the nature/culture dichotomy altogether, though his critique is articulated from a scientific rather than an historical perspective. He writes:

Of all the baleful false dichotomies that stymie our understanding of the world's complexity, nature vs nurture must rank among the top two or three . . . We will not get this issue straight until we realize that the "interactionism" we all accept does not permit such statements as "Trait x is 29 percent environmental and 71 percent genetic." When causative factors . . . interact so complexly, and throughout growth, to produce an intricate adult being, we cannot, in principle, parse that being's behavior into quantitative percentages of remote root causes.

Gould doesn't simply criticize our reliance upon the nature/nurture dichotomy, he also offers an alternative. He says that instead of trying to ascertain whether certain behaviors or identities are formed primarily by nature or culture, we should try to determine to what extent those behaviors or identities are malleable. As he puts it, the "truly salient issues are malleability and flexibility, not fallacious parsing by percentages . . . A twenty-dollar pair of eyeglasses from the local pharmacy may fully correct a defect of vision that is 100 percent heritable."[14]

The second major argument of this book is an historically inflected version of Gould's point. While it would be impossible to determine the extent to which gender identity was actually malleable during the early modern period, or even to determine whether it was seen as being more malleable than it is today, what I do hope to show is that masculinity and femininity were often conceptualized as being malleable. By contrast, in contemporary western culture, gender identity is generally imagined to be "fixed" by biology.[15] This is yet another side-effect of the sex/gender schema. According to Diana Fuss's *Essentially Speaking*, the sex/gender schema encourages us to think of sexual characteristics as things which are natural, "hardwired," and therefore largely immutable: as she puts it, we tend to assume that "nature and fixity . . . go together."[16]

In sixteenth- and early seventeenth-century England, biological sexual features were certainly considered to be "natural" or essential, but they were not therefore imagined to be fixed or immutable. In fact, it was proverbial in the period to say that what "God makes . . . man shapes."[17] One reason why "sex" and the body were understood in this way was the influence of the Galenic medical tradition. Within this tradition, male and female bodies were not understood to be two discrete entities that were fundamentally different from one another; instead, they were viewed along a continuum. Moreover, on account of the homology between male and female bodies, it was always possible for individuals to move in one direction or the other along this gradated continuum, and even, in some cases, to be transformed from one sex to the other.[18] In *Making Sex*, Thomas Laqueur illustrates this point by discussing early modern medical accounts of women who were spontaneously transformed into men.[19] According to Laqueur, the notion that "sex" was (at least potentially) malleable went hand-in-hand with the notion that male and female bodies were structurally homologous: since both males and females were thought to have the same underlying corporeal structure (males had their private parts on the outside, and females had theirs on the inside), changes in humoral makeup and/or corporeal structure could move an individual along the gendered continuum.

So within this schema, it is as if gender was viewed as a kind of balance or scale, and as if masculine and feminine features were like "weights" that were placed on one side or the other. The configuration of these weights was not entirely fixed: they could be altered spontaneously or through human intervention. And if enough of the weights were shifted, then the overall balance of the scales would tip. Moreover, although some physical features undoubtedly "weighed" more than others, they all "weighed" something and had an impact on the equilibrium. It therefore makes sense to say they were constitutive.

Masculinity and femininity tend to be viewed quite differently in the post-Enlightenment world. Male and female bodies are usually seen as structurally dimorphic – this is what Laqueur calls "the two sex model" – and this dimorphism is imagined to be to some extent "hardwired" by nature. In practice, moreover, corporeal form tends to be equated with genital form so that genital morphology effectively becomes *the* "primary sexual characteristic" rather than simply *a* "primary sexual characteristic." This is suggested by the largely genito-centric procedures I discussed above that are used to "determine" whether an intersexed individual should be male or female. In this modern conceptual schema, "secondary" or "tertiary" features tend to be regarded as little more than peripheral "signs" that point to the underlying genital "truth." Fergus's quip about Dil in Neil Jordan's *The Crying Game* exemplifies this modern thinking. After having seen Dil's penis, Fergus insists that she is "not a girl." For her part, Dil refuses to accept this phallocentric logic, replying – "Details, baby, details." Dil's repartee works on two levels. On the one hand, she suggests that her penis is nothing more than a "detail" and she therefore implicitly mocks Fergus for placing so much emphasis on it. On the other hand, she calls attention to the "details" that materialize her femininity such as her hair, her clothes, her voice, and her fingernails. But despite the wonderful élan of Dil's response, it is ultimately Fergus's view that is dominant.[20]

The differences between modern and early modern notions of gender identity can be further clarified by looking at how "sex change" is understood in the two periods. Today, since male and female bodies are imagined to be dimorphic, "sex change" is often understood as a radical and decisive shift from one state of being to another. Moreover, given the cultural centrality of the genitalia, it is hardly surprising to find that "sex change" is frequently conflated in the popular imaginary with the surgical procedure that alters the genitalia. This operation is assumed to act as a "switch" that moves the individual from one distinct category of being to the other, and until the genital morphology is transformed, the sex change is not "really" effected.[21]

During the Renaissance, sexual transformations were understood quite differently. First, they were often said to occur spontaneously or "naturally" – while the individual was jumping over a ditch or playing with a sexual partner. Even more important for my purposes is the fact that they were often said to involve a range of physical transformations. Indeed, early modern accounts of sexual metamorphosis frequently include information about changes in the person's non-genital features as well as information about changes in their "privities." Take the well-known case of the French peasant Marie/Germain as an example. This case was discussed by writers like Michel de Montaigne, Ambroise Paré, and others during the Renaissance; it has also been analyzed by modern critics like Thomas Laqueur and Stephen Greenblatt.[22] The story goes something like this: in France, a fifteen-year-old girl named Marie was chasing after her swine in a wheat field one day. In midpursuit, she leapt over a ditch only to find that the sudden exertion had caused a set of male genitals to pop out of her body. Marie was subsequently examined by a group of physicians who concluded that she had become a man, and she was eventually rebaptized as Germain.

If this is the version of events that has circulated in contemporary criticism, it omits what I take to be a crucial detail of the story: namely, the fact that Marie was, before her metamorphosis, "remarkable for having a little more hair about her chin than the other girls; they called her bearded Marie." Moreover, after the genital transformation, Germain is said to have developed "a big, very thick beard."[23] Almost all the early modern writers who discuss this case make some sort of reference to Marie/Germain's facial hair (although Montaigne is the only one who notes that Marie had a beard *before* her genitals were altered). Paré, for example, indicates that Germain had "a thicke and red beard," and also describes how he was brought before an assembly called by the bishop and "he received the name and habite of a man."[24] Similarly, the seventeenth-century Italian monk Francesco Maria Guazzo states that a "beard grew upon her chin."[25] Finally, in England, George Sandys mentions this case in his commentary on the story of Iphis and Ianthe in his translation of Ovid's *Metamorphoses*, and he also says that Germain "ha[d] a long beard."[26]

The growth of Marie/Germain's beard is not simply a superfluous detail in these accounts, as is implied by its omission by modern historians and literary critics; instead, it was part of Marie's transformation. In fact, the growth of facial hair on women was commonly thought to be the opening stage of a sexual metamorphosis. The English anatomist Helkiah Crooke points out that many people believe that "women whose voyces turne strong or have beards and grow hairy do presently also change their parts of generation."[27] The thinking that Crooke describes here is of interest because it implies that the alterations of the beard, voice, and genitalia were believed to go together – they were all components of the "sex change."

There is another story of sexual metamorphosis that suggests that changes in the length of the hair on the head could also be considered part of the "sex change." This is an instance of a girl who was transformed into a boy, and during her transformation, her "curles" supposedly "shorten[ed]" to the point where they "scarce h[u]ng beneath her eares."[28] Another version of the same story simply stipulates that the girl's "heare grew shorter."[29] In both of these texts, the length of the girl's hair changes spontaneously during her sex change. It would therefore appear that just as the growth of Marie's beard was considered to be a part of her metamorphosis, the "shortening" of this girl's hair was also considered to be a part of hers.

By calling attention to the role of the beard and the hair in these sexual transformations, I do not mean to downplay the importance of the genitalia or to imply more generally that they were not crucial for determining an individual's gender. On the contrary, if we think of physical features as "weights" on a scale, then genital morphology was clearly a massive weight, and may even have been "heavier" than all of the other features combined. Nonetheless, features like beard growth and hair length did matter. They not only helped to tip the overall balance of the gender scales in one direction or the other, they also helped to move an individual along the gender continuum after the balance had been tipped. In other words, these parts might make a female who had been transformed into a male more or less masculine, or a male who had been transformed into a female more or less feminine. The case of the Portuguese woman Maria Pachero illustrates this point. When "she was at the age when a woman's monthly courses usually begin, instead of a fluid excretion there broke or otherwise grew from those parts a virile member; and so, from being a girl, she suddenly became a public young man endowed with virility." At the same time, however, "he remained unbearded and with a feminine cast of countenance, these being indications of imperfect virility." Although facial hair again features prominently in this account, it works in a negative way: the lack of facial hair pulls the gender of this newly minted "public young man" toward the feminine side of the continuum, and thus he is said to have only an "imperfect virility."[30]

A similar logic seems to inform the cases of spontaneous sexual transformation described by the Spanish physician Juan Huarte in his *Examinations of Men's Wits* (a text which was translated into English in 1594 and went through three more editions in England by the mid seventeenth century). Huarte's text is of interest for several reasons. First, he discusses sex changes that occur while the individual is still in the womb as opposed to those that occur after birth. Moreover, he contends that sex changes can take place in directions – from female to male and male to female. For my purposes, however, the crucial thing to note is that he indicates that the individuals who undergo these metamorphoses may be inconsistently gendered. First, he recounts how "divers times . . . nature hath made a female child, and she hath so remained in her mothers belly for the space of one or two months: and afterwards, plentie of heat growing in the genitall members, upon some occasion they have issued forth, and she become a male." He goes on to note, however, that "To whom this transformation hath befallen . . . is afterwards plainly discovered, by certain motions they retaine, unfitting for the masculine sex, being altogither womanish, & their voice shrill & sweet." Conversely, he talks about how "nature hath sundrie times made a male with his geneotries outward, and cold growing on, they have turned inward, and it became female." But again, he maintains that "This is knowen after she is borne, for she retaineth a mannish fashion, as well in her words, as in all her motions and workings."[31] Thus, according to Huarte, although in each of these cases the gender scales have shifted, some parts or features remain that continue to pull in the opposite direction and as a result the individual's gender identity is somewhat mixed: the female who has been reconstituted as a male still has, for instance, a "shrill & sweet" voice, while the male who has been reconstituted as a female has "a mannish fashion . . . in her words," "motions," and " workings."

If the influence of the Galenic medicine helps to explain why "secondary" corporeal features like beards and hair might have been considered more essential in the early modern period, it also helps to explain why accessories of dress like codpieces and handkerchiefs might have been accorded a similar status. Interestingly, clothing features prominently in many of the cases of sexual transformation mentioned above. For example, when Marie/Germain appeared before an assembly called by the bishop, s/he was given both "the name *and habite* of a man." Paré also records a similar action taking place in another case – that of a fourteen-year-old girl named Joane. Her male "members started forth and unfolded themselves" while she was "lay[ing] in the same bed" as a maid and "play[ing] somewhat wantonly with her." Joane's parents recognized the change and "by helpe of the Ecclesiasticke power," they "changed his name from *Joane* to *John, and put him in mans apparell*."[32]

Even more complex is the case of Thomas(ine) Hall, an indentured servant born in England but who lived in Virginia during the early seventeenth century. Although Hall came to the colonies as a man, his/her gender identity subsequently came into question and the issue ultimately had to be decided by a judicial inquiry. The court ruled that Hall was both a "man and a woeman" and stipulated that this fact should be announced to the entire community: "that all the Inhabitants . . . may take notice thereof." Tellingly, however, this public pronouncement about his/her gender was not enough. The authorities also forced Hall to wear articles of both male and female dress, presumably so that the clothes would materialize his/her contradictory gender. They note that "hee shall goe Clothed in mans apparell, only his head to bee attired in a Coyfe and Corsecloth with an Apron before him."[33] The clothes mentioned in this verdict establish Hall's gender in a finely calibrated way. Although Hall is generally classified as both "man and woeman," the dominant gender seems to be male since the court decision consistently uses the masculine pronoun as in the quote above – "*hee* shall goe Clothed." The clothes assigned to Hall figure this judgment exactly: s/he is supposed to "go Clothed in mans apparell" just as her/his predominant gender seems to be male, but at the same time, s/he is to wear some feminine articles – namely, a female headdress and an "Apron." A similar solution was adopted in England in the mid seventeenth century. The Reverend John Ward, a physician and natural historian, notes in his diary that he saw "An hermaphrodite at a place 4 miles of Worcester" and that "Hee goes dressed upward as a woman in a kind of waistcoat and Bodies; but Breeches on."[34]

Modern readers might be tempted to see the clothes mentioned in these accounts as gendered "signs" that simply indicate the type of body that lies beneath, but in early modern English culture, clothing was often seen as integral to a person's identity. Ann Rosalind Jones and Peter Stallybrass provide the most thoroughgoing articulation of this thesis in *Renaissance Clothing and the Materials of Memory*. They contend that clothes were thought to have the power to "deeply make" an individual, and that they "inscribe themselves on a person who comes into being through that inscription."[35] Similarly, Stephen Greenblatt notes that it is frequently "as if identity resided in clothing,"[36] and Jonas Barish maintains that for early modern writers, "Distinctions of dress, however external and theatrical they may seem to us . . . virtually belong to our essence, and may no more be tampered with than that essence itself."[37] Finally, Dympna Callaghan claims that "essence resides in apparel rather than in what lies beneath it."[38]

The work of Stephen Orgel and Jean Howard is particularly relevant for my project because they suggest that clothing was often understood to confer *gender* identity. Stephen Orgel observes that the ending of Shakespeare's *Twelfth Night* implies that Viola "is not a woman unless she is dressed as one . . . Clothes make the woman, clothes make the man: the costume is of the essence."[39] Jean Howard makes a similar point, asserting that dress was "part of the apparatus for producing and marking gender difference."[40] In what follows, I build on the work of Orgel and Howard by looking at clothing and its relationship to gender in a detailed way. In chapters 1 and 2,

I will analyze how particular accessories of dress – the handkerchief and the codpiece – materialized specific forms of masculine and feminine identity.

I also want to flesh out the cultural logics that lay behind these beliefs. To do so, I turn to yet another account of sexual metamorphosis. This is the story of a Spanish woman who turned into a man. It circulated widely in early modern Europe, and was included by the English writer Nathaniel Wanley in his section on "Persons as have changed their Sex" in *Wonders of the Little World* (1678). Wanley explains that the woman was married to a farmer who physically abused her, and therefore she decided to leave him one night. She dressed herself in her husband's clothes and

stole out of the House, to seek out a more peaceable fortune elsewhere. And having been in divers services, whether the conceit of her mans habit, or whether Nature strangely wrought in her, but she found a notable alteration in her self; insomuch, that she who had been a Wife, desired to perform the office of Husband. She marry'd a Woman in that place, where she had retired her self.[41]

In this account, Wanley provides two possible explanations for the woman's sex change: he says that either the transformation was caused by nature having "strangely wrought in her" or it was caused by "the conceit of her mans habit." These same two explanations are also offered by Francesco Maria Guazzo in his discussion of the case. He writes that the woman "found she had actually turned into a man" and that this was either because of "the efficacy of her natural heat" or because her "imagination" was "induced and strengthened by her continuous masculine clothing and work."[42] These two explanations are not necessarily mutually exclusive, but it is the latter that is of particular interest to me here. In this scenario, the clothing is the catalyst for the woman's change of sex. The "conceit" of wearing masculine clothes "induce[s]" and "strengthen[s]" her imagination, and this quite literally transforms her into a man. It is significant, moreover, that in Wanley's version the woman is said to wear her husband's clothes because it is as if wearing his clothes produces in her the desire to "perform the office of *husband*."

When viewed in relation to this story, the polemical literature on clothing and gender from early modern England begins to resonate in new ways. Take the *Hic Mulier* (1620) pamphlet as an example. In it, the author contends that the mannish women of the time "mould their bodies to every deformed fashion" and that they are "man-like not only from the head to the waist, but to the very foot, & in every condition: man in body by attyre, man in behaviour by rude complement . . . man in wearing weapons, man in using weapons: And in briefe . . . man in all things."[43] While it is clear that the author is not suggesting that these women have actually been transformed into men by their apparell and "weapons," we need to acknowledge that it was possible for clothing to "mould" a person's body, or for a woman to become a "man in body by attire." The author of the *Hic Mulier* pamphlet may even be deliberately raising the specter of such a sexual metamorphosis in order to regulate or restrict women's fashion(ings). Another seventeenth-century writer uses similar language, asserting that men's codpieces "unfashion" the "gracious parts" that "God fayre fashion'd."[44] We should resist assuming that statements like this are completely figurative or metaphorical; they may also hint at clothing's ability to "unfashion" or "mould" sex and the body.

But why is it that clothing was considered constitutive? Why did people believe that it had the power to "deeply make" gender identity and even transform an individual from a woman to a man? Some scholars have suggested that these beliefs need to be understood in relation to the Hippo-cratic or Galenic conceptions of the body. They argue that because there was only "one sex" during the period, masculinity and femininity had to be secured through other, non-corporeal, means, and therefore differences in dress were deemed more essential. Mark Breitenberg, for example, contends in *Anxious Masculinity in Early Modern England* that there was no "bio-logical, essentialist basis for [gender] identity" and consequently that it was necessary "to assert the naturalness and immutability of [gender] categories from other sources" such as dress.[45] Some scholars have even gone so far as to state that before the Enlightenment, there was "confusion about sexual difference" and that "[t]here was no clear cut grasp of the sexual differences between men and women."[46] While claims like this are relatively common,[47] they are, in my opinion, misleading. Sources from the period like Paré's advice to his fellow physicians demonstrate quite conclusively that early modern writers had a "clear cut grasp" of "the sexual differences between men and women." In fact, they articulated more differences between male and female bodies than we typically do today. Just because those differ-ences were not thought to be absolute and were not thought to be completely fixed does not mean that they were therefore less culturally significant or essential.[48]

So instead of saying that clothing served as a compensatory mechanism that secured gender in the absence of corporeal difference, I believe that it would be more accurate to say that clothing materialized gender along with other, more corporeal, features, and both were essential. Thus, the "cultural" distinctions materialized through clothing were not as radically differentiated from the "natural" distinctions materialized through the body as they are today. But this still doesn't explain how clothing might have worked to make the man or woman. Humoral theory and Galenic conceptions of the body are invoked here, not as an explanatory device, but as something that must be compensated for. What I want to suggest, however, is that humoralism also provides a means of accounting for clothing's power to "deeply make" identity. The mechanism for this is alluded to in the case of the Spanish woman who was transformed into a man by wearing her husband's clothing. Both Wanley and Guazzo suggest that the woman's imagination was stimulated by "the conceit of her man's habit" and this transformed her into a man. Or, as Guazzo puts it, the sex change was effected "through imagination induced and strengthened by her continuous masculine clothing and work." In these passages, Wanley and Guazzo invoke a belief that was popular at the time: namely, that the imagination had the power to precipitate changes in the material world. Lorraine Daston has recently studied these beliefs in some detail, insisting that they continued to have purchase well into the eighteenth century.[49] The most widely discussed examples of this phenomenon involved women whose imaginings were imprinted onto the fetus they were carrying. There is, for instance, an account of a woman who spent too much time looking at a portrait of a priest wearing fur during her pregnancy and who consequently gave birth to a hairy child, or another who had longed for lobster at Leadenhall market and who later bore a child who was "boiled and red." If people believed that the imagination could modify the fetus, they also believed that it could modify the body of the imaginer. One such case was that of Cyppus, a king of Italy, whose imagination was said to have brought forth horns on his head after he "had attended and assisted at a bull baiting and had 'dreamed of hornes in his head'."[50]

Montaigne's discussion of the transformation of Marie/Germain appears in his essay "Of the power of the imagination." Moreover, immediately before his analysis of the case of Marie/Germain, Montaigne mentions another similar story: Ovid's Iphis and Ianthe. Iphis is a girl who was raised as a boy and engaged to be married to Ianthe. Her "secret" is eventually discovered and the marriage is in jeopardy, but at the last minute she is transformed into a boy on account of her mother's prayers. Montaigne maintains that these metamorphoses demonstrate the imagination's power: he states that "the imagination has power in such things" and that if "it is so continually and vigorously fixed on the same subject . . . in order not to have to relapse so often into the same thought and sharpness of desire, it is better off if once and for all it incorporates this masculine member in girls."[51] Although Montaigne doesn't delineate how Marie/Germain's "imagination" might have led her to "incorporate" a "masculine member," it is clear that it was not through wearing masculine clothing since she was only given new attire after her transformation. Was it perhaps instead through the activity of chasing after the pig? When seen from this perspective, it is worth noting that in Guazzo's account of the Spanish woman's metamorphosis, he suggests that her "work" along with her masculine attire helped "induce" and "strengthen" her imagination. Thus, it would appear that there were a variety of means through which the imagination might be fired, and wearing masculine clothing was just one of them.

The material power of the imagination was a humoral phenomenon involving the animal spirits. John Sutton describes the physiological mechanism at work here in *Philosophy and Memory Traces*. As he puts it, an individual's imaginings were thought to be "imprinted" on them "by resemblance and through spirits and fluids."[52] Lorraine Daston adds that the imagination was "fired up" through the animal spirits, and that this affected both memory and the material body itself. She notes that Francis Bacon thought that these "subtle spirits" were behind not only the power of the imagination, but also other puzzling phenomena like electricity, magnetism, gravitation, contagion, and perception.[53]

While the influence of Galenic medicine and humoral theory helps to explain why both clothing and peripheral parts of the body like hair and beards might have been considered more constitutive in early modern English culture, there are other factors that need to be considered as well. One of these is the centrality of religious authority. Put simply, we might say that all distinctions between men and women – whether they were natural or cultural, sex or gender – were understood to be fundamental because they were part of "God's holy order in nature." The extent to which the ideologies of gender were underpinned by religious belief becomes evident when we look at texts from the period. In *Spiritual Armour to Defend the Head from a Superfluity of Naughtiness*, Thomas Wall asserts:

Woman God made for Man . . . She also was made in subjection to Man, her earthly Lord and Husband . . . This being that holy Order God created Man and Woman in . . . it was therefore the pleasure of God to give unto the Woman a sign in nature differing from Man, to teach her subjection to Man whose Glory she is, namely long hair.[54]

Wall tellingly begins his comments here with the "fact" of divinely created patriarchal order – with the "fact" that God made women "for Man . . . [and] in subjection to Man."[55] He then goes on to discuss the physical features that God supposedly "gave" to women to "teach" them their place in this hierarchy. The progression of the argument thus implies that the patriarchal hierarchy is primary and established by God, and that the material differences in men's and women's bodies are manifestations of that hierarchy, not the basis for it.[56] A similar logic underlies Helkiah Crooke's description of the beard in his anatomy book, *Microcosmographia*. He says that women do not have beards because they "needed no ensigne of majesty [i.e. beard] because they were born to subjection." For Crooke, as for Wall, the physical feature is taken to be a sign of the more primary, God-given order: as he puts it, women are beardless "because" they are subordinate to men. The modern version of this argument would almost certainly reverse the logical order and claim that women do not have beards (the "ensigne of majesty"), and *therefore* they are subordinate to men.

Early modern writers use a comparable logic when discussing differences in men's and women's attire. In *Hic Mulier*, for example, the author enjoins mannish women to "Remember how your Maker made . . . our first Parents coates, not one coat, but a coat for the man, and a coat for the woman; coates of several fashions, severall formes, and for severall uses: the mans coat fit for his labour, and the womans fit for her modestie."[57] In this passage, clothing is said to "fit" the social roles of men and women, and those roles, like the "coats" themselves, are said to be given by God. Thus, the clothes God gave to the woman are "fit for her modestie," which means primarily "fit for her subordinate role in society." Clothing is not, therefore, unlike other physical markers of gender difference such as long hair, beardlessness, or genital morphology; in the end, all of these things simply give expression to "God's Holy Order in Nature."

Since God supposedly instituted all of these physical differences as "signs" of his holy order, there was less of a need to distinguish sharply between what we would today call "sexual characteristics" and "gendered characteristics." Moreover, these religious beliefs also made it easier to acknowledge or accept that these "signs" were malleable or alterable. This is because these physical features were not thought to provide the main foundation for the patriarchal hierarchy in the way they do in the modern world. Instead, the hierarchy was also anchored by God's word.

But even though early modern writers acknowledged that physical features were thus potentially malleable – or that "man" might "shape" what God had "made" – this did not mean that they thought it was acceptable for people to alter God's holy order in nature in whatever way they liked. The diatribes of writers like William Prynne and Phillip Stubbes against "unnatural" clothing and hairstyles demonstrate this quite clearly. The poem about codpieces that I quoted above also reinforces this point since it stresses that individuals must not "unfashion" the "gracious parts" that "God fayre fashion'd." At the same time, it is important to recognize that these writers are not necessarily condemning all human "fashioning." This is evident in another passage in the *Hic Mulier* pamphlets. At one point, the Hic Mulier character speaks and defends herself for her "mannish" sartorial excesses. She says

Nature to everything she hath created hath given a singular delight to change: as to the Herbs, Plants, and Trees, a time to wither and shed their leaves, a time to bud and bring forth their leaves, and a time for their Fruits and Flowers . . . To the Beasts, libertie to chuse their foode, liberty to delight in their food, and liberty to feed and grow fat with their food . . . But to man, [she has given] both these and all things else, to alter, frame and fashion . . . as his will and delight shall rule him.[58]

Given that this argument is placed in the mouth of the demonized Hic Mulier figure, we are clearly meant to see it as being spurious. But what is considered wrongheaded about the argument is not what modern readers might expect: it is not the idea that Nature "delight[s] in change" or that man has the ability to "alter, frame, and fashion" nature. As we have seen, these ideas were widely accepted, even proverbial. Instead, Hic Mulier's mistake is in thinking that man can "alter, frame, and fashion" nature *in whatever way "his will and delight shall rule him."* This becomes even more evident in the passage that follows. When Hic Mulier's interlocutor contests her reasoning, s/he cites the poet "C.M.," who writes that "A stronger hand restraines our wilfull powers, / A will must rule above this will of ours."[59] This passage implies that "fashioning" is only "sinful" if it is not guided by the "stronger hand" of God's "will."

Religious beliefs and the influence of Galenic medicine and humoralism are thus the two main factors that we need to consider in order to comprehend why early modern gender was, in important ways, "prosthetic." Their influence helps to explain, first and foremost, why the modern conceptual distinction between sex and gender wouldn't have been fully operative. They also help to explain why "secondary" or "tertiary" parts like beards, hair, codpieces, and handkerchiefs played such an integral role in materializing masculinity and femininity. Finally, their influence helps to explain why malleable features could be considered to be constitutive in the first place; or, put differently, why gender was prosthetic.

In *Simians, Cyborgs, and Women*, Donna Haraway charts the emergence and development of the sex/gender schema. She maintains that it was first conceived by feminists in the 1960s "within the framework of the biology/culture distinction, such that sex was related to biology (hormones, genes, nervous system, morphology) and gender was related to culture (psychology, sociology)."[60] Although this paradigm is still dominant today, Haraway points out that feminists have started to come up with new ways of thinking about gender that circumvent the problems inherent in the sex/gender model. She notes that by "the mid-1980s a general suspicion of the category of gender and the binarism sex/gender entered the feminist literature" (136). Feminists have therefore begun to explore things like how the body and sexual characteristics might be constructed, and how construction itself might be essential. In *Essentially Speaking* (1989), Diana Fuss proposes that "it may be time to ask whether essences can change and whether construction can be normative."[61]

My own work seeks to contribute to this feminist project. I believe that examining early modern thinking about masculinity and femininity is useful in this regard because our modern assumptions about "essences" and "construction" were not fully in place at that time. Moreover, the physical features that I will be focusing on here are also particularly apt for the theoretical project that Fuss outlines. Beards and hair, for example, are a part of the body and are "natural" or "essences," but they are nevertheless also clearly "constructed": they are alterable and subject to acculturation in the form of tonsure and shaving. Similarly, although codpieces and handkerchiefs are cultural artifacts, I will argue that they are, in a sense, auxiliary organs of the body – they work to shape the body and might therefore be considered essential to it.

If the project of rethinking the sex/gender schema is already well under-way, the central figure of this revisionist process has undoubtedly been Judith Butler. In *Gender Trouble* and *Bodies that Matter*, Butler provides a compelling rearticulation of our ideas about "sex" and "the body." She claims, for instance, that the sexed body should not be understood as a natural entity that is simply bound up in an irreducible tension with cultural norms and ideals. Instead, as she puts it, sex, or the body, *is* that tension. Moreover, Butler maintains that our current model for understanding the formation of gender identity is inadequate. If we have tended to see masculinity and femininity as being formed through a process in which "natural" differences are modified by "culture," she maintains – as the pun in her title *Bodies that Matter* implies – that in reality sexual differences between male and female bodies only "matter" (that is to say, come into being physically) through the process of being made to "matter" (being made socially significant). Consequently, the body is best understood as "a process of materialization that stabilizes over time to produce the effect of boundary, fixity, and surface we call matter."[62] Butler's point about sexual differences needing to be "materialized" is powerfully illustrated by items like beards and hair since it is only through cultural practices such as depilation and tonsure that sharp and dichotomous distinctions between men's and women's hair can be produced in the first place. In the case of beards, for example, a clear dichotomy can only be created if men allow their facial hair to grow and women remove theirs. As a result, we might say that the sexual differences in facial hair are only brought into being (or made "matter") when they "matter" socially speaking.

The hair of the head is possibly even more interesting. Like the beard, the length of an individual's hair was often considered an essential element of gender identity in early modern England. As a result, writers from the period sometimes argued that women's hair was naturally longer than men's. In other words, they said that if women and men allowed their hair to grow indefinitely without ever cutting it, most women's hair would grow to be longer than most men's. Modern hair scientists suggest that these claims are actually true (although this is not common knowledge). But if there is thus a biological difference between men's and women's hair, it is quite odd that hair length is not generally considered to be part of the apparatus of sex today. It is not, for example, listed as a primary or secondary sexual characteristic. When it is classified, it is almost always as a gendered characteristic. There are several possible explanations for why this sexual difference doesn't "matter." One is that the difference between male and female hair is not sharp and dichotomous: that is to say, even if most men's hair does not have the biological capacity to grow as long as most women's hair does, there would inevitably be some men whose hair would be longer than some women's and vice versa. Another explanation for why the biological difference between male and female hair doesn't "matter" is that it is almost entirely malleable, and it cannot therefore really be imagined to "fix" gender in any meaningful way. Another way of putting this is to say that the biological differences are superseded by culture in this instance: it is barbers rather than biology that usually determine the length of an individual's hair. Thus, we might say that part of the reason why tonsorial differences do not "matter" physically today, to return to Butler's formulation, is because they don't matter socially – they don't materialize gender in the "right" way.

If feminists like Butler have therefore done much to reconceptualize sex and the body, less theoretical work has been done with regard to thinking about the ways in which elements of gender (like clothing) might materialize masculinity and femininity. In fact, some feminists have rejected the notion outright. Butler, for one, claims that she does not believe that gender is "like clothes or that clothes make the woman."[63] There are, however, others who have recognized this as a crucial intervention. It is implicit, for example, in the second half of Fuss's proposition when she says that we need to consider the possibility that "construction might be normative" or even essential. I hope to contribute to the revisionist project by concentrating on accessories of dress like codpieces and handkerchiefs and demonstrating how these cultural artifacts work to "fashion" the sexed body and produce masculinity and femininity.

There are several contemporary theorists who can help us to think about the "clothes-make-the-man/woman" proposition in a theoretically sophisticated way. Anne Hollander's *Seeing through Clothes*, for instance, argues that the images and ideals that we have of our bodies are fundamentally constituted by clothing. To make her point, Hollander looks at nudes from different epochs – from the statuesque figures of Titian to the fleshy Courbets – and notes the drastic variations in body shape across the range of images. She then explains the reason for these differences by juxtaposing nude figures from each period with contemporaneous representations of clothed figures, and pointing out the similarities between the form of the garments and the stylized form of the body. So, for example, she contends that the bodies of the women in portraits by Tintoretto or Bronzino – with their small, flattened breasts and cylindrical torsos – have shapes which are quite similar to the shape of dresses at the time: these garments often featured stiff, tube-like bodices which pressed the breasts tightly to the body. Similarly, Hollander shows how Courbet's nudes – "with their enormous buttocks and ripe breasts . . . minimal neat bellies and tiny waists" – correspond with the idealized form produced by the popular clothing of the mid nineteenth century: dresses at that time often featured tightly laced corsets that held the stomach in, padding to enlarge the bosom, and "puffy folds of a full skirt bursting out below the . . . corset."[64] In each of these instances, the nude body has the same shape as the clothed body popular at the time, despite the fact that the clothes are no longer "there."[65] Hence, when we look at a representation of the nude body, it is as if we are seeing through (the invisible) clothes (figures 1 and 2). Hollander's observations have radical implications for the way in which we conceptualize the body: although we tend to think of the body as a "natural" entity that precedes its cultural inscription, Hollander powerfully demonstrates that our ideas about the natural/nude body are in some ways a backformation from the acculturated/clothed body.[66] While Hollander never considers the gendered dimension of this process and focuses almost exclusively on women, I use her work in my third chapter to argue that the codpiece shaped ideas about the masculine body, and by extension, ideas about masculinity itself. Indeed, the specific forms of the codpiece – one which was baglike and the other more phallic – can be said to correspond to two of the notions of masculinity competing for hegemony at the time: one which was articulated around reproduction and the other around phallic (heterosexual) penetration.

If Hollander thus analyzes the ways in which clothing "fashions" ideas and perceptions of the body, Michel de Certeau looks at clothing's relationship to the body in an even more materialist way. In *The Practice of Everyday Life*, he argues that bodies are quite literally formed by the items that are attached to them. He also claims that this process of corporeal formation is a normalizing one – that the "activity of extracting [from] or adding on" to the body is "carried out by reference to a code that keeps bodies within the limits set by a norm." As a result of this,

clothes [and other detachable parts] . . . can be regarded as instruments through which a social law maintains its hold on bodies and its members, regulates them and exercises them through changes in fashion as well as through military maneuvers. The automobile, like a corset, also shapes [bodies] and makes them conform to a model of correct posture; . . . Glasses, cigarettes, shoes, etc., [all] reshape the physical "portrait" in their own ways . . . Where does the disciplinary apparatus end that displaces and corrects, adds or removes things from these bodies, malleable under the instrumentation of so many laws? To tell the truth, they become bodies only by conforming to these codes.[67]

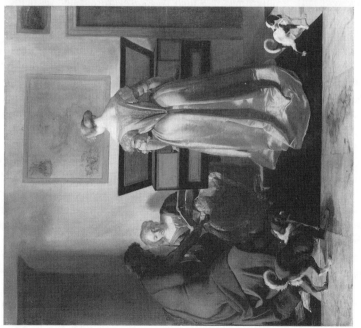

Figures 1 and 2. Paintings illustrating Anne Hollander's thesis in *Seeing through Clothes*. Left: Jacob Ochtervelt, *A Woman Playing a Virginal* (1675–80). Right: Jacob Jordaens, *King Candaules of Lydia showing his Wife to Gyges*, 1646.

In this passage, de Certeau contends that the body is "regulated" and "shaped" by a whole range of detachable items – clothing, shoes, glasses, cigarettes, and even automobiles. He maintains that all of these objects have the power literally to (re)form the "physical portrait." Moreover, de Certeau explicitly acknowledges the role that society and "social laws" play in this process. He points out that bodies are always fashioned "in reference to a code that keeps [them] within limits set by a norm," and thus that the detachable parts themselves might be understood as "disciplinary apparatus[es]" or "instruments through which the social law maintains its hold on bodies." Although these "social codes" remain relatively abstract and indefinite in de Certeau's formulation, it is easy to extrapolate from his comments and imagine how bodies might be shaped according to *gender* norms, for instance. This is essentially what I want to argue in my first chapter with regard to the handkerchief. There, I suggest that this newly popularized object quite literally produced a new "physical portrait" in the early modern period by absorbing sweat and other bodily fluids from the hand in which it was carried. While this "drying" may seem like a relatively minor transformation for us today, it had profound gender implications in a culture in which humoral theory was still popular, and in which women were defined as being more "watery" than men.

Theorists like Hollander and de Certeau can thus help us to imagine how clothing might work to materialize gender identity. Nevertheless, it is worth acknowledging that other theorists reject this notion entirely. As I noted above, Butler claims that even "[t]hough the publication of *Gender Trouble* coincided with a number of publications that did assert that 'clothes make the woman,' I never did think that gender was like clothes, or that clothes make the woman." She clarifies her position by explaining that one does not "put on" gender as if it were clothing or "a mask or persona"; there is "no 'one' who precedes that 'putting on,' who is something other than gender from the start." Instead, the "miming," or "impersonating" that Butler speaks of "precede[s] and form[s] the one, operating as its formative precondition rather than its dispensable artifice." If gender is performative, it is not necessarily a performance that individuals are in control of, and gender is certainly not put on or taken off at will. Butler's observations here about the fantasies of unlimited agency that often accompany the "clothes make the woman/man" argument are trenchant. She is certainly correct to stress that the process of assuming a gender is not voluntaristic: as she puts it, "the practice by which gendering occurs, the embodying of norms, is a compulsory practice, a forcible production, but not for that reason fully determining."[68]

Literary critics and historians working on the early modern period would do well to consider Butler's point. It is often assumed that during the Renaissance, the influence of humoral theory and the structural homology between male and female bodies meant that masculinity and femininity were fluid, or that they could be easily altered and transformed. This is true not only with regard to dress, but even with regard to the body itself. Thomas Laqueur, for instance, says that the early modern "body could move *easily* from one [gendered] category to the next" and that "the body with its one elastic sex was *far freer to express theatrical gender*."[69] While it is certainly true that sex and the body were conceptualized as being malleable in a way that they no longer are in the modern world, Laqueur's formulation here is, I think, misleading. It does not follow from his more general observations about the potential malleability of the male and female bodies to say that gender identity was "theatrical" or that it could be put on or taken off with "ease" (like costumes in the theater). Moreover, individuals were certainly not completely "free" to materialize their bodies or to perform their gender in any way they pleased. As I will argue in this book, there were important cultural apparatuses in place that worked to articulate ideals regarding both dress and the body and that attempted to insure that gender was "properly" materialized.

I would nevertheless stress that the voluntarist subject who "freely" performs his or her gender is by no means a necessary component of the clothes-make-the-woman/man argument. Decisions about dress are often actively compelled. This is not to say that individuals have no agency in the process, but rather that putting on a gender-specific type of clothing is an ideological act. It is often an unconscious act – an act that takes place "without anyone having made a decision" – but it is an ideological act all the same.[70] Another problem with Butler's critique is that she assumes that clothing is, and can only be, a "dispensable artifice." She fails to consider the possibility that it, or any other detachable part, might be constitutive. By contrast, the theoretical writings of Hollander and de Certeau help us to see how clothing might actively form or materialize gender. It is particularly ironic that Butler compares clothing to a "persona" in disavowing its power to fashion gender (she says that gender is not put on as if it were "a mask or persona") because the conceptual and etymological trajectory of the term "persona" is exactly the opposite of what we might expect, and of the way in which Butler dismissively uses it here. In *Keywords*, Raymond Williams points out that the word "persona" went through "a remarkable development, from its earliest meaning of a mask used by a player, through a character in a play and a part that a man acts, to a general word for a human being."[71] Thus, our sense of a "person" grows out of our sense of a "persona," and not vice versa. The "persona" or "mask" is a "formative precondition," to use Butler's terminology, not a "dispensable artifice."

By rejecting the clothes-make-the-woman/man argument altogether, Butler effectively dismisses the possibility that there might be a productive parallel between that position and her own. Such a parallel is precisely what I have been trying to suggest here. I believe that de Certeau's schema for thinking about the production of the body through its various auxiliary organs is ultimately quite similar to the one that Butler uses for thinking about the materialization of the sexed body. Both of these thinkers also develop an alternative to the notion of "modification" that underlies so many theories of identity formation. As Haraway suggests, the typical feminist narrative of gender formation stipulates that a person begins with essential biological characteristics that are then *modified* by culture as the individual develops. In rethinking sex and the body, Butler provides an alternate way of viewing this process: she insists that the "sexed" body is not simply "modified" by culture, but rather that it is brought into being (or "materialized") in the process of being formed by culture.

The concept of modification has also been used to understand how clothing and other prosthetic attachments might transform the body. Marshall McLuhan, for example, contends in his *Understanding Media: The Extensions of Man* that the physical body is "perpetually modified" by its various technological extensions. He writes:

[a]ny invention or technology is an extension . . . of our physical bodies, and such extension also demands new ratios or new equilibriums among the other organs and extensions of the body . . . Physiologically, man in his normal use of technology (or his variously extended body) is perpetually modified by it.[72]

If this is the usual way of understanding the relationship between individuals and their prosthetic "extensions," the passage from de Certeau cited above provides an alternative vision. He states that physical bodies are not simply "modified" by their various extensions and thereby made to conform to "social codes"; instead, as he puts it, *"they become bodies only by conforming to these codes."* In other words, "orthopedic and orthopractic instrument[s]" are not incorporated into a pre-existing "natural" body (thereby altering it and making it conform to social norms), rather, it is through the process of modification that the body (and, for that matter, the social norms themselves) comes into being.

In the end, we might therefore say that the relationship between sex and gender in Butler is analogous to the relationship between the body and its auxiliary organs in de Certeau. Moreover, both of these theorists argue that these processes are governed by a mechanism of materialization. Following them, I will use the language of "materialization" throughout this study. In part, this is to suggest that when, for example, a handkerchief is added to the hand, or when the hair of the head is cut short or allowed to grow long, the gendered body is quite literally reformed or reconstituted.

If the primary theoretical engagement of this book is thus with feminism and the sex/gender debate, I also draw heavily upon new forms of histori-ography. Historians have increasingly come to believe that we should not, as Virginia Woolf once warned, "take it for granted that life exists more fully in what is commonly thought big than in what is commonly thought small."[73] Over the past three decades, there have been a number of important historical studies that have examined the minutiae of " everyday life" in earlier epochs, including Philippe Ariès' *History of Private Life*, Fernand Braudel's *Structures of Everyday Life*, Daniel Roche's *A History of Everyday Things*, and *Renaissance Culture and the Everyday*.[74] This research is indebted to the ground-breaking work of Henri Lefebvre and Norbert Elias.[75] The assump-tion behind this work is that exploring the particulars of people's quotidian existence can reveal important information about society. As Braudel puts it, "[t]he ways people eat, dress, or lodge at the different levels of society are never a matter of indifference."[76]

I would add that examining the details of everyday life in previous eras is also a useful way of analyzing the workings of ideology. This is, in effect, an historically inflected version of one of Michel Foucault's central insights since he contends that the "minute details" of dress and bearing can encode an entire "micro-physics of power." In *Discipline and Punish*, for instance, Foucault charts the way in which the modern disciplinary regime was instituted through seemingly innocuous things such as the archi-tectural layout of a prison or a guide to posture. According to Foucault, these "meticulous, often minute, techniques" were a means of "defin[ing] . . . a certain mode of detailed political investment in the body."[77] These observations are relevant to my project because they suggest that a "small" item like a handkerchief or beard can do serious ideological work.[78] We might, however, refine Foucault's formulation and say that these "small" items do not perform their cultural work *despite* their size, but rather *because of* it. In other words, these parts often have a powerful ideological impact *precisely because* they are commonly thought to be "small" or "superfluous." As a result, they slide beneath the radar of con-scious consideration or concern. Pierre Bourdieu makes a comparable point in *Outline for a Theory of Practice* when he claims that the "trick" of ideology lies "in the way it exhorts the essential while seeming to demand the insignifi-cant." Thus, for Bourdieu, minor "details of dress, bearing, physical and verbal manners" are "the most visible and at the same time the best-hidden (because most 'natural') manifestation[s] of submission to the established order."[79]

Fernand Braudel similarly notes the ideological work performed by the seemingly trivial details of dress and bearing in his *Afterthoughts on*

Material Civilization and Capitalism (which is a precursor for his *Structures of Everyday Life*). Braudel is interested in

those aspects of life that control us without our even being aware of them: habit or better yet, routine – those thousands of acts that flower and reach fruition without anyone having made a decision, acts of which we are not even fully aware. I think mankind is more than waist-deep in daily routine. Countless inherited acts, accumulated pell-mell and repeated time after time to this very day, become habits that help us live, imprison us, and make decisions for us throughout our lives.[80]

Braudel brilliantly captures the way in which people can be interpellated by the "thousands of acts that flower and reach fruition without anyone having made a decision." Not surprisingly, his account here closely parallels Louis Althusser's account of being hailed by ideology, at least insofar as the "acts" are said to take hold at the level of the pre-reflective unconscious, and insofar as they come to define the "lived relations" between an individual and society.[81] In what follows, I will concentrate on the "acts" or "habits" that were part of people's everyday lives in early modern England – carrying a handkerchief, putting on or taking off a codpiece, growing or cutting the hair on the face or head – and will argue that these "acts" or "habits" played a crucial role in the ideological construction of masculinity and femininity.

Throughout this book, I refer to beards, hair, codpieces and handkerchiefs as "prostheses."[82] I have decided to use this term primarily because it helps to highlight the fact that these items are both integral to the subject's sense of identity or self, and at the same time resolutely detachable or "auxiliary."

The prosthesis is a classic post-structural item that does not fit easily into the binary rubrics that structure much of our thinking about identity formation and subjectivity: it is neither clearly nature or culture, essential or constructed, body or artifact, self or other, inside or outside. As Allon White puts it, the prosthesis "occup[ies] and occlude[s] a disturbing middle ground, disrupting the clear mediation of subject and object. Ontologically unstable, [it] can be definitively claimed by neither the body nor by the world." The prosthesis is, he continues, "marked by a uniqueness, a 'thingy-ness' which makes each *more than object*, unassimilable either to other objects or to the body itself . . . [It is n]either fully 'out there' nor fully 'in here'."[83]

Given the uncanny nature of the prosthesis, it is hardly surprising to find that there are two Derridian concepts that serve as analogs for it. The first is the *supplément*.[84] This is Derrida's term for an originary or constitutive addition: that is to say, an *addition* which is also a *replacement* (in that it compensates for a lack in the thing to which it is added). One oft-cited example is the "supplement" for a dictionary, but the prosthesis is equally apt. Moreover, clothing – as described by Hollander and de Certeau – might also be described in this way.[85] It is, on the one hand, a *mere* addition, and yet it is also a *necessary* addition (or an *integral* part of the whole) since it reconstitutes what the whole is. It is also worth emphasizing that this point about the prostheses is a correlative of the point I made earlier about the ideas of modification and materialization: the prosthesis is not a simple form of modification since it reconstitutes the entity to which it is added. As a result, it makes more sense to see it as a materialization of that entity – one that quite literally brings it into being.

The Derridian notion of the *supplément* is conceptualized almost entirely in terms of addition: it is something-to-be-added. The prosthesis, however, can also be imagined in the inverse sense: it can be seen as a detachable part, or something-to-be-subtracted. When seen from this perspective, the pros-thesis might be compared to the Derridian *parergon*.[86] The *parergon* is the term Derrida uses to describe things such as the frame of a picture, the clothes on a statue, or the colonnades of a palace. Beards and the hair of the head could easily be added to this list. These are detachable parts that are integral and yet also alienable: they are "a hybrid of outside and inside, but a hybrid which is not a mixture of or a half-measure. [They are] an outside which is called to the inside of the inside *in order to constitute it as an inside*."[87] Finally, the term that Freud applies to prosthetic items – "auxiliary organs" – is also quite apt in that it encodes these contradictory relations. On the one hand, describing these items as "organs" implies that they are integral parts of the body and self – parts which serve a function vital to the life of the individual. But on the other, to say that they are "auxiliary" is to suggest that they are detachable, ancillary, even dispensable.

I will therefore be using terms like "prosthesis" and "auxiliary organ" to refer to the items under scrutiny here in order to foreground their liminality. There is, nevertheless, a tendency to reassimilate these parts into the traditional categories and see them as either simply parts of the body or objects; as nature or culture. There is a similar tendency regarding false limbs or medical prostheses: they are often considered to be either simply objects or parts of the body – either autonomous entities or integral parts of the self. Take the *OED*'s definition of the "prosthesis" as an example. It says that the prosthesis is "an artificial replacement for a part of the body."[88] While this may at first glance seem both clear and accurate, there are some problems with it that become apparent if we examine the issue further. First, in order to say that the prosthesis is a "replacement for a part of the body," we must assume that we know what is properly "a part of the body" and what is not.[89] Indeed, we must assume that there is such a thing as "the" body in the first place.[90] None of this is as self-evident as it might at first seem. For example, although the hair of the head is generally considered to be "a part of the body," it is sometimes not present – it can be removed through cutting or shaving, or through some "natural" process like male pattern baldness or *alopecia areata*. If the hair is not there, it cannot really be considered a part of the body. Similar difficulties arise with regard to the idea of the "prosthesis." For example, should wigs, false beards, or merkins be called "prostheses"? In order for the answer to this question to be "yes," we would have to assume, first, that hair is indeed part of the body and, second, that the "natural" hair is missing, for it would not really make sense to call these things "replacement[s]" if the "natural" hair were not there to start with, or if it still was there and the "prosthesis" was simply worn on top of it.

The conceptual problems with the *OED*'s vision of the prosthesis become even more evident if we look at its definition of "prosthetics." This is defined as "the part of surgery which consists in supplying deficiencies." The assumptions underlying this definition follow from, and reinforce, those of the earlier definition. Once we assume that there is such a thing as "the" body, then bodies that do not conform to this model can be labeled "deficient." I would argue, by contrast, that in reality there is no such thing as "the body," only *bodies* in their seemingly endless morphological variety. By extension, there is no such thing as a "whole" body or a "deficient" body. When we speak of "the body," we are in fact speaking of a normative social ideal which must be actively produced. In other words, at any particular historical moment or in any particular culture, specific features or a certain kind of morphological variation are idealized and held up for imitation and materialization. This idealized somatic form eventually comes to be seen as "the body." It is then in reference to this corporeal norm that actual bodies are adjudged to be either "whole" or "deficient."

By questioning the concept of "the" body and the idea that there is a clear cut distinction between the body and its attachments, I hope to suggest that this somatic schema is not only idealized, but also potentially pernicious. The same cultural logic that says that the prosthesis "corrects" a "deficiency" also says that people born with only one arm or leg, for instance, are in some way "incomplete." Indeed, one of the scholarly contributions of disability studies has been to elucidate the ways in which certain corporeal variations have been pathologized.[91] It should be said, moreover, that balding men – and even women as a group – have at times been figured as somehow incomplete or "lacking." It is therefore partially in order to counteract these problems that I have decided to adopt a more free-ranging definition of "the body" and a more free-ranging definition of the term "prosthesis." Once the notion of "the body" is called into question, the notion of "prosthesis" must change accordingly. In fact, we might use this term to refer to any detachable part that is part of the physical portrait, including things like handkerchiefs, codpieces, beards and hair. I don't mean to downplay the specific problems encountered by those with disabilities, but it is crucial that we recognize that we are differently able and are all in some sense prosthetic gods. Rethinking our notion of "prosthesis" will help us to see this, but it is possible even if we continue to use the *OED*'s definition. Although everyday items such as shoes are not normally thought of as prostheses, they might well be viewed as such since they are "an artificial replacement for a part of the body": namely, the calluses that would otherwise form on the bottom of the feet. This is, of course, still slightly problematic in that it assumes that calluses themselves are "part of the body," but it nevertheless may help us to recognize the extent to which we all are reliant upon our own prostheses.

The *OED*'s definition of the term "prosthesis" is typical of modern discourses about "auxiliary organs" in that it tries to assimilate this item into a conceptual framework where the body and the outside world are imagined to be distinct and diametrically opposed entities or spaces. Indeed, given this framework, it is hardly surprising to find that most modern representations of the prosthesis can be put into one of two antithetical camps: first, there are those that figure the prosthesis as an object that stands apart from the body and is simply attached to it, and second, there are those that view the prosthesis as an entity that is completely absorbed or assimilated into the body.

In the first of these modern fantasies, the auxiliary organ stubbornly is imagined to resist any kind of incorporization and interiorization. Often, the prosthesis is simply considered a superfluous object that is completely independent from the individual who wears it. In its most extreme form, this fantasy may even entail the prosthesis "taking over" the subject and objectifying or dehumanizing them in the process. The "Borg" from the television series *Star Trek* and the humans cocooned in virtual-reality pods in the machine-dominated world of *The Matrix* are two recent pop-cultural examples of this cultural fantasy, but the conception can, like its counterpart, be traced back at least as far as the nineteenth century. Edgar Allen Poe's "The Man that Was All Used Up" (1839) is a narrative that is powerfully shaped by this fantasy/anxiety.[92] In Poe's tale, the central character is a soldier who has lost many parts of his body in battle and is therefore composed almost entirely of prostheses: he has artificial limbs and eyes, a false shoulder, tongue, scalp, and palate. Poe's narrative subtly implies that although the General's body has been "repaired," he has been reduced to an object or machine in the process. The grammatical shift in the title hints at the General's dehumanization: rather than "The Man *who* Was All Used Up," the story and the protagonist himself are known as "The Man *that* Was All Used Up." In addition, this objectification brings about a correspondent loss of individuality or identity. This is perhaps most powerfully registered by the General's name: Brevet Brigadier General A. B. C. John Smith. It implies that the General has become just that, "general" or nondescript. Indeed, his proper name is simply the generic "John Smith." Although the titles attached to his name (such as "Brevet," "Brigadier," and "General") endow him with the appearance of a distinct personality, the story suggests that if we begin to unravel the name (and the correspondent person), there is ultimately no "there" there.[93] Prostheses have erased the supposedly "real" body and self.

If one modern fantasy of the prosthesis is thus that it is an object that is added onto the body but not really incorporated into it, we need to recognize that there is another equally powerful (if virtually antithetical) way of representing this item. Prostheses are also often depicted as entities that are completely and unproblematically absorbed into the bodies of their wearers, and that simply become a part of the individual. According to Erin O'Connor's research on the history of prosthetics, this particular cultural fantasy has its roots in the Victorian period. She claims that at the very moment that industrialization (and in America, the Civil War) was increasingly mutilating workers' bodies, a recuperative fantasy was constructed about technology's ability to repair and recreate the body.[94] Indeed, A. A. Mark's *Treatise on Artificial Limbs* claims that prostheses allow Victorian limb-makers to rebuild amputees and make "new men" of them, "remov[ing] . . . disabilities for all practical purposes." As Marks puts it, "What is done can be done again."[95] Freud's initial characterization in *Civilization and its Discontents* is similarly idealized: he claims that "when [man] puts on all of his auxiliary organs, he is truly magnificent." More recently, the "bionic" man from the television program *The Six Million Dollar Man* was presented along similar lines. The opening segment of the show – which is about an astronaut whose body has been severely damaged in an accident – includes the lines: "We have the technology. We can rebuild him." It is also worth noting that this fantasy often appears in contemporary theoretical writing on "prostheses" and on "cyborgs" where various technological or prosthetic extensions are imagined to be magnificent expansions of the self.[96] Donna Haraway's "Cyborg Manifesto" adopts this fantasy in order to imagine the gender trouble that prostheses might generate, though it does so in what I take to be a subtly ironic way.[97]

In the end, these two modern fantasies about our auxiliary organs are inverted versions of one another: in the first, the prosthesis remains entirely distinct from the individual, and may even begin to take over the person's sense of identity, whereas in the second, the prosthesis is completely absorbed into the individual and is itself taken over in the process. It should also be noted that in these different scenarios, the prosthesis is either figured as something that is completely alien to an individual's identity or sense of self (as in the Poe story) or as a simple part of that self (as in Freud's initial characterization). Indeed, the two fantasies are mapped onto one another so that to the extent that the prosthesis remains outside the body, it also remains outside the self (or even takes the self over), and to the extent that it is absorbed into the body, it becomes part of the self. Furthermore, the crucial thing to note is that in *both* of these cultural fantasies, the notion of "the body" as distinct from "the object" remains firmly in place, as does the concept of the stable "self" as distinct from the outside world.

It should by now be clear that neither of these cultural fantasies is entirely adequate. Interestingly, Freud seems to draw on *both* of them in the passage from *Civilization and its Discontents*. Freud describes the "auxiliary organs" as alternately subject and object. At first, he posits a melding of man and machine that echoes the discourse of nineteenth-century limb-makers: he writes "Man has. . .become a kind of prosthetic god. When he puts on all his auxiliary organs, he is truly magnificent." Having said this, however, Freud retreats, like Poe, to the position that prostheses are exterior and not "really" part of the body or the individual: as he puts it, "Man's" auxiliary organs have not "grown onto him," they "still give him much trouble at times."

It is important to hold on to this complexity, not only for theoretical reasons, but also for more practical ones. When people who have false limbs speak about them, they often use similarly multivalent strategies to describe them. Indeed, the editors of the volume *Artificial Parts, Practical Lives: Modern Histories of Prosthetics* insist that the "material and social tales of prosthetics provide a[n] . . . intimate and compelling history of embodied technology."[98] More specifically, people often describe their prostheses as both body and object, self and other. For example, one man wrote to the limb-maker A. A. Marks in the nineteenth century saying, "My leg is my best friend; it is what I love the most, and without it my life would be miserable."[99] In this single sentence, the prosthesis is envisaged as part of the subject ("my leg"), an object ("what"), and finally as a subject in its own right ("my best friend").[100]

This multivalence seems to derive in part from the peculiar status of the items themselves. Although prostheses are in a sense objects that can be removed from the body, they also shape or materialize the body and self in important ways. To understand how this works, we first need to recognize that when a limb is lost, the amputee usually develops what is known in the medical community as a "phantom limb" – a kind of spectral memorialization of the lost part.[101] A patient described by Oliver Sacks in one of his case studies explains his "phantom limb" as follows:

There's this thing, this ghost foot, which sometimes hurts like hell . . . This is worst at night, or with the prosthesis off . . . It goes away, when I strap the prosthesis on and walk. I still feel the leg then, vividly, but it's a good phantom, different – it animates the prosthesis, and allows me to walk.[102]

As this testimony makes clear, the prosthesis eventually fuses with the phantom and is "animated" by it, becoming, in effect, part of the wearer: "I have become so accustomed to [my false leg]," another patient explains, "that *it has become a part of me*."[103] Similarly, a man with two artificial legs wrote to A. A. Marks saying "your labors have restored me to *my feet*, and I am, for all practical purposes, *myself* again."[104] As part of the individual, the artificial limb may even become "sentient": according to William James, a prosthetic foot can "sympathize with the foot which remains. If one is cold, the other feels cold. One man writes that whenever he walks through puddles and wets his sound foot, his lost foot feels wet too."[105]

If the prosthesis is thus a multivalent item that slides back and forth between many of the categories that we use to think about subjectivity, then this will perhaps explain my desire to use this term to refer to the items under scrutiny in this study. Throughout, I endeavor to hold on to the conceptual tensions that surround "prosthetic" parts like handkerchiefs, codpieces, beards, and hair, and resist seeing them as either simply superfluous objects or as things that are unproblematically assimilated into the body and self. This is not an easy task. Indeed, scholars who write about clothes and identity in early modern England often end up falling into one of the two modern "fantasies" that I have outlined with regard to the prosthesis. That is to say, they tend to view early modern clothing as if it were either simply an integral part of the subject or a dispensable object. For example, Stephen Greenblatt insists, as I noted earlier, that during the Renaissance "it is often as if identity resided in clothing," but at another point, he argues that identity also "paradoxically" came from the "inward realm beyond costumes." He writes, "the belief in a complex inward realm beyond costumes and status is a striking inversion of the clothes cult."[106] Greenblatt titles this part of his discussion "The Paradoxes of [early modern] Identity" and thus suggests that these two modes of subject formation are to some extent incompatible or mutually exclusive. So, within this formulation, identity is either produced through clothes from the outside and impressed onto the individual, or it is generated from the inside in a way that is entirely independent of those "outside" influences.

Not all modern critics speak of identity in this "paradoxical" way. Ann Rosalind Jones and Peter Stallybrass circumvent the problem in *Renaissance Clothing and the Materials of Memory* by claiming that clothes had the power to "deeply make" the individual and that they "permeate[d] the wearer fashioning him or her within."[107] When viewed in this way, "the clothes cult" and interiority need not be seen as completely antithetical.

The organizational structure of this book is meant to emphasize the continuity between interior and exterior, as between nature and culture, sex and gender. I begin with the chapters on cultural artifacts (handkerchiefs and codpieces) and move on to items that are part of the body (beards and hair). In the process, I hope to demonstrate that during the Renaissance all of these prosthetic parts were much more similar than we might expect today.

The first chapter focuses on the handkerchief, a cultural artifact that was popularized in England in the fifteenth century, and that eventually became a means of negotiating various kinds of social interaction. In this chapter I build on the theoretical insights of Norbert Elias by claiming that the handkerchief not only helped to form class distinctions (through the system of manners), but that it helped to produce gendered distinctions as well. Put simply, this item helped to construct the "female" form by absorbing sweat and other bodily fluids from women's hands (where it was usually carried). This relatively minor change must be understood in relation to humoral theories of femininity, which insisted upon women's "watery" nature. It is within this context that I propose to read Shakespeare's *Othello*. The play and its title character become obsessed not only with the handkerchief, but with Desdemona's "sweaty" palm. Indeed, this reading suggests that the hand and handkerchief form a single symbolic unit. Shakespeare's play thus dramatizes the ideological production of the female body as a "leaky vessel" and suggests the role the handkerchief played in this process. Although my focus throughout this chapter is therefore on how the handkerchief might have helped to rearticulate or reinforce normative ideals about femininity and the female body, I want to stress that the item itself was manifestly prosthetic and transferable, and as a result, the ideals produced through it were necessarily open to rearticulation. While this is in fact true of all the items under consideration in this book, it is particularly crucial to point out here because it allows for the possibility of women's resistance – both collectively and individually – to normative gender formations.

Chapter 2 examines one of the most striking accessories of dress in early modern England: the codpiece. When this masculine appendage was first introduced in the early fifteenth century, it was a bag-like triangular frontispiece that covered the genital area of men's hose or breeches, but over the course of the next two centuries, it also came to take the form of an ornate – sometimes even jewel-encrusted – phallic object. This conspicuous accessory was the subject of much discussion and debate during the Renaissance. Even after it went out of fashion at the end of the sixteenth century, it did not completely disappear from the cultural imaginary: indeed, Henry VIII's codpiece was on display in the Tower of London throughout much of the seventeenth and early eighteenth centuries, attracting attention and comments. The main argument of the chapter is that codpieces, like handkerchiefs, helped to constitute gender identity. Indeed, writers from the period sometimes claimed that wearing a codpiece essentially made an individual into a man. But in addition, I want to suggest that the different physical manifestations of the codpiece helped to constitute different modes, or ideologies, of masculinity. Thus, the two forms of the codpiece worked to figure the male genitalia as distinctly phallic or distinctly scrotal, and hence worked to emphasize either primarily sexuality (i.e. penetration) or reproduction. At the same time, however, the detachability of this object added yet another layer of complexity to the situation. It meant, most crucially, that these ideologies were necessarily subject to dislocation, appropriation, change, and rearticulation.

The third chapter marks a shift from cultural artifacts to malleable or prosthetic parts of the body. It analyzes the role that facial hair played in constituting gender and builds upon Judith Butler's insights in *Bodies that Matter* by suggesting that the sexual differences that "mattered" in early modern England were not the same as those that "matter" today. The centrality of the beard in English Renaissance culture is powerfully demonstrated by evidence from a whole range of sources: portraiture, anatomy and physiognomy books, tracts on gender, religious debates, and theatrical texts and practices. But if facial hair ultimately provided a means of constructing differences between men and women, it also provided a means of constructing differences between men and boys. Thus, a second contention of this chapter is that boys were quite literally a different gender from men during this period. Finally, we need to bear in mind that if facial hair thus served as an important means of materializing masculinity, it was also crucially malleable and prosthetic. As a result, both masculinity and the beard itself had to be constantly made (to) matter.

Finally, chapter 4 looks at the hair of the head, and argues that it too was an essential means of materializing both masculinity and femininity during the Renaissance. As with beards, there is an astonishing amount of early modern writing on the subject, including sermons, pamphlets, and even full-length books that are entirely devoted to discussing hair and hair fashions. What is most striking about this tonsorial discourse (apart from the fact that many of the books are hundreds of pages long) is the extent to which the hair of the head is imagined to be gendered. Indeed, writers from the Renaissance often claimed that long hair is a "natural" characteristic of women and short hair a "natural" characteristic of men. But if hair thus played a crucial role in helping to form masculinity and femininity, I argue that its role in this process was interestingly mediated by the revolutionary politics of the period. Political differences between the Roundheads and Cavaliers were also constructed through hair length. Parliamentarians were called "roundheads" on account of their closely trimmed locks. They were, in turn, contrasted with Cavaliers who were known for their flowing tresses. The political discourses and practices regarding hair sometimes reinforced gendered norms (as when Roundheads figured themselves as masculine and Cavaliers as feminine) and at other times undermined them (as when Cavaliers claimed that women and men could both have long hair, but that women must bind their hair and men must not).

If most of the book is synchronic in its focus and examines aspects of the early modern sex/gender system that challenge modern preconceptions, the conclusion is more diachronic. It sets out to address the question of how prosthetic elements of the physical portrait came to be somewhat deemphasized during the course of the seventeenth century. The chapter examines the rise of the notion of "the individual" as it was articulated in the works of Hobbes and Descartes, and argues that "the individual" increasingly came to be conceptualized as an entity that was quite literally in-dividual (in the sense of indivisible). In other words, it had no prosthetic or detachable parts. This notion of the individual was also spurred by developments in science, especially by the burgeoning popularity of the concept of the atom. As we shall see, the indivisible atom often served as an analog for the individual human being.

1   That Shakespearean rag: handkerchiefs and femininity

I begin with a story from early modern England about a handkerchief. It is a tale of intrigue and jealousy involving a man anxious about a woman's purity and some impertinent trifling. The plot is quite simple. First, one of the two male protagonists steals the handkerchief from the principal female character. Then, when the second man eventually sees the woman's napkin in the hands of his rival (and even touching his face), he becomes enraged and initiates a struggle that ends in a violent confrontation. While this story may sound familiar, it is not the one told by William Shakespeare. Shakespeare's version would not be written for another forty years. Instead, it is Sir Thomas Randolph's account of an incident that occurred at Hampton Court in 1565, involving Queen Elizabeth and two of her most influential courtiers at the time, Leicester and Norfolk.

One day in March of 1565, the Queen watched as her favorites played tennis for her amusement. The weather was warm and Leicester had apparently become "hot" and was "sweating." During a break from the action the two men came over to the area where the Queen was sitting, and Leicester suddenly snatched "the Queen's napkin out of her hand and wiped his face" with it. When Norfolk realized what had transpired, he was incensed. He "said that [Leicester] was too saucy" and "swore that he would lay his racket upon his face." Following this threat, there "rose great trouble" and blows eventually ensued. In the end, "the Queen [was] offended sore with the Duke" for his behavior.[1]

In order to better understand this incident, there are two things that we need to bear in mind. First of all, the conflict takes place relatively early in Elizabeth's reign, and Leicester was, at the time, actively vying for the Queen's hand – and perhaps even her handkerchiefs – despite Norfolk's opposition. In fact, only a year before the affair at Hampton Court, Leicester had a portrait of himself painted (figure 3) in which he gently caresses a handkerchief tucked away in his purse. In a recent article on the portrait, the art historian Jacob Voorthuis suggests that this napkin may well have been a token of affection from the Queen herself.[2] This is certainly a possibility, given that the Queen was in the habit of both giving and receiving

Figure 3. Unknown artist, *Robert Dudley, 1st Earl of Leicester* (*c.* 1564).

handkerchiefs as gifts. Inventories indicate that on New Year's Eve of 1561–2, for example, Elizabeth was given seventy-two handkerchiefs from various "Ladyes" and "Gentlewomen" of the court: a "Lady *Lane*," for instance, gave her "sixe handkercheves, four of them black silk and gold and two red silk" and "Mysteris *Astley*, Chief Gentlewoman of the Pryvy Chamber" provided another "twelve handkercheves edged with gold and silver."[3]

If these examples show that handkerchiefs often served as gifts in Elizabeth's court, they also suggest that she usually exchanged them *with women*. This may have been to avoid the appearance of impropriety since handkerchiefs were often used as tokens of affection and even signs of matrimonial contract, as Diana O'Hara has shown in her article "The Language of Tokens and the Making of Marriage."[4] When seen from this perspective, the Queen's gift of a handkerchief to Leicester takes on added significance. Moreover, we should also note that Leicester's portrait of himself with Elizabeth's handkerchief is virtually identical (in terms of spatial composition) to a portrait Norfolk had painted of himself in the previous year, 1563. In Norfolk's portrait (figure 4), he too fingers a handkerchief in his purse, and his body is posed in almost the same position as Leicester's.

The second thing that we need to bear in mind in relation to the incident at Hampton Court is that the handkerchief itself was a relatively new cultural artifact, and therefore the conflict may well have been fueled by the fact that the object's social connotations and the rules governing its use were still in process of being defined. Fashion historians often point out that the handkerchief was an "invention" of the Renaissance. While this is probably something of an overstatement (in that it implies that items like this were completely unknown in the middle ages), it is certainly true that handkerchiefs became much more widespread in England during the course of the fifteenth and sixteenth centuries, reaching a peak during the reign of Elizabeth. The evidence from the *OED* provides some validation of this genesis insofar as it indicates that the term "hand-kercher" was first used in print during the 1530s. As the etymology "hand" + "kerchief" suggests, the Renaissance handkerchief was seen as a variation of the Medieval "kerchief" specifically intended for the "hand." Although we now tend to associate this item with other parts of the body (like the nose and the eyes), the link between the handkerchief and hand was much stronger during the early modern period. According to the fashion historian Katherine Morris Lester, "The handkerchief, which in earlier times was carried in the hand, today seeks the seclusion of purse or pocket."[5] This difference can be explained, in part, by the fact that handkerchiefs were often quite decorative and used as fashionable accessories. M. Braun-Ronsdorf's *The History of the Handkerchief* explains that these items were at times even scented with perfumes and "were carried in the hand in the most conspicuous manner possible . . . like a fragrant fan."[6]

Stowe's *Chronicle* provides a detailed description of the "handkerchiefs" popular in England in the sixteenth and seventeenth centuries:

Figure 4. Hans Eworth, *Thomas Howard, 4th Duke of Norfolk* (1563).

[they were] about three or four inches square wrought round about, with a button or tassel at each corner, and a little one in the middle, with silke and threed; the best edged with a small gold, lace, or twist, which being doubled up in foure crosse foldes, so as the middle might be seen . . . Some cost six pence apiece, some twelve pence, and the richest sixteen pence.[7]

An item fitting this description appears in the seventeenth-century portrait of the Countess of Arundel. Many napkins from the period were, however, of an even larger format. In fact, one surviving handkerchief measures 16 ins (40 cm) by 15 ins (38 cm) and is embroidered with a border of flowers and the initials "P. E."

I begin with this story about Elizabeth and her courtiers as a means of initiating a discussion about handkerchiefs in early modern England, and in particular the role they played in the formation of gender identity. My work here draws heavily upon the research of Norbert Elias, for he has brilliantly demonstrated how everyday objects like handkerchiefs can be linked to larger social and cultural processes. In fact, Elias mentions the handkerchief in his *History of Manners* and argues that the popularization of this object and others like it (the fork, separate bowls for eating, etc.) played an important role in what he calls "the civilizing process": in other words, in the process of forming new rules of etiquette and new types of social interaction.[8] But "concessions of *politeness*" are always, as Pierre Bourdieu would point out, "*political* concessions," and as such, they have broader ideological ramifications.[9] Indeed, this point is implicit in Elias's argument itself, for he ultimately suggests that the utensils of polite society helped to establish distinctions between different social groups and map out differences of social status. When seen from this perspective, we might say that the handkerchief aided in the production of a new – more "civilized" – body, since it created a somatic form purified of "base" fluids like sweat and snot.[10]

But if Elias has given us an incisive analysis of how a specifically early modern form of status was materialized through the development of a new system of manners and through new cultural artifacts like the handkerchief, I want to consider the possibility that these processes might also have had a gendered dimension as well. Scholars doing research on Renaissance handkerchiefs have been quite attentive to the ways in which gender factored into the equation. The art historian Stephanie Dickey, for example, claims that "in history painting, theater, and portraiture" from the period, "the handkerchief remains almost exclusively a female attribute."[11] Similarly, Juana Green points out that many Elizabethan, Jacobean, and Carolinian paintings "depict noble and gentry women holding large lace-edged handkerchiefs."[12]

What I want to do in this chapter is to combine these two approaches, and to explore the way in which the handkerchief helped to produce notions of femininity and the female body. It is worth saying, however, that because of the handkerchief's prosthetic nature, it could never be linked exclusively to women or to femininity. As a matter of fact, we have already seen two instances where napkins were carried by men as opposed to women. Nevertheless, if the handkerchief was, as Dickey suggests, usually *represented* in "history paintings," "theater," and "portraiture" as an accessory used exclusively by women, then it becomes apparent that these representations were performing the ideological work of establishing a link between the object and femininity. In other words, they were working to code handkerchiefs as "female attribute[s]."

The link between the handkerchief and femininity functioned not only on a semiotic register, but also on a more material one. Indeed, we might say that the handkerchief was a kind of prosthesis since it was to some extent "incorporated" into the (female) body, and, in the process, reformed the physical portrait. Although the "drying" that it performed by absorbing sweat and other bodily fluids may seem like a relatively minor change, it had important implications in a culture where humoral theory was popular, and where women were often figured as being more "watery" than men. Gail Paster has brilliantly demonstrated the pervasiveness of the trope of women as "leaky vessels" during the Renaissance, noting that "medical texts, iconography, and proverbs of oral culture" all portray women as being more "watery" than men.[13] These descriptions of women's humoral "nature" are not neutral; they have encoded within them pejorative ideas about women's character and behavior. According to Paster, the images of "leaky" women "reproduce a virtual symptomatology of woman, which insists on the female body's moisture, secretions, and productions as shameful tokens of uncontrol" (52). Moreover, as a result of their inherent uncontrolability, women were seen to "threaten. . .the acquisitive goals of the family and its maintenance of status and power" (25).

The handkerchief was ultimately one of the ways in which this gender ideology was made manifest and reinforced. Insofar as the hanky was carried by women rather than men, it would have implied that they were more "watery" and that they needed a special accessory to absorb and control their bodily fluids. Thus, the item itself might be seen as a "disciplinary apparatus" (to use the term of Michel de Certeau) since it provides a means of keeping women's bodies "dry" and "within the [implicitly masculine] limits set by a norm."

My argument about the handkerchief's role in materializing gender identity is somewhat similar to the one made by Douglas Bruster in *Drama and the Market in the Age of Shakespeare*. Although Bruster does not focus explicitly on gender identity, he does maintain that new cultural artifacts like handkerchiefs participated in a process that he labels "the commercial inscription of identity" – this is the "culturally and historically determined process by which identity is constructed by being 'written' into or onto objects."[14] But if Bruster thus astutely examines how early modern identities were projected onto newly minted objects and how those articles might have been understood as extensions of the self, my own project differs from his in two important ways. The first is theoretical. Instead of thinking of identity as something which is pre-existent and which is projected onto an artifact, I prefer to think about the way in which identity is materialized or formed through the process of "projection." This is a correlative of the point I made at some length in my introduction. There I discussed how writers like de Certeau reject the notion of " modification" and instead suggest that identity and the body are brought into being in the process of prosthetic addition.

The second major difference is that whereas Bruster looks primarily at the ways in which personal identity was projected onto things, I will be examining how objects work to shape the identities that they help to construct. I don't mean to attribute some sort of magical agency to objects, but rather to suggest that the material form of these items mediates the types of identity that are brought into being through them. I therefore believe that we would do well to attend to how different objects (such as handkerchiefs, chains, or shoes) might materialize identity differently on account of their distinct physical forms and functions.

I have already begun to indicate some of the ways in which the material form of the handkerchief might have influenced the types of gender identity that were produced through it when I indicated that this item needs to be understood in its relationship to the hand, and that it needs to be understood in its role of absorbing and controlling bodily fluids. We can begin to get a sense of how this might work in practice if we return to Randolph's account of the incident at Hampton Court. First of all, the handkerchief in that story is clearly associated with Elizabeth's purity. Indeed, Norfolk's anger about Leicester's decision to wipe his sweat on it is, at least in part, a displaced reaction to Leicester's attempts to "soil" the Queen's virtue by forming a marital (or sexual) alliance with her. It is not particularly surprising to find that Norfolk was anxious about protecting Elizabeth from being "tainted" by Leicester's since the chastity of the Virgin Queen was a widespread cultural preoccupation. Nor, for that matter, is it particularly surprising to find that Elizabeth's handkerchief was the locus for Norfolk's anxieties. Handkerchiefs were, as I said earlier, well-known tokens of love. But more importantly, for my purposes, they were also a means of regulating the body's fluids and keeping it "pure."

Interestingly, Elizabeth often constructed her own purity in precisely these terms. The most notable example of this is the sieve portraits that she had painted of herself starting in about 1579 (figure 5). The sieve that Elizabeth holds in these images is a symbol of her virginity – an allusion to Petrarch's

Figure 5. Quentin Metsys the Younger, *Elizabeth I: 'The Sieve Portrait'* (*c*. 1583).

Triumph of Chastity where the Roman Vestal Virgin Tuccia proved her chastity by carrying water in a sieve without spilling a drop. The crucial point for my purposes is not simply that Elizabeth had herself represented as a "pure" virgin, but rather that her virginity was symbolically linked to her ability to control leakage. In other words, in these portraits Elizabeth's sexual control is figured through the Vestal Virgin's miraculous ability to control the flow of water from the sieve. When seen in this context, the Queen's handkerchief emerges as yet another instrument for materializing her body as a classical body (to use Bakhtin's terms) – for materializing it as an entity that is closed-off and under-control. Indeed, both the handkerchief in Randolph's account and the sieves in the portraits are associated with Elizabeth's purity, and in both cases that purity seems to be associated with a type of corporeal continence.

But if the handkerchief was an instrument of self-fashioning for Elizabeth and, more generally, an artifact that helped to materialize the patriarchal ideology figuring women as "leaky" vessels, its role in these processes was necessarily complicated by its prosthetic nature. Just as the handkerchief could move from hand to hand, so the ideology of incontinence was to some extent unstable. This meant, among other things, that it could (at least potentially) be transferred from one group to another. The incident at Hampton court beautifully illustrates this point since the handkerchief in Randolph's account migrates from Elizabeth's hand to Leicester's. Accordingly, the story complicates the gendered stereotypes of the day insofar as it is a man who is here described as a "leaky vessel." This latter shift can be explained in part by Leicester's status: the upstart courtier is figured as sweaty and out-of-control. In fact, Norfolk's comment that Leicester was "too saucy" implies both of these things – that he had been "impertinent" with a social superior and also that he was quite literally too leaky.[15] For Norfolk, Leicester's excessive perspiration ultimately demonstrates that he is an inappropriate partner for the Queen: it is a sign of both his excessive heat (his indecorous sexuality) and his inherent "baseness" (his "lowly" class status).

In the end, the events that took place at Hampton Court indicate how the handkerchief might have helped to contribute to the ideological figuration of women as "leaky vessels," but they also demonstrate the ideological instability that arises on account of the handkerchief's detachability.

At this point, I want to turn to another early modern story that revolves around a handkerchief and that treats this new cultural artifact in a similar manner. Although written later than Randolph's account and for a very different purpose, Shakespeare's *Othello* nevertheless has much in common with its predecessor. Not only does a handkerchief figure prominently, but in both instances this item is linked with the female protagonist's sexual continence, and more specifically with male anxiety about that continence.

Othello, however, is unique in that it provides a sustained and detailed representation of the handkerchief and its social functions. While there are many other works of literature from the period that include handkerchiefs, there are none in which the handkerchief takes center stage as it does in *Othello*.[16] Viewers and critics alike have long noted the importance of this prop in Shakespeare's play. In fact, Thomas Rhymer made a remark about its centrality at the end of the seventeenth century in one of the earliest extant commentaries on the text: he facetiously quipped that *Othello* should have been called *The Tragedy of the Handkerchief* because there was "so much ado, so much stress, so much passion and repetition about an Handker-chief!"[17] Over the last three decades there has been an increasing amount of critical writing about this accessory. The resurgence of interest in the napkin was initiated by Lynda Boose's groundbreaking article "Othello's Handker-chief,"[18] and includes more recent work by critics such as Harry Berger, Douglas Bruster, Natasha Korda, Karen Newman, Edward Snow, Andrew Sofer, and Peter Stallybrass.[19]

In what follows, I hope to contribute to this critical discussion in two primary ways. First, I want to put the play's treatment of the handkerchief in a broader social context, by offering a historical account of the handker-chief in early modern England and exploring the kinds of cultural work that this object would have performed at that time. Secondly, I want to suggest that the play's focus on the handkerchief might be productively understood in relation to its obsession with the *hand*. Although critics have done much to explain the symbolic resonance of the handkerchief, the fact that many of Iago's machinations also focus on hands – and especially on Desdemona's hand – has gone largely unremarked. In what follows, I will discuss the handkerchief and the hand in relation to one another because I believe that they are ultimately meant to form a single (though not indivisible) syntag-matic unit. In fact, Iago himself foregrounds the connection between these two parts when he asks Othello: "Have you seen a handkerchief spotted with strawberries *in your wife's hand*?" (3.3.439–40).[20]

Although the relationship between the handkerchief and the hand in *Othello* has remained largely unexamined, there has been a lot of more general research about the significance of hands in early modern English culture. This research has demonstrated, as Michael Neill puts it, that the hand had "a density of semiotic suggestiveness [during the Renaissance] that the modern hand has lost," and that "for Shakespeare and his contemporaries" this member was "a primary site of meaning. . .[and] the conduit for extraordinary energies."[21] Indeed, the hand was both an important site for the inscription of character (as Jonathan Goldberg has shown) and a means of figuring agency (as Katherine Rowe demonstrates).[22] I draw upon this work extensively, but at the same time I will be taking it in a slightly different direction for I will be analyzing how a new morphological form of the hand was produced in the sixteenth century with the popularization of the handkerchief, and, more importantly, exploring the complex gendering of that process.

From the very beginning of Shakespeare's *Othello*, Iago's schemes center on hands. For example, when Cassio and Desdemona meet for the first time in Cyprus, Iago notes to himself that Cassio "takes [Desdemona] by the palm" and gloats that "with as little a web as this will I ensnare as great a fly as Cassio" (2.1.168–9). He then comments upon Cassio's gesture of hand-kissing: "if such tricks as these strip you out of your lieutenantry, it had been better you had not kissed your three fingers so oft . . . Very good; well kissed! an excellent courtesy! 'tis so, indeed. Yet again your fingers to your lips? would they were clyster-pipes for your sake!" (171–6). In these asides, Iago reveals the strategy that he will use in the ensuing scenes: he will play on the ambiguities surrounding the conventions of courtesy and specifically with the ambiguities surrounding courtly gestures such as hand kissing and hand shaking. Moreover, in his final comment – where he imagines Cassio's as "clyster-pipes" (enema tubes) – he demonstrates how easily a courtly gesture can be transformed into something indecent.

In 1644, John Bulwer published his *Chirologia, or the Natural Language of the Hand*. This was a book that explained the significance of all sorts of hand rhetoric. Perhaps unsurprisingly, it also attempted to disavow the potential ambiguity involved with these sorts of everyday gestures. In Bulwer's section entitled "TO KISSE THE HAND," he writes that this is an "obsequious expression who would adore & give respect by the courtly solemnity of a salutation or valediction . . . There is no expression of the *Hand* more frequent in the formalities of civil conversation, and he is a novice in the Court of Nature, who doth not understand a *basiér de la main*."[23] The gesture that Bulwer describes here is slightly different from the one that Cassio performs in the play, but the crucial thing for my purposes is that these courtly gestures are the types of interaction that Iago will ultimately try to use to "prove" Desdemona's infidelity. Although Bulwer insists upon the transparency of these gestures, Iago's tactic is to take these customs of politeness and to bring out their erotic potentiality.

If this is the strategy that Iago eventually uses to persuade Othello, it is worth saying that he does not go to work immediately on his commanding officer; instead, he begins by trying to convince *Roderigo* of Desdemona's incontinence. Iago asks Roderigo "Didst thou not see her paddle with the palm of his [Cassio's] hand? Didst not mark that?" (2.1.245–6). When Roderigo claims that this gesture "was but courtesy," Iago counters that it was "[l]echery, by this hand; an index and obscure prologue to the history of lust and foul thoughts / They met so near with their lips that their breaths embraced together" (2.1.247–9). Iago describes Desdemona's gesture here as a "paddling" in order to give it an erotic overtone. The *OED* lists "To play or dabble idly or fondly with the fingers" as one of its definitions, and this is, in fact, the only way that Shakespeare uses the word in his writing, as when

Hamlet upbraids Gertrude: "And let him [the King] for a pair of reechie kisses, Or paddling your necke with his damn'd fingers, Make you to ravell all this matter out" (3.4.168–70). It is, moreover, significant that Iago uses the oath "by this hand" (which was common at the time). His statement thus takes on a second meaning, with the ambiguity of the phrase perhaps echoing the ambiguity of the gesture. In this particular instance the phrase can be understood to mean not only "lechery, I swear" but also "lechery, [enacted] by this [Desdemona's] hand." Moreover, in making this oath, Iago implicitly contrasts his own (supposedly) truthful hand with the deceptive hands of Desdemona and Cassio. Finally, the following line contains a complex bibliographic pun on the word "index": the term "index" was used to refer not only to what we would now call a "table of contents," but also to the pointing hands printed in the margins of early modern texts to mark important passages.

The references to Cassio taking Desdemona "by the palm" and to Desdemona "paddling with the palm of his hand" recall the exchanges that take place in two other Shakespearean plays – *The Winter's Tale* and *Romeo and Juliet*. The exchange in *The Winter's Tale* echoes the one in *Othello* not only in emphasizing the hand, but also in the role this member plays in the story. In that play, Hermione's hand becomes the focal point for Leontes' jealousy; he too mistakes the gestures of everyday courtly interaction for indications of his wife's infidelity. In the opening scenes of the play, Hermione offers her hand to Polixenes in friendship in order to persuade him to stay on at the court, and it is at precisely this point that Leontes becomes suspicious of their relationship: he says that his "bosom likes not" (1.2.121) that they are "paddling palms and pinching fingers, and making practiced smiles" (116–17). These courtesies ultimately lead Leontes to claim, like Othello, that his wife is "Too hot, too hot" (1.2.110). The focus on hands continues throughout the play, culminating in the final scene. As Jean Howard puts it, "joined hands. . .are an important and recurring visual motif."[24]

But even though both Othello and Leontes are mistaken in convincing themselves of the erotic overtones of their wives' social exchanges, we need to recognize that it was certainly possible for these courteous interactions to be eroticized. This is demonstrated quite clearly by the first meeting of the lovers in Shakespeare's *Romeo and Juliet*:

ROMEO   If I profane with my unworthiest hand
         This holy shrine, the gentle fine is this:
         My lips, two blushing pilgrims, ready stand
         To smooth that rough touch with a tender kiss.

JULIET   Good pilgrim, you do wrong your hand too much,
          Which mannerly devotion shows in this;
          For saints have hands that pilgrims' hands do touch,
          And palm to palm is holy palmers' kiss.

                                                        (1.5.90–7)

In this case, the courteous greeting between Romeo and Juliet does in fact turn out to be a "prologue to . . . lust." At this stage, however, the interactions of the lovers are delicately poised on the border between the courteous and the carnal, the sacred and the profane. If they at times begin to slide into the register of the erotic, this is precisely what Iago wishes to suggest has transpired between Cassio and Desdemona. But it is worth noting that even though Iago attempts to code this language – and its attendant gestures – as being entirely profane, Cassio, for his part, almost always uses the rhetoric of the sacred when addressing Desdemona: for example, just before they meet in Cyprus, he refers to her as "the divine Desdemona" (2.1.74), and when they do meet, he says "Hail to thee, lady! and the grace of heaven / Before, behind thee, and on every hand, / Enwheel thee round!" (2.1.86–8). Thus, in *Othello*, the sacred and the profane are split between two characters – Cassio and Iago – rather than being conflated in one as in Romeo's case.

If the hand is the focal point of Iago's machinations with Roderigo early in the play, it also becomes the key component of his later scheming with Othello himself. It figures prominently, for instance, in the scene where Iago tells Othello about Cassio's supposed dream. According to Iago, while he and Cassio slept together, Cassio dreamt of Desdemona, and "In sleep I heard him say 'Sweet Desdemona, Let us be wary, let us hide our loves;' And then, sir, *would he gripe and wring my hand*, Cry 'O sweet creature!' and then kiss me hard" (3.3.423–6). In this passage, Iago's description of how Cassio "gripped and wrung his hand" is meant to recall, and rearticulate, Cassio's earlier interactions with Desdemona's hand. It is, moreover, in this context clearly a "prologue" to lust – a precursor to his making declarations and "kissing him hard." Interestingly, Bulwer writes at length in *Chirologia* about the very gesture that Iago describes. He states that "TO PRESSE HARD AND WRING ANOTHERS HAND, is a naturall insinuation of love, duty, [and] reverence."[25] He goes on to explain that men "doe much use this speaking touch of the hand" in "preferring their *amorous insinuations*." He explains that it is

a piece of covert courtship whereby they seem to strive to imprint their mistresses *Hand* a tacit hint of their affection, suggested in this preferring flattery of the *Hand*; for lovers, I know not by what amorous instinct . . . [often] direct their *passionate respects* to the *Hand* of those they *love*; to this part they most usually accommodate their significant expressions; this they devoutly wring and embrace, and by the discoursing compressions thereof, intimate and suggest the *eagernesse of desire*. (116–17)

If Bulwer was earlier reluctant to call hand-kissing anything more than a courtesy, at this point, he seems to take an almost antithetical position, claiming that it is impossible for this gesture *not* to have obscene connotations: "this . . . gripping of anothers *Hand* was never held a safe or warrantable expression in the *Hand* of any man, taken for the most part for a *wanton essay* or *sly proofe* of a tractable disposition, and a *lascivious prologue* and *insinuation of lust*" (117). But if Bulwer is thus clearly invested in separating the courteous and the erotic, Iago exploits the inherent difficulty of doing so. He here describes Cassio making what Bulwer would call a "profane" gesture (wringing the hand), in part, in order to recode the earlier "polite" gesture (kissing his fingers). Moreover, it is worth pointing out that the language that Iago used in the earlier scene to describe Desdemona and Cassio's "polite" handclasp is almost exactly the same that Bulwer uses here: wringing the hand is, for Bulwer, a "lascivious prologue" and an "insinuation of lust."

Given all of Iago's scheming, it is perhaps overdetermined that Desdemona's hand – and its ensign the handkerchief – would become a site of fixation for Othello. Indeed, Othello focuses his attention on this member immediately after Iago has told him about Cassio's supposed dream and his hand-wringing:

OTHELLO   How do you do, Desdemona?
DESDEMONA   Well, my good lord.
OTHELLO   Give me your hand: this hand is moist, my lady.
DESDEMONA   It yet hath felt no age nor known no sorrow.
OTHELLO   This argues fruitfulness and liberal heart:
             Hot, hot, and moist: this hand of yours requires
             A sequester from liberty, fasting and prayer,
             Much castigation, exercise devout;
             For here's a young and sweating devil here,
             That commonly rebels. 'Tis a good hand,
             A frank one.
DESDEMONA   You may, indeed, say so;
             For 'twas that hand that gave away my heart.
OTHELLO   A liberal hand: the hearts of old gave hands;
             But our new heraldry is hands, not hearts.
                                              (3.4.33–45)

This exchange begins, like those between Desdemona and Cassio, with a courtly greeting which involves Othello taking Desdemona by the hand. In this instance, however, the polite gesture is immediately transformed from a greeting or a display of affection to an act of surveillance. Othello tries to discern whether Desdemona has remained faithful to him by looking at her palm.

It is hardly surprising that Othello fixates on this member, given that it was often linked to "character" (as Jonathan Goldberg's work on handwriting and graphology indicates). In this particular scene, however, the more relevant cultural practice is the art of palm-reading, or " palmistry." This was a popular activity in early modern England and there were numerous books published on the topic during the sixteenth and seventeenth centuries. Richard Saunders's *Palmistry*, for example, is a book-length manual that promises to "disclose" the "secrets" of palm reading.[26] While most of Saunders's book explains how to decode the meaning of various lines of the hand in order to predict things such as the length of time the person will live, the manner of their death, or the amount of money they will make, it also contains a remarkable section on women's hands – and more specifically, on how to discern a woman's character (which in this case means her sexual character or fidelity) by examining her palm. The heading for the section reads: "The following Aphorisms, and answerable Characters. . .*in the hands of Women*, denote Lust and commonly Whoredome" (120).

Like Saunders, Othello focuses on Desdemona's hand in his search for signs of "lust" and "whoredom," but instead of reading the lines of her palm as Saunders does, he concentrates on its moisture, or liquidity. He notes "This hand is moist, my Lady" (3.4.34). He repeats this characterization several times in the lines that follow. He describes her hand as "Hot, hot, and moist" (3.4.37) and later declares "here's a young and sweating devil here" (40). According to E. A. M. Coleman's *The Dramatic Uses of Bawdy in Shakespeare*, a "moist hand" implied lust and "amorous desire" among the Elizabethans.[27] This is certainly true in Shakespeare's *Venus and Adonis*, where Venus is represented with "Smooth moist hand," "soft flesh," and "burning marrow" – all of which are meant to be signs of her licentiousness and sexual availability. Similarly, the "Curtizan" Imperia in Thomas Dekker's *Blurt Master-Constable* (1602) swears by "the moyst hand of love."[28] These associations derive, in part, from humoral theory, where people with "moyst compleccyons" were said to be "often moved to coeate or to the lust of the body."[29]

Othello's description of Desdemona's "moist palm" and his subsequent depiction of her as a "sweating devil" resonate with the other moments in the play where her "watery" nature is emphasized. In fact, as the play progresses, the figurations of Desdemona as a "leaky vessel" become more and more pronounced (especially once the handkerchief has been lost). They also begin to take on added meanings. We can get a sense of how this works by looking at the references to Desdemona's weeping and tears.[30] Drying tears was, of course, another important use of the handkerchief. In fact, Stephanie Dickey claims that it was "the principal implied use of the handkerchief" in seventeenth-century portraiture.[31] Othello initially sees Desdemona's crying as a sign of her compassion for him (after their courtship, he claims he "beguiled her of her tears"), but he later comes to associate it with her supposed insincerity and changeability: he notes that "she can turn, and she can weep, sir, weep" (4.1.251). Still later, he claims that the earth is "teeming" with women's "crocodile" tears, using imagery that not only eroticizes her weeping, but is full of sexual revulsion.[32] Finally, when Desdemona cries on her deathbed, Othello finds these tears to be a confirmation of her infidelity because he interprets them as being for Cassio (whose death he has just told her about) rather than about her fate or about his failure to trust her: he says "Weep'st thou for him to my face?" (5.2.84). The crucial point I want to make about these references to Desdemona's crying is not only that they become more and more conspicuous as they are repeated, but also that Othello comes to give them meanings which are more and more in line with the ideology that figured women as "watery" and untrustworthy. In the course of the play, Desdemona's tears become a sign of her lack of control and her changeability, and eventually even a sign of her infidelity. These characterizations culminate in Othello's pronouncement that Desdemona is "false as water."[33] This strange simile resonates profoundly with all of the other descriptions of Desdemona's superfluidity, and through it, Othello ultimately suggests that Desdemona is changeable, formless, and unreliable.

There are two important cultural resonances of hands that may help to explain why Othello focuses so much attention on this part of the body. First, the hand – and especially the handclasp – was a powerful symbol of love and marriage during the Renaissance. It had, for example, a prominent place in visual rhetoric used to denote the marital union. Every Anglican wedding ceremony required the bridal couple to ritually join hands three times.[34] *The Booke of Common Prayer* notes that at the end of the ceremony "the Minister ioyne their right hands together" and, uniting word and deed, speak the familiar injunction, "Those whom God hath ioyned together let no man put asunder." The minister then turns to the congregation and says that because the couple has consented to holy wedlock, pledged their troth, given and received a ring, and joined hands, "I pronounce that they be man and wife together."[35] The marital hand-in-hand symbolism is ubiquitous: it also occurred, for example, in many betrothal and spousal rings of the day. These fede rings – whose name derives from *mani in fede*, meaning "hands clasped in faith" – were one of the most popular love-rings in early modern England.[36]

There are numerous examples of this association in Shakespeare's works. In *Twelfth Night*, when the priest describes the marriage ceremony between Olivia and Sebastian, he conspicuously notes that their "contract of eternal bond of love" was "confirmed by the mutual joinder of [their] hands" (5.1.153–4). Similarly, when Marina unveils herself to Angelo in *Measure for Measure*, she states "This is the hand which, with a vow'd contract, / Was fast belock'd in thine" (5.1.204–5). Finally, in *Much Ado About Nothing*, Benedict swears "good Beatrice, by this hand I love thee" (4.1.319).

If the hand's role as an emblem of love and marriage is implicit in Othello's preoccupation with this organ, these connotations become explicit when Desdemona states that this is the same hand that "gave away [her] heart" (3.4.43). The link Desdemona makes here between her hand and her heart was not simply symbolic. According to traditional folk beliefs that came down to the Renaissance from the Middle Ages, these two organs were connected physically by either a nerve or vein that ran directly from the third finger of the left hand – where the wedding ring was to be worn – to the heart.[37] But while Desdemona attempts to bind the two parts together irrevocably, Othello is attentive to the possible disjunction between inside and out (thanks primarily to Iago's tutoring). He claims that this linkage is no longer certain: "the hearts of old gave hands; / But our new heraldry is hands, not hearts" (3.4.45).

When Desdemona insists that this is "the hand that gave [her] heart away," she calls to mind not only her courtship and the marital handclasp, but also her *agency* in the process. This is the second crucial cultural resonance of the hand in this scene. Indeed, within the Western tradition, the hand is "the preeminent bodily metaphor for human action" as Katherine Rowe has convincingly demonstrated in *Dead Hands: Fictions of Agency, Renaissance to Modern*.[38] In this particular instance, however, the issue of agency cannot be isolated from the issue of gender, for it matters deeply that it is a *woman*'s hand that performs this action. In other words, what is remarkable about Desdemona's marriage is precisely the fact that it was her own hand that gave her heart away. According to traditional patriarchal strictures, it should have been her father's hand that performed this action. Thus, even though Desdemona reminds Othello of her role in their courtship in order to reassure him of her continued affection, she also inadvertently evokes the very thing that he has come to fear: her erotic agency. As Michael Neill notes, her "liberal hand" has become, for Othello, a sign of her "liberal [libertine] heart."[39] So despite the fact that Othello had previously benefited from Desdemona's "liberality," he now feels threatened by it. He therefore suggests that her hand (and by extension her agency) now needs to be constrained: he says, "this hand of yours requires a sequester from liberty." In essence, Othello has come to believe that if Desdemona's agency is not regulated, she will become uncontrollable – a position which again resonates with the stereotypes about women's watery nature.

If Desdemona's hand is thus a figure of her agency in *Othello*, the same can be said of Hermione's hand in *The Winter's Tale*. In that play, Hermione does not give her own heart away as Desdemona does, but she uses her hand as an instrument of (sexual) expression.[40] In the final scene of the play, Hermione comes to life again after having been turned into a statue, and she "take[s]" her husband "by the hand" (5.2.89) and "embraces him" and "hangs about his neck" (5.3.112–13). It is clear that Hermione is meant to be the active participant here and Leontes, for his part, is reduced to a passive role: he is told to "present [his] hand" (5.3.107) for Hermione to take. One of the other participants in the scene comments on this dynamic, stating that "When she [Hermione] was young, [Leontes] wooed her. Now, in age" she has "become the suitor" (5.3.108–9). It is worth noting, moreover, that Leontes' earlier wooing of Hermione had also concentrated on her hand: he comments that he had to wait for three months, "Ere I could make thee [Hermione] open thy white hand / And clap thyself my love" (1.2.105–6). In addition, Hermione's hand was, as we have seen, the focal point of Leontes' anxieties about his wife's constancy. So it is therefore appropriate that in the reconciliation scene at the end of the play, her hand again takes center stage. It is also appropriate that her (erotic) agency is expressed through this member since that is precisely what Leontes had feared.

The actions of Desdemona and Hermione can be contrasted with those of Katerina in *The Taming of the Shrew*. In Kate's final lines, she tells her fellow wives to "place [their] hands below [their] husband's foote" as a sign of subjection, commenting that her own "hand is ready, may it do [Petruchio] ease" (5.2.177–9). Katerina's gesture here seems to draw upon and transform the hand-in-hand symbol of the marital union. Indeed, Lynda Boose provides several examples of the hand-under-foot gesture being used in marriage ceremonies from the period. She maintains that "[n]ot only do [Kate's] words represent [a bride's wedding vows] . . . her body re-enacts them. For what transpires onstage turns out to be a virtual representation of the ceremony that women were required to perform in most pre-Reformation marriage services throughout Europe."[41] In the end, Katerina's gesture alludes to the ritual performances of her wedding, and perhaps even becomes a figure for her agency. But in Katerina's case, unlike that of Desdemona and Hermione, this is a thoroughly *renounced* agency.

It should be evident by now that in *Othello* the hand is as central as the handkerchief. In fact, part of what I have been trying to suggest in looking at Othello's description of Desdemona's hand is that in the play, the hand and handkerchief fuse into a single unit. Desdemona's "moist," "hot," and "sweat[y]" hand might therefore best be described as *a hand-without-a-handkerchief*. It is as if, at some earlier moment in the story, the handkerchief had become part of her physical portrait, and now even though the auxiliary organ is no longer physically present, Othello can only view Desdemona's "moist palme" by contrasting it with its earlier, sweatless state. Thus, the handkerchief continues to mold perceptions of Desdemona's hand much as the clothes in the portraits examined by Anne Hollander continued to shape perceptions of the nude body even when they were no longer present.[42] As a result,

Desdemona's hand appears to be incomplete without its auxiliary. This phenomenon has been labeled "prosthetic backlash" by Harry Berger in a recent article. What Berger means by this is that after a prosthesis is incorporated into the body, there is often a "backlash" – or a sense of deprivation – that occurs when the object is then removed. In other words, the "natural" body ultimately comes to be perceived as incomplete or wanting.[43] The examples that Berger mentions are things like eyeglasses or even cars, but I want to suggest that a similar phenomenon occurs with the handkerchief in *Othello*. The implications of this are ultimately quite radical. It means that although we tend to think of the body as a natural entity which precedes its cultural inscription, it might also productively be seen as a backformation. Or, returning to *Othello*, we might say that Desdemona's nude hand comes to be seen as backformation from her handkerchiefed hand.

There is, therefore, a sense in which the handkerchief in *Othello* is a "prosthesis" which both is and is not a part of the body. This liminality is consistently evoked in the play through the conflicting accounts of the object itself. On the one hand, the handkerchief is repeatedly imagined to be integral. Othello "conjures" Desdemona that "she should ever keep it" (3.3.298) and "make it a darling like [her] precious eye" (3.4.64). In this last analogy, he accords the handkerchief a kind of corporeal status by linking it symbolically with her "precious eye." Desdemona, for her part, also sees the item as being integral. She supposedly "reserves it evermore about her" (3.3.299). But at the same time, she treats the object as if it were itself a living being or a doll: she "kiss[es]" it and "talk[s] to [it]" (3.3.300). The ways in which Desdemona views and treats her handkerchief are identical to the ways in which people view and treat their false limbs. As I noted in my introduction, patients at times see their prostheses as part of their bodies, at others as objects, and sometimes as subjects in their own right. In this last regard, it is worth recalling that people (and especially children) often give their prostheses names and sometimes even sleep with them. But if Desdemona and Othello speak of the handkerchief in ways that are similar to the way in which people speak of their prostheses, this is offset in the play by instances where the item is called a "trifle." Emilia, for example, says that the hanky is a "trifle" unworthy of "earnestness" and Iago calls it a "trifle . . . light as air" (3.3.226), implying that it is insubstantial and without weight or mooring.

In the aggregate, these conflicting valuations of the object work to stress its transitional status and its liminality. Othello's account of the object's material construction has a similar effect. He indicates that the handkerchief melds both subject and object insofar as it incorporates remnants of the human body into its web: it was supposedly "dy'ed in mummy [the fluid removed from corpses] which the skillful conserved of maidens' hearts" (3.4.72–3). It is worth saying that a mummy – like the corpse itself – is already liminal; it both is and is not a body. Moreover, the fluid removed from such an entity would appear to be even more liminal or cryptic. It is also worth pointing out that this "mummy" is "conserved of maidens' hearts." Whereas Othello had earlier envisioned a disjunction between Desdemona's hand and heart, he here constructs a compensatory link between the handkerchief and the "maidens' hearts." In essence, Othello imagines that the napkin – stained with this virginal liquid from the most integral of bodily parts – provides a means of correcting and purifying Desdemona's "sweaty" hand which he fears has become dissociated from her heart. The handkerchief's role in this scenario is ultimately not that different from the role that ordinary handkerchiefs played: as we have seen, Braun-Ronsdorf's *The History of the Handkerchief* suggests that this accessory was often perfumed in order to cover over unseemly odors.[44] In this case, however, the "perfume" has an incredibly rich symbolic resonance, implying not only that Desdemona should have a maiden's heart (and hand), but also possibly hinting at her death.

In this chapter, I have argued that Shakespeare's *Othello* dramatizes the ideological production of the female body as a "leaky vessel," and that it begins to suggest the role that the handkerchief played in this process. I want to stress, however, that the ideology of femininity that I have been examining is entirely normative, even stereotypical. It is therefore hardly surprising that it is articulated in Shakespeare's play primarily by the character Iago, since he often ventriloquizes dominant ideologies. Indeed, Iago consistently invokes ideological beliefs – that is to say, beliefs that are taken-for-granted or that are commonsensical. With these beliefs as his weapons, Iago is able to manipulate other characters in the play. For example, in the opening scenes, Iago draws upon racial stereotypes regarding black men's sexuality as part of his attempt to turn Brabantio against Othello. Later, he concentrates on rehearsing patriarchal notions of women's changeability and their propensity to infidelity. To Roderigo, he says that Desdemona's love for Othello had "a violent commencement" and it will therefore have "an answerable sequestration" (1.3.337–8). And at another point he says that "It cannot be long that Desdemona should continue her love to the Moor" (335–6). This second statement contains embedded within it not only an assumption about women's inevitable disloyalty, but also an assumption of racial inferiority: (Desdemona's) love for "the Moor" cannot continue because he lacks, as Iago later reveals, "manners," "beauties," and "sympathy" (2.1.224). Iago articulates similar ideas about women's inconstancy when he speaks with Othello later in the play. He says, for example, that in Venice, women's "best conscience / Is not to leave't undone, but to keep't unknown" (3.3.207–8). He also implies that even Desdemona herself has been deceitful, when he says that "She did deceive her father, marrying you" (3.3.210). This pronouncement is clearly meant to echo and reinforce Brabantio's earlier warning that Desdemona has "deceived her father, and may thee" (1.3.292). While it is true that in the play all of Iago's pronouncements and insinuations turn out to be false, I would argue that part of the reason why they are able to take hold in other characters is because they are commonplace slanders.

Othello not only buys into the ideology of women's incontinence promulgated by Iago, he also associates that incontinence with women's "watery" nature. This may help to explain why he is so insistent about attaching the handkerchief firmly to Desdemona's hand. Indeed, Othello's increasing doubts about women's fidelity in general, and Desdemona's fidelity in particular, directly correlate with his obsessional behavior regarding the handkerchief, and with his attempts to police Desdemona's "leaky" body. In the end, it is as if Othello has come to imagine the napkin as his lieutenant: he sees it as a "disciplinary apparatus" (to use the phrase of Michel de Certeau) that will regulate Desdemona's "moist" hand and give it a "sequester from liberty." What I want to suggest, moreover, is that Othello's attempts to put the handkerchief in the hands of his wife and keep it there mirror the more general attempt to put handkerchiefs into the hands of women in early modern England. Indeed, we have already come to understand that this is part of the cultural work performed by "history painting" and "portraiture" as well as "theater."

But if Othello sees the handkerchief as an integral part of Desdemona's hand and a necessary means of controlling her "watery" nature, the play as a whole nevertheless insists upon the accessory's detachability and transferability. This is not surprising given that these were often-acknowledged characteristics of the item. The speaker in John Taylor's *The Praise of Cleane Linnen* (1624), for instance, states that "I have often knowne unto my cost, / A *Handkerchiefe* is quickly found, and lost."[45] In Shakespeare's play, as in Taylor's poem, the transferability of the handkerchief is foregrounded. Indeed, the entire plot revolves around the object's displacement. Moreover, Othello himself is aware of the napkin's ability to circulate between different hands (and even differently gendered hands) as his stories about its provenance indicate. At one point, Othello tells Desdemona that the handkerchief was given to him by his dying mother (3.4.61), and at another he claims that it was "an antique token / My father gave my mother" (5.2.224). When seen from this perspective, Othello's later attempts to stop the circulation of the handkerchief and attach it irrevocably to Desdemona's hand can be seen as his desperate attempt to disavow this transferability.

The detachability of the handkerchief has important ramifications for the ideology of femininity materialized through it. On the one hand, the prosthetic nature of the handkerchief might be seen as an indication of the precariousness of the ideology itself. That is to say, removing the handkerchiefs from the hands of women might be seen as a means of undermining ideas about women's "watery" nature, and by extension their incontinence. Although this would definitely be true in the long run, it is important to recognize that the detachability of the handkerchief does not *necessarily* lead to the subversion of normative ideas about gender in the short run. After the handkerchief has been incorporated into the physical portrait, it has, as we have seen, a ghostly afterlife and it can therefore continue to shape or constitute ideas about the body even when it is no longer physically present. To further illustrate this point, I would note that in *Othello*, Iago highlights the detachability of the handkerchief in order to *reinforce* the dominant ideas about women's profligacy. He says that if a husband gives his "wife a handkerchief . . . Why then, 'tis hers . . . and being hers, she may . . . bestow't on any man" (4.1.10–13). Othello does not fail to comprehend the implication of Iago's remark: he notes that she is "protectress of her honor too" and asks "may she give that?" (4.1.14–15). In this case, removing the handkerchief from Desdemona's hand does not lead either of these characters to question their ideas about women's incontinence; instead, it is taken as proof of that incontinence. Iago manages to put this particular spin on the events, in part, by imaginatively putting the handkerchief into the hands of another man whom he has constructed as Othello's rival. He thus places the love token within a masculine economy of (erotic) competition, and as a result, the loss of the handkerchief is not seen as an act of resistance to patriarchal norms or patriarchal power itself, but as a transfer of that power to the hands of another.

If the handkerchief's prosthetic nature does not, then, *necessarily* compromise the gender ideologies constructed through it, it does nevertheless signal that those ideologies need to be constantly (re)produced. In terms of this chapter, this means that handkerchiefs had to be put into the hands of women over and over again, since this was, as I've tried to suggest, one of the ways in which the ideas about women's watery nature were reinforced. But since this cultural work had to be performed continually, the ideology itself was always open to dislocation and rearticulation. While this is true of any ideology (and is particularly true of ideologies materialized through prosthetic parts), I want to emphasize it here because the instability is what allows for the possibility of women's resistance – both collectively and individually – to the normative gender formations that I have been discussing.

An analogous point can be made about the handkerchief itself. Although the napkin served as a disciplinary apparatus that regulated bodily excretions and helped to materialize the ideology of the "leaky woman," it was also an instrument that helped to establish women's agency, and particularly their erotic agency. In fact, handkerchiefs were considered to be one of the household properties that were legally under women's control even after they were married (the rest of their property was effectively commandeered by their husbands through coverture).[46] Moreover, women often gave handkerchiefs as tokens of their affections. Juana Green's article on the representation of the handkerchief in *The Faire Maide of the Exchange* focuses on this role for the object, not only in Heywood's play, but also in a number of other plays from the period.[47] The point I want to make here is that the handkerchief therefore served both as a means of enacting social control *and* as a means of enacting individual agency. While we usually tend to assume that a "prosthesis" is an instrument of either one or the other of these – and indeed that the two forces are themselves largely juxtaposed with one moving from the outside in and the other from the inside out – we are now, I hope, in a position to recognize the limitations of these assumptions, and to begin to articulate a better model for understanding the complex ways in which agency and social control are bound up with one another.

If, in the previous chapter, I examined the role that the handkerchief played in forming gendered identity, in this chapter, I turn to one of the most distinctive elements of early modern dress: the codpiece. The *Oxford English Dictionary* describes this accessory as "a bagged appendage to the front of the close-fitting hose or breeches worn . . . [in England] from the 15th to the [beginning of the] 17th century." Codpieces were first introduced, according to fashion historians, as a means of concealing the genital area in masculine apparel. Earlier, this task had been performed by knee-length surcoats, but when shorter doublets were adopted at the beginning of the fifteenth century, the genital area was left at least partially exposed, and the codpiece was created as a way of dealing with this problem.[1]

The definition from the *OED* provides a good overview of what the codpiece was. It is, however, a bit misleading in that it gives the impression of a simple, uniform object. The truth is that codpieces came in a variety of shapes and style. One common style was, as the *OED* implies, a "bagged appendage." This particular type of codpiece was essentially a triangular flap or gusset that was attached to the front of the hose or breeches (figure 6). The bottom corner of the triangle was sewn to the inseam of the garment and the top two corners were attached near the hips with either buttons or laces called "codpiece points." One writer from the late seventeenth century describes this style of codpiece in his account of "the Suits that [were] generally worn heretofore in *England*": he says the codpiece "came up with two wings fastened to either side with points." The writer notes, moreover, that this "large and ample Codpiss supplied the want of Pockets" for when the points were "unknit," they "made way to the Linnen bags tyed to the inside between the Shirt and Codpiss, these Bags held every thing they carried about them."[2]

But if the codpiece was sometimes a "bagged appendage," it also took other forms as well. The most common of these was an ornate (sometimes even jewel-encrusted) phallic sheath that protruded conspicuously from the front of the outfit.[3] This second type of codpiece was constructed out of layers of woven cloth with inner padding and stays (figure 7). According to the fashion historian Aileen Ribeiro, the "modest codpiece of the late fifteenth

Figure 6. Albrecht Dürer, *The Standard Bearer* (1498), wearing a scrotal codpiece.

Figure 7. Agnolo Bronzino, *Portrait of Guidobaldo della Rovere* (1532), wearing a phallic codpiece.

century . . . assumed the shape of a permanent erection."[4] John Bulwer's proto-anthropological text, *Anthropometamorphosis* (1654), compares the people who wear this second version of the codpiece to the "*Indians* of the Island of La Trinidad" who "beare their members in a Gourd or Reed, as it were in a sheath, letting their stones hang out."[5] (See figure 8.)

This chapter sets out to analyze the gendered work performed by the codpiece, but it will not offer a semiotic analysis of this accessory. Instead, I hope to provide a more materialist account, considering the way in which the codpiece quite literally helped to fashion manhood. Indeed, I will argue that when this artifact was incorporated into the physical portrait in the fifteenth century, it helped to remake the male body, and by extension, the ideologies of gender circulating at the time.

Anne Hollander's *Seeing through Clothes* provides the theoretical frame-work for this chapter insofar as it demonstrates the extent to which clothing can shape perceptions of the human body. As I noted in my introduction, Hollander's art-historical study begins by looking at nudes from many different time periods and noting the drastic variations in the corporeal form of the women depicted therein. She then argues that the stylized form of the body presented in each painting corresponds roughly to the form of the garments popular at the time. So, for example, she observes that the bodies of women in paintings by Tintoretto or Bronzino have small, flattened breasts and cylindrical torsos, and simultaneously notes that this corresponds to the shape of dresses from the period. Hollander thus convincingly concludes that it is as if the nude bodies in these paintings are quite literally "shaped" by the "absent" clothing, and as a result, it is as if we are "seeing through" the invisible clothes when we look at them.[6]

Following Hollander, I want to suggest that the codpiece shaped the vision of the body (and specifically the male genitalia) in early modern England. But I also want to add another dimension to Hollander's analysis by insisting that there are important gendered aspects to this process that need to be considered. Thus, I don't simply want to contend that the codpiece formed ideas about the body in general, but rather that it formed ideas about *the male body*. Moreover, I hope to show how these ideas related to the early modern ideologies of masculinity.

Although the argument I will make in this chapter about the codpiece is ultimately somewhat similar to the argument I made in the last chapter about the handkerchief, there is also a significant difference between the two and between the two artifacts themselves: whereas the handkerchief reformed the body on a physical level by absorbing sweat and other bodily fluids, the codpiece reformed the body on a more ideational level. Nevertheless, I believe that the corporeal changes instituted through the codpiece were just as "real" as those instituted through the handkerchief. Even though we might be tempted to say that the codpiece only helped to alter the *psychic* contours of the body, it is actually almost impossible to divorce people's ideas about the body from the body itself. As Judith Butler puts it, the body is not only

540   *The Pedigree of*

Ribband-bufhes that our moderne Gallants hang
at their Cod-piece, want nothing but Bells inftead
of Tags, to be allied in their Phanfie to the yard-
balls of thofe of *Aga, Pegu, Siam,* and the *Bramas,*
who delight in fuch gay bables and Codpiece
mufique. Bombafted paned hofe were, fince
I can remember, in fafhion, but now our hofe
are made fo clofe to our Breeches, that, like
Irifh Trowfes, they too manifeftly difcover the
dimenfions of every part.

What would Turkes fay to an Englifh man
thus ftrictly cloathed, who deteft our little and
ftreight breeches as difhoneft, becaufe they too
much expreffe our fhamefull parts.

At

Figure 8. Wood engraving from John Bulwer, *Anthropometamorphosis*
(1654).

bound up in an irreducible tension with culturally constructed ideas about it, but rather, the body *is* that tension.[7]

Texts from early modern England that discuss the codpiece tend to perform two types of cultural work with regard to this object, and with regard to gendered ideologies of the era. First, many of them work to figure the accessory as an integral element of masculinity. For example, a character in Henry Medwall's *Fulgens and Lucrece* claims that "a new man of fascyon now a day" must have a "codpiece before almost as large, and therein restith the greatest charge."[8] Medwall's play – the earliest existent secular drama – was first staged at the end of the fifteenth century when codpieces were just coming into fashion. This may help to explain why the character claims that the codpiece is necessary for the "*new* man of fascyon."

Dramatic texts from later in the period also contain similar pronouncements about the codpiece's role in constituting masculine identity. In the play *Wiley Beguiled* (1606), for instance, the character William Cricket provides a catalog of his masculine features, pointing out that he has "a fine beard, [a] comely corps, And a Carowsing Codpeece." He is so proud of these attributes that he challenges "All England if it can / [to] Show mee such a man / . . . As William Cricket is."[9] There are two primary things I want to note about these statements. First, I simply want to point out the centrality of the "Carowsing codpiece" as a guarantor of masculinity. But in addition, it is worth noting that this part is listed alongside more corporeal features such as the "fine beard" and the "comely corps." While modern readers might be tempted to place more emphasis on the body than on dress, these items seem to carry equal weight here. Given this emphasis placed on the codpiece, it is hardly surprising to find that later in the play, Cricket "swear[s] . . . by the round, sound, and profound contents . . . Of this costly Codpeece," claiming that it makes him "a good proper man as yee see" (48).

Another seventeenth-century text that attempts to establish the codpiece as a constitutive component of masculinity is an epigram by Richard Niccols. He writes:

> T'is strange to see a Mermaide, you will say,
> Yet not so strange, as that I saw to day, . . .
> One part of this was man or I mistooke,
> The other woman, for I pray (sirs) looke,
> The head is mans, I iudge by hat and haire,
> And by the band and doublet it doth weare,
> The bodie should be mans, what doth it need?
> Had it a codpiece, 'twere a man indeed.[10]

In this passage, Niccols describes an ambiguously gendered figure who is reminiscent of those portrayed in the *Hic Mulier* and *Haec Vir* pamphlets. Although the individual that Niccols depicts already has a number of masculine attributes such as the "hat," "haire," "band," and "doublet," Niccols implies that without the *pièce de résistance*, the "bodie" remains feminine, and hence the whole is a "monstrous" amalgam of contraries. With the codpiece, however, the scales would be tipped and the individual would become definitively masculine. Thus, for my purposes, the crucial thing to note is that even though the codpiece does not act alone, it seems to have the power to constitute the gendered identity of this individual – to help to make him/her into "a man indeed."

Like Medwell and Niccols, the satirist John Marston suggests that the codpiece establishes the masculinity of the person who wears it. Indeed, the normally satirical Marston is at first surprisingly restrained in front of this artifact. He states that he will

> . . . never raile at those
> That weare a codpis, thereby to disclose
> What sexe they are, since strumpets breeches vse,
> And all men's eyes save Linceus can abuse.[11]

In these lines, Marston suggests that the codpiece has the ability to "disclose" the "sexe" of its wearer. Although he acknowledges that "strumpets" might "use" breeches to "abuse" men's eyes, he implies that they could not do the same with the codpiece. In this sense, Marston's description is quite similar to that of Niccols: both writers intimate that even when other gendered items ("breeches," "hats," "hair") fail to secure masculinity, the codpiece nevertheless serves as an incontrovertible anchor.

Finally, Shakespeare's *Two Gentlemen of Verona* has much in common with these other texts. It too stages the codpiece as a necessary element of masculine attire and identity. But there is also a crucial difference in Shakespeare's play, and that is that in it, the item is worn by a *female* character. When Julia decides to dress herself as a man, Lucetta first tells her that she must wear a pair of "breeches." She then adds that she "must needs have them with a codpiece" because "A round hose . . . now's not worth a pin, Unless you have a codpiece to stick pins on" (2.7.49–56).[12] The codpiece thus occupies a central place in this scene. It seems to carry even more cultural weight than the breeches/hose alone. Lucetta states that, without the codpiece, the hose alone are "not worth a pin" (with the obvious phallic pun). Also, it is worth saying that in the exchange Lucetta gradually works her way up to suggesting that Julia don a codpiece, with the implication being that her recommendations are becoming more and more outrageous.

Julia, for her part, is reluctant to appropriate this accessory. She responds to Lucetta's suggestion that she wear a codpiece by insisting "Out, out, that would be illfavored" (2.7.54). This scene therefore seems to be structured by a logic similar to that found in Marston's text: it indicates that even though women might "use" breeches to deceive "men's eyes," they would not use the codpiece. In this case, however, Julia *does* eventually adopt the codpiece, and consequently Shakespeare, unlike Marston, ends up foregrounding the transferability of the item. Whereas Marston draws a distinction between the breeches and the codpiece, Shakespeare's play emphasizes that both objects can be appropriated. This point will, I hope, help us to recognize not only the uniqueness of the Shakespearean text, but also the cultural work performed by the other texts that I have been discussing. Those texts forge a connection between the codpiece and masculinity, and when they are viewed in relation to Shakespeare's play, it becomes evident that this connection was not something "natural" or unremarkable, but rather something they labored to establish. This was done, in part, by downplaying the codpiece's detachability/transferability and hence fastening the object firmly to men.

But early modern texts do not simply characterize the codpiece as a crucial attribute of masculinity, they also work to conflate this part with the male genitalia. Indeed, these two interventions are related to one another. This is evident if we return to the play *Wiley Beguiled*. As I noted earlier, at one point in the play, the character William Cricket declares that his "carowsing codpiece" is one of the things that establishes his masculinity. Later, he "swear[s] . . . by the round, sound, and profound contents . . . Of this costly Codpeece" and insists that this makes him "a good and proper man." In these passages, Cricket seems to elide the difference between his "carowsing codpiece" with its "round, sound, and profound contents" and to imply that the two are virtually identical. This conflation is reiterated in a different form later in the play when Cricket "sweare[s] by the blood of [his] codpiece." This remarkable oath seems to confer a measure of corporeality to the codpiece.

This is not to say that the codpiece was always melded with the male genitalia in early modern texts. As we saw earlier, one of the characters in Medwall's *Fulgens and Lucrece* distinguishes between the item and its corporeal contents when he indicates that the "new" man's "greatest charge" still rests "within" his codpiece. Nevertheless, there are many texts that do actively conflate the two. For example, at the beginning of the seventeenth century (after the codpiece had already gone out of fashion), the playwright Barten Holyday writes nostalgically of "that Cod-piece-ago, when the innocency of men did not blush to shew all that Nature gaue them."[13] In this passage, Holyday implies that the codpiece "shew[ed]" the genitals, much as Marston implied that it "disclosed" the "sex" of the wearer. Holyday suggests, moreover, that this was done with an almost prelapsarian innocence. Indeed, he somewhat paradoxically insists on the "Naturalness" of the fashion, claiming that the men that wore this accessory "did no more, then, that [sic] nature taught them."

Other seventeenth-century writers, like John Bulwer, had a less nostalgic view of the accessory and the era in which it was worn. Bulwer describes the

"Breeches" of the previous century as being "filthy and Apish" and claims that they "openly shew'd our secret parts, with the vaine and unprofitable modell of a member which we may not so much name with modesty."[14] Although Bulwer's *evaluation* of the codpiece is thus radically different from Holyday's, his description of the item is remarkably similar: just as Holiday says that the codpiece "shew[s] all that Nature" gave men, Bulwer says that it "shew[s]" men's "secret parts." For Bulwer, however, this is an index of the item's unnaturalness rather than its naturalness. In fact, he subtly emphasizes the indecency of the codpiece by using the term "secret parts" to refer to the genitalia – thus indicating that they ought to be hidden from public view rather than "openly" displayed.

Bulwer's condemnation of the codpiece seems to echo the polemical literature from sixteenth-century Germany. Andreas Musculus' *Hosen Teuffel*, for instance, was a book-length invective against youthful fashions that reserved some of its sharpest criticism for the codpiece.[15] Musculus' text, and others like it, have been perceptively analyzed by Lyndal Roper in *Oedipus and the Devil*. Roper maintains that "moralists like Musculus . . . condemned the codpiece not because it paraded the phallus, but because it was a form of nudity. It displayed the penis to . . . lascivious eyes."[16] These German denunciations clearly resemble Bulwer's diatribe: whereas the German writers claim that the codpiece "displayed the penis" and that it "was a form of nudity," Bulwer asserts that it "openly shew'd our secret parts." It is worth saying, however, that in the process of articulating their objections to this item, these writers ironically perform some of the same cultural work as those writers with a more favorable opinion of the codpiece like Holyday and Medwall: they all effectively fuse the codpiece and the male genitalia. Consequently, I would argue that even though moralists like Bulwer and Musculus condemn the wearing of this accessory, they also unwittingly construct it as a masculine feature.

It should, I hope, be clear by now that the codpiece was an article of clothing that helped to make early modern individuals "men in body by attire" (to return to the phrase I discussed in my introduction). What we have seen here, moreover, are some of the steps through which this fashioning was achieved: first, attaching the accessory to male bodies, then, conflating it with the male genitalia, and also insisting that it made the individuals into "men indeed." But if many early modern writers maintained that the codpiece "showed" all that "Nature" gave men, and that it could establish the masculinity of its wearer, these cultural fantasies have too often been taken at face value by modern historians.[17] Leo Steinberg, for example, discusses the vogue for codpieces in his *Sexuality of Christ in Renaissance Art and Modern Oblivion*.[18] He contends that this accessory was meant to indicate "a permanent state of erection" and that it was therefore a "token of [sexual] prowess."[19] Moreover, Steinberg maintains that the codpiece was also an "instrument of power" and that the "conceit of the phallus as a manifestation of power" (90) was "constant" throughout Renaissance culture. While it may seem pretty straightforward to say that the codpiece was a priapic stand-in for the penis beneath it, I would argue that this description does not achieve enough metacritical distance on the accessory or on the discourses about it, and therefore does not adequately acknowledge the problem of representation posed by it. In reality, of course, the codpiece did not "show" anything; on the contrary, its purpose, as we have seen, was to conceal. Nor for that matter did this elaborately decorated cultural artifact have any transparent connection with nature.

Marjorie Garber is much more attentive to the ambiguous status of this accessory. In *Vested Interest*, she emphasizes the detachability of the codpiece and insists that the item bears no necessary relationship to the body beneath. In fact, she goes so far as to assert that the codpiece is a "sign of gender undecidability." As she puts it, the object "confounds the question of gender, since it can signify yes or no, full or empty, lack or lack of lack."[20] If Garber provides a much needed corrective to critics like Steinberg who assume the accessory to be transparently related to the body, I would argue that her emphasis on the indeterminacy of this item, while true, is also ultimately somewhat problematic in that it fails to adequately acknowledge the cultural work that the object itself performed.

What I therefore hope to do in this chapter is to find a theoretical middle ground between Steinberg and Garber. Instead of seeing the codpiece either as a simple indication of what nature gave men, or, conversely, as an empty cipher, I want to suggest that it was an item through which male bodies and masculinity were culturally constructed. Put differently, we might say that although early modern writers like Bulwer claim that the codpiece was simply a "model of" the male genitalia, it was in reality as much a model *for* the genitalia as a model *of* them.

But if this was the case, then we need to be especially attentive to the codpiece's material manifestations. In particular, it seems crucial to recognize that the codpiece was not always phallic, and did not always suggest, as Steinberg maintains, a "permanent state of erection." The codpiece came in a range of styles and many of them were distinctly non-phallic. Indeed, the very name "codpiece" implies that there is a link between this accessory and the scrotum/testicles rather than the phallus. The word "cod" was, of course, a slang term for the "scrotum" and the plural form "cods" almost always referred to the "testicles." One seventeenth-century anatomist described the testicles as being "seated externally in Men in their *Cod* or Covering."[21] Another said they "hang . . . without the Abdomen . . . in the cod."[22] Thus, even though early modern writers often conflate the codpiece with the male genitals, it is not always entirely clear exactly what is being conflated. For example, when the character in the play *Wiley Beguiled* speaks of the "round, sound, and profound" contents of his codpiece, he could be referring to either the phallus or the testicles (or, for that matter, both or neither of these).

What I am trying to suggest here is that these two forms of the codpiece worked to fashion slightly different versions of the male genitals and, by extension, slightly different versions of masculinity. Recent research has suggested that in the early modern period, the concept of manhood underwent a significant shift. According to Jean Howard and Phyllis Rackin's *Engendering a Nation*, "a man's identity" had, prior to the Renaissance, been "defined on the basis of patrilineal inheritance" and linked with his ability to reproduce himself, but over time, an "emergent culture" of "performative masculinity" developed in which masculine identity was secured through the sexual "conquest" of women.[23] So if the older model of masculinity emphasized reproduction as a key to establishing a masculine identity, the newer "performative" one emphasized sexuality and especially phallic penetration. Howard and Rackin suggest that the dark underside of this emergent ideal can be glimpsed in changing ideas about rape. They insist that in older texts "where the logic of patrilineal feudal succession is privileged, rape is [not usually] associated with military conquest or valorized as the 'natural' instinct of men. Instead, it serves to separate 'low' from their betters" (198). By contrast, in texts which exemplify the new "performative masculinity" rape sometimes serves as a "model of masculine dominance" and even a "gatekeeper for the gendered hierarchy" (196).

Gary Taylor's work on castration corroborates many of the assertions made by Howard and Rackin. In *Castration: An Abbreviated History of Western Manhood*, Taylor points out that although the term castration originally referred to the surgical process of removing the testicles, it increasingly came to be associated with the amputation of the penis as is typified by the term's use within Freudian psychoanalysis.[24] These changing ideas about castration are, for Taylor, indicative of a larger shift in the notions of manhood that had its roots in the Renaissance. Taylor labels the earlier ideology of masculinity "the regime of the scrotum" and the newer one "the regime of the penis." Rebecca Ann Bach similarly refers to the older model of masculinity as "testicular" and says that it "values breeding for itself and not for the sexual act."[25]

If both of these "regimes" of masculinity were operative in early modern England and stood in tension with one another, the gradual displacement of the former by the latter is suggested by the changing accounts of the testicles in anatomy books from the period. According to the anatomical tradition, the "coddes" were considered to be one of the "principal parts" of the body, along with organs such as the heart, the liver, and the brain. In fact, Galen claims that the testicles are not simply *one* of the principal parts, but rather they are *the* principal part, edging out even the heart. As he puts it, *"The Heart is indeede the author of living; but the Testicles are they which adde a better-nesse or farther degree of perfection to the life*, because if they be taken away, the jollity and courage of the Creature is extinguished."[26]

During the sixteenth and seventeenth centuries, however, the traditional centrality of the testicles began to wane. Nicholas Udall's 1553 translation of Thomas Gemini's *Compendiosa Totius Anatomie Delineatio* still claimed that the testicles are a principal part: it states that they are "numbered amongst the generative membres, ye it is a priyncipal membre, for withoute it is no gener-ation."[27] Similarly in 1586, Thomas Vicary asserted that "The Coddes . . . is called a principal member."[28] In 1615, however, Helkiah Crooke acknow-ledged that there were "adversaries who would thrust them out of this ranke of dignity." According to Crooke, these "adversaries" claimed that "the testicles do not give life at all" and therefore "there is no necessity of them, for *Eunuches* live without them." Crooke, however, did not agree with these writers: he admits that the testicles "are not necessary for conservation of the life of the *individuum* or singular man," but nevertheless claims that they are "an absolute necessity" for "the propagation of the whole species, or of mankinde." As he puts it, "they are principall parts in respect of mankinde, not in respect to this or that particular man."[29]

By the mid seventeenth century, the "adversaries" seem to have been gaining ascendancy. In 1668, Nicholas Culpepper no longer felt compelled to include the testicles in his list of principal parts: Culpepper writes that "The *Principal* [parts] are the Liver, Heart, [and the] Brain." He acknowledges that "Others add the Testicles," but claims that this is "without any need, because they make nothing to the Conservation of the Individual."[30] Interestingly, the rubric of "principal parts" was completely abandoned by anatomists in the eighteenth century. This may have been done for scientific reasons – as the profession became increasingly empirical, perhaps anatomists decided that the category itself was not scientifically necessary or useful. Nonetheless, the timing of this decision also seems significant. It may be that the designation was dropped instead of establishing a new pantheon of principal parts that excluded the testicles. But whatever the rationale behind this decision, the crucial thing is that, in the aggregate, these anatomical texts suggest that there was a gradual erosion of the cultural centrality of the testicles over the course of the early modern period. Indeed, these texts helped to instantiate it.

The codpiece helped to materialize both of the competing "regimes" of masculinity. While some forms of this accessory worked to construct the male genitalia as distinctly phallic, others worked to construct them as scrotal/testicular. The tension between these two models becomes apparent if we

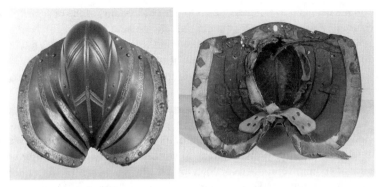

Figure 9. Two views of Henry VIII's codpiece from the Tower of London.

look at the writing about the codpiece of one of the most important masculine
icons from the period – Henry VIII. Apparently, during the seventeenth
century, one of Henry's codpieces was put on public display in the Tower
of London (figure 9). It remained there until the middle of the eighteenth
century, when it was finally removed as an "offence to decency." The letters
of a French visitor, César de Saussure, provide a detailed description of the
layout of the display in the Tower. First, he says that there was a large hall
"containing statues and figures of a score or so of ancient English Kings," and
"near the entrance of the hall is the figure of Henry VIII" who is "represented
standing in his royal robes." According to de Saussure, there was also some
sort of mechanical contrivance in place to reveal the king's codpiece. He
states that "If you press a spot on the floor with your feet, you will see
something surprising with regard to this figure, but I will not say more and
leave you to guess what it is."[31]

This mechanized display codes the king's codpiece as something that is
quite literally ob-scene – that is to say, something that cannot be seen in
public. A similar strategy is used to deal with the codpiece by Thomas
Boreman in his account of the "curious figure of king Henry the eighth"
in *Curiosities in the Tower*. At the end of his description, Boreman writes
"I have now told my young readers all the fine things that I know of in this
pompous place, excepting one,

> And that's a secret
>   Which king Harry has
>   to show;
> And so it must remain,
>   Till they to men and
>   women grow."[32]

Boreman's decision to relegate the codpiece to the status of the obscene or the "open secret" was undoubtedly a consequence of the fact that his book was written primarily for children, but it nevertheless replicates, on a verbal level, the strategy used for exhibiting the item itself.

John Dunton and Ned Ward provide more "adult" accounts of the Tower display. Dunton, in his *Voyage Round the World* (1691), declares that "the most remarkable thing I saw [in the Tower] was *Old Hary's Cod-piece.*" He notes that it was "such a sizeable one that I shall never more wonder there belong'd *so many Wives to't.*"[33] This quip clearly associates Henry's codpiece with his virility. It also, I want to suggest, imagines that virility to be sexual rather than reproductive. First of all, the very size of the codpiece seems to be an index of Henry's gargantuan sexual appetite. Moreover, that appetite is figured, not in terms of the number of children Henry sired, but in terms of the number of women he married (and by extension, had sexual relations with). In the end, Dunton's comment implies that Henry needed these multiple partners to satisfy his "sizable" sexual desire.

Similar assumptions about Henry and his codpiece underlie Ned Ward's account of his visit to the Tower of London published in 1699 in *London Spy*. Ward mentions that he saw "the *Codpiece* of that Great Prince who never spar'd a *Woman* in his *Lust.*"[34] In this formulation, Henry's codpiece is again associated with his "lust." In this case, however, that "lust" is not only directed at his five wives (and crudely quantified by them); instead, it is directed at any and all women.

Strangely, Ward then goes on to explain that the codpiece was "Lin'd with Red" and that it "hung gaping like a *Maiden-Head* at full Stretch, just Consenting to be Ravish'd" (321). If earlier, the codpiece seemed to stand in for Henry's phallus as an index of his "lust," here it is figured as a vaginal receptacle for the phallus itself. It is as if Ward first viewed the codpiece from the outside, and then viewed it from the inside. Consequently, the codpiece emerges as what Freud would eventually label a "bisexual" artifact: that is to say, an artifact that can be associated with either "the male or female genitalia according to context."[35] For my purposes, the thing to note about this latter description is that it still clearly links Henry's masculinity with sexual penetration by comparing the codpiece to a "maidenhead" that he could "ravish." In fact, this metaphorical comparison associates Henry not just with sexual penetration in general, but more specifically with the penetration of virgins. This is an extreme form of penetrative sexuality insofar as it involves the rupture of the hymen/maidenhead.

Finally, it must be said that Ward seems to evoke the specter of rape in his text, both in the comparison of Henry's codpiece to a maidenhead that he could "ravish" and in the comment that Henry "never spared a woman in his lust." He papers over the unseemly implications of this by representing the codpiece/maidenhead in typically sexist form as a "consenting" participant in the "rape." According to Ward, the codpiece/maidenhead is "just consenting to be ravished." Nevertheless, it might seem odd that Ward would risk referring to rape at all in the context of the monarch's masculinity and sexuality. This can perhaps be explained by returning to the observation made by Howard and Rackin: namely, that within the emergent regime of performative masculinity, rape is not only a demonized practice but also a "model for masculine dominance." The point, then, is not that Ward is suggesting that Henry is a rapist, but rather that in describing Henry's penetrative masculinity, Ward consistently evokes this act.

Although all of these seventeenth-century accounts of Henry's codpiece in the Tower of London thus imagined the king's masculinity in distinctly penetrative terms, it should be noted that the older reproductive model had not completely disappeared. Indeed, Ward repeats a story about Henry's codpiece that characterizes the object in more reproductive terms. He says that, according to his guide

in [Henry's codpiece], to this Day, remains this Vertue, That if any Married Woman, tho' she has for many Years been Barren, but sticks a *Pin* in this *Member-Case*, the next time she uses proper means, let her but think of her *Tower Pin-Cushion* and she needs not fear *Conception*.[36]

Henry's codpiece thus seems to have served as a kind of fertility talisman. There are, however, a number of somewhat unorthodox elements about this practice. First, the codpiece serves as a reproductive aid for women rather than men. Second, this scenario inverts traditional gender roles insofar as it is the women who stick phallic "pins" into the vaginal "Pin-Cushion." And finally, it is strange that the object became a fertility symbol in the first place, given Henry's well-known reproductive tribulations.

The practice of sticking pins into Henry's codpiece is also mentioned in a seventeenth-century ballad from the Pepys collection entitled "The Maids new All-a-mode Pincushing." One of the verses states that "People in the tower / stick forty in an hour / Upon an old Pincushing there . . . For Codpiece does never cry, forbear, forbear, forbear."[37] Although these verses allude to the custom of sticking pins in Henry's codpiece, they do not mention that this was a fertility rite. Instead, the practice is sexualized through an extended allusion to prostitution and sticking "pins" into this "pincushion": this secondary meaning is signaled most clearly in the lines explaining that "for a pence a piece the Rabble-Rout / May stick 'em [pins] in and take 'em out."[38]

If, in this ballad, the codpiece is returned to a sexual and, more specifically, penetrative economy, the fact that it was sometimes used as a fertility symbol means that the cultural work it performed was somewhat uneven or contradictory. Indeed, it would appear that both of the ideologies of masculinity circulating at the time were in one way or another articulated through this object. This situation might be explained in part by the odd shape of the Tower codpiece itself (it seems to meld both phallic and scrotal elements), but it also indicates that the ideologies of masculinity didn't necessarily get materialized in an entirely schematic way.

The representations of Henry VIII's codpieces from his own lifetime also illustrate this point. Most of them, no matter what their form, seem to have been used to construct a more "testicular masculinity." For example, the well-known Holbein mural at Whitehall portrays Henry with a somewhat phallic codpiece, but at the same time, the portrait emphasizes genealogical concerns. Indeed, Louis Montrose argues that "The prominence and ample proportions of the king's codpiece . . . are especially appropriate to the dynastic theme of this particular painting, which commemorates the birth of Prince Edward, thus guaranteeing (so it seemed) the continuity of the Tudors in the male line."[39] This same theme and trope is repeated in a portrait of Henry's son. This image of Edward VI mirrors the painting of his father in many of its compositional elements, from the hat down to the codpiece and dagger. The art historian Karen Hearn notes that "the positioning of [Edward's] left hand draws attention to his codpiece." She claims, moreover, that this gesture is meant to assure "the viewer of the future continuance of the dynasty."[40] Thus, both of these paintings (and the codpieces in them) construct masculinity in largely reproductive terms.

In the end, it would thus appear that Henry's codpiece was alternatively figured as both penetrative and reproductive. Nevertheless, there does seem to be a pattern with regard to those figurations: in his lifetime, Henry's codpiece was usually (though not always) associated with reproduction and "testicular masculinity," but later it was usually (though again not always) a means of articulating the newly emergent "performative masculinity."[41] In the end, both of these ideologies of masculinity were competing with one another in early modern England, and both of them were materialized through the codpiece. Indeed, I have tried to suggest that these two ideologies corresponded roughly with the two most common forms of the codpiece. While these correspondences aren't entirely schematic, it does seem clear that both forms of the codpiece were doing important cultural work in relation to the ideologies of gender.

So far, I've been analyzing the cultural construction of masculinity in early modern England and the role that the codpiece played in this process. But I now want to return to something that I mentioned at the beginning of this chapter: namely the fact that the codpiece disappeared from general usage sometime around the turn of the seventeenth century. Signs of its decline began to appear as early as 1594. Thomas Nashe describes a man wearing a "codpiece" in *The Unfortunate Traveller* and notes parenthetically that "they were then in fashion."[42] The implication, of course, is that they no longer are. In 1600, another writer insisted that the "codpeece breech" was "cleane out of fashion."[43] And finally, in 1628, Robert Hayman celebrated the demise of this fashion in a poem entitled "Two Filthy Fashions." He writes

> Of all fond fashions, that were worne by Men,
> These two (I hope) will ne'r be worne againe:
> Great Codpist Doublets, and great Codpist britch,
> At seuerall times worne both by meane and rich:
> These two had beene, had they beene worne together,
> Like two Fooles, pointing, mocking each the other.[44]

As Hayman's verses begin to suggest, the codpiece was not only out of fashion, but also increasingly disarticulated from masculine identity. In Hayman's poem, the codpiece is no longer a guarantor of masculinity or an indication of what "nature" has given men; rather, it is a ridiculous "fool."

We might therefore say that the codpiece eventually became a failed means of establishing masculinity. But how did this transformation occur? First of all, we need to recognize that it did not happen overnight and was not simply a whimsy of fashion. Instead, it too had to be culturally enacted or produced. So if, throughout much of the early modern period, the codpiece had often worked to make the man, the link between the two then had to be actively disarticulated. This disarticulation was, moreover, an "uneven development."[45] That is to say, despite the overall trend, there were early texts that distanced the codpiece from masculinity in one way or another (such as Shakespeare's *Two Gentlemen of Verona*), and there were later ones that continued the productive investment in it long after it had gone out of fashion (such as the discussions of Henry VIII's codpiece).

In the remainder of the chapter, I will be analyzing some of the seventeenth-century writing that helped to divorce the codpiece from masculine identity. This is of particular interest in the context of my larger project because it is the only instance where I will have the opportunity to look at the systematic *disarticulation* of a prosthetic part from gendered identity. All of the other items included in this study were also in some sense "new" to the Renaissance: they were all either introduced during the period or took on important new meanings or forms. As a result, I primarily concern myself with the ways in which these parts were incorporated into the physical portrait and how they worked to materialize gendered identity in the process. But these items were also, apart from the codpiece, relatively stable over the course of the early modern period (or at least from the mid sixteenth to the mid seventeenth century). Thus, the codpiece provides a unique opportunity to study not only the social and cultural processes whereby an item can be fashioned into a component of gender, but also how those processes can be undermined or reversed.

I should begin by saying that some of the texts that I discussed at the beginning of this chapter are actually somewhat more complicated than they might at first appear. The best example of this is the verses by Marston. As I noted earlier, Marston says:

> . . . I'll never raile at those
> That weare a codpis, thereby to disclose
> What sexe they are, since strumpets breeches vse,
> And all men's eyes save Linceus can abuse.

If these lines seem to suggest that the codpiece is a necessary means of securing masculine identity, their meaning is radically altered by the lines that follow. Marston goes on to say

> Nay, steed [instead] of shadow, lay the substance out,
> Or els faire Briscus I shall stand in doubt
> What sex thou art, since such Hermaphrodites
> Such Protean shadowes so delude our sights.[46]

Here Marston essentially reverses himself and advises men who wear codpieces (emblematized in the foppish figure of "faire Briscus")[47] to "lay the substance out." In doing so, he implicitly acknowledges that the codpiece is not any different from the "breeches" he mentioned earlier – both of these things could be used to "abuse" or "delude our sights." Moreover, Marston, like Hayman, ultimately suggests that the codpiece is ridiculous. He does this, in part, through the humorous pun on "steed." The two possible readings of the line are thus: "Nay, *instead* of shadow, lay the substance out" and "Nay, *steed* of shadow, lay the substance out." In the second, Marston addresses men who wear codpieces directly, referring to them as "steed[s] of shadow." This moniker implies that they are trying to turn themselves into "steeds," or "stud horses,"[48] by means of the "shadow[y]" codpiece. When seen from this perspective, the "nay" at the beginning of the sentence also takes on a humorous equine resonance. But Marston does not simply ridicule the codpiece-wearing men by comparing them to horses, he also does so by comparing them to the "strumpets" who use "breeches": all of these people are, he implies, trying to become something they are not. Indeed, in an ironic reversal, Marston suggests that the foppish men who wear codpieces are actually feminine. Therefore, unless they "lay the substance out" he will still "stand in doubt" of "what sex" they are.

For my purposes, the important thing to notice about Marston's text is that he at first ventriloquizes the discourses on the codpiece that I analyzed at the beginning of this chapter in claiming that the item "discloses" the "sex" of the wearer, and then later turns and undermines them when he says that it is only the genital "substance" and not its "shadow" that can "remove" his "doubts" about "what sexe" these individuals are. Marston thus questions the codpiece's role as a constituent element of masculinity, in part, by producing a disjunction between the object ("shadow") and the genitals ("substance").

The discussion of the codpiece in *The Minte of Deformities* (1600) – written by "C. G., Gent." – does some of the same cultural work as Marston's verses. C. G. writes:

> A codpeece breech. . .
> is used of all: oh spightfull forgerie.
> When God fayre fashion'd partes, vnfashioning,
> they both deforme those gratious parts, & him.[49]

These fascinating lines portray the codpiece, first and foremost, as a "forgerie" of the "partes" God created. This description implicitly counters the claim put forward by writers like Holyday that the codpiece was a transparent manifestation of those parts. Indeed, we might say that C. G. drives a conceptual wedge between the codpiece and the genitals in much the same way as Marston had, though obviously to less humorous effect.

Even though C. G. condemns the use of the codpiece, he tacitly acknowledges the power that this item had to constitute or "fashion" the body. He says that "God . . . fashion'd partes," and that by wearing the codpiece, men "unfashion" or "deforme" them. The assumption the author makes about clothing's ability to "deforme" the body might be compared to the theoretical point made by Anne Hollander in *Seeing through Clothes*: whereas Hollander maintains that clothes can shape the body, C. G. gives this idea negative spin, saying that they "deforme" or "unfashion" it.[50] If C. G. thus recognizes the constitutive power of the codpiece, it is hardly surprising to find that he also endeavors to distance the object from the male body. He does this in both a literal way (by insinuating that it should not be worn) and in a more figurative one (by labeling it a "forgery"). He was not alone in this. Other seventeenth-century writers also challenged the seemingly transparent connection between the codpiece and the male "parts." They did so, not only by referring to the codpiece as a "forgerie," but also by revealing the contents of the codpiece to be almost anything but the male genitals. In other words, if, in earlier texts, characters like William Cricket boast about the "contents" of their codpieces and claim that this is what makes them "good and proper" men, in later ones, the "round, sound and profound contents" of the codpiece are revealed to be an object like an orange. This is precisely the object that Panurge is said to carry in his codpiece in a mid seventeenth-century translation of Rabelais' *Pantagruel*.[51] In other seventeenth-century texts, codpieces are said to hold things such as ballads, bottles, napkins, pistols, hair, and even a looking glass.

And in Thomas Middleton's *Your Five Gallants* (1608), several of the characters joke about a "great codpiece with nothing in't."[52]

These descriptions of people revealing the contents of their codpieces are almost invariably humorous. Nevertheless, the fashion-historian Max von Boehn "explains" these representations by noting that the codpiece "served as a pocket in which a gentleman kept his handkerchief, purse, and even oranges." He also points out, moreover, that gentlemen would often pull these items "out before the ladies' eyes and hand them to them."[53] The "joke" involved in this gesture is quite similar to the humor that arose from revealing the contents of the codpiece in the texts I mentioned above. Both follow the typical pattern described by Freud in *Jokes and their Relation to the Unconscious*: first, anxiety is created by the potential exposure of the genitals, and then it is dispelled by revealing the alternative object.[54] But if the humor involved in all of these "revelations" is predicated upon the assumed connection between the codpiece and the male genitalia, I want to stress that the social practices and the texts that describe them would ultimately have worked to disarticulate that connection insofar as they suggested that it was not the male genitals that were actually contained in the codpiece.

Another way in which seventeenth-century writers worked to dissociate the codpiece from the male body and from masculinity was by highlighting the transferability of the accessory. If, as we have already seen, Marston recognizes the possibility that women might "use" the codpiece to "abuse men's eyes," there are a number of other instances in drama and poetry from the period where this is precisely what happens. I have already discussed Julia's decision to don a codpiece in Shakespeare's *Two Gentlemen of Verona*, but perhaps the most well-known codpiece-wearing-woman from the period was Moll Frith. In Middleton and Dekker's play *The Roaring Girl* (1611), they coin the term "codpiece daughter" to refer to Moll and other women like her.[55] Another such "codpiece daughter" is Constantina in Lording Barry's play *Ram Alley*, published the same year as *The Roaring Girl*. Finally, Francis Kynaston's narrative poem *Leoline and Sydanis* (1642) describes the Princess Sydanis,

> Who without scruple instantly put on
> The cloathes Prince Leoline on's wedding day
> Had worne, and drest her selfe without delay:
> Nor were the Breech, or Codpiece to her view
> Unpleasing . . .

The contrast between the descriptions of Julia and the Princess Sydanis is, I believe, striking and is undoubtedly a function of the fact that the first appeared in the sixteenth century and the latter in the mid seventeenth. Although both of these characters are the heroines of their respective stories, they behave very differently with regard to appropriating the codpiece. Whereas Julia is uncertain about using the item and has to be convinced by Lucetta, Sydanis adopts the item "without scruple" or hesitation. Kynaston reiterates this point later, saying that she "drest her selfe without delay." Moreover, whereas Julia initially states that it would be "illfavored" for her to wear the codpiece, the Princess has no such misgivings. In fact, she supposedly does not find the item "unpleasing." The contrast between these two stories indicates that the item had, in the intervening years, lost some of its cultural power, and it was therefore no longer quite as transgressive for a woman to appropriate the object. Moreover, more generally, what I have tried to suggest here is that the various representations of women wearing codpieces would have contributed to this development insofar as they highlighted the transferability of this item, and helped to disarticulate it further from masculinity.

A scene from Middleton and Dekker's *The Honest Whore, Part I* indicates that, by 1604, the codpiece had already been substantially disarticulated from masculinity. In it, a servant refuses admission to a messenger because he fears that he might be a woman: he states "I would not enter his man, tho' he had haires at his mouth, for feare he should be a woman, for some women have beardes, mary they are halfe witches. Slid you are a sweete youth to weare a codpeece, and haue no pinnes to sticke upon't."[56] This passage demonstrates, on the one hand, the continued cultural centrality of the beard and codpiece simply by virtue of the fact that the servant looks to these items to evaluate the masculinity of the messenger. But, on the other hand, the servant also clearly questions the reliability of those very items. He does so primarily by drawing attention to their transferability. First, he observes that although the messenger has "haires at his mouth," "some women have beardes."[57] He also questions whether the codpiece guarantees masculinity even more forcefully. He says that the messenger is "a sweet youth" to "wear a codpiece, and have no pinnes to stick upon't." First of all, it is important to note that in calling the messenger a "sweet youth," the servant implies that s/he is not a man. Even if s/he is not a woman, s/he is only a "youth" or "boy."[58] As evidence of this, the servant points to the fact that s/he "wears a codpiece" without any "pinnes to stick upon't." On the surface, this comment simply means that the messenger is a somewhat naive or unsophisticated gallant in that s/he does not have pins to stick in his codpiece (as was the custom).[59] But it also has other resonances that again undermine the masculinity of the figure. Most obviously, the servant seems to be questioning whether the messenger has a "pin" (in a phallic sense), but this quip may also have a more sexual significance as well. Apparently, bestowing a pin on someone was slang for having intercourse with them.[60] A servant in *Misogonus* says that "As for my pinnes, ile bestowe them of Jone when we sit by ye fier and rost a crabb. [S]he and I have good sporte when we are all alone."[61] When seen from this perspective, the servant would be indicating that the messenger is unmasculine, not only because s/he does not have a pin/penis, but also because s/he does not have sexual experience. Indeed, as I suggested earlier, both of these were increasingly emphasized as constituents of masculinity.

Other writers from the period pushed this idea a step further and suggested that if the codpiece was detachable/transferable, so then patriarchal power itself must be open to appropriation. For example, in the play *Apius and Virginia* (1575), the character "Haphasard" describes several potential scenes of the-world-turned-upside-down. He warns not only that "wives" might "wear the Codpeece, and maydens coy strange," but also that "maides would be masters by the guise of this country."[62] In this formulation, the idea of women wearing the codpiece goes hand-in-hand with them being masters. Indeed, it is "by the guise of this country" that women seem to become "masters." If this fantasmatic description was meant primarily as a warning against women's appropriation of the codpiece, it was also potentially subversive in that it acknowledged the transferability of both the codpiece and patriarchal power.

At first glance, William Gamage's "On the feminine Supremacie," written in 1613, seems quite similar to *Apius and Virginia*. Gamage writes

> I often heard, but never read till now,
> That Women-kinde the Codpeeces did weare;
> But in those Iles, the men to women bow . . .
> I should therefore the woman iudge to be
> The vessell strongst, but Paule denies it me.[63]

In this poem, as in *Apius and Virginia*, the transferability of the codpiece is foregrounded and is again taken as a correlative of the transferability of patriarchal power: Gamage says that he has heard that "Women-kinde" wear "the Codpeeces," and that in the "Isles" where this happens, the men "bow" to women. It might thus seem as if Gamage is warning against English women appropriating the codpiece and thereby inverting gendered relations, much as in *Apius and Virginia*. I believe, however, that Gamage is actually questioning the use of the codpiece altogether, rather than playing with its potential appropriation. Even though Gamage initially highlights the transferability of both the codpiece and patriarchal power, he later makes an effort to (re)secure the latter, but he does so without the former. This is a crucial point of departure from the scenario described in *Apius and Virginia*, and one which might be related to the fact that Gamage's text appears after the codpiece had gone out of fashion. Whatever the reason, Gamage says that while he might be tempted to generalize based on the social arrangements of this fantasmatic

"Isle" and judge women to be "the vessell strongest," "Paul denies" him this possibility. With this all-important qualification, Gamage attempts to guarantee the legitimacy and stability of the patriarchal order in the British "Isles" by grounding it in biblical authority – and specifically in Paul's pronouncements about gender relations in Corinthians. We should note, however, that Gamage conspicuously avoids rehabilitating the codpiece. In the end, his comments (re)assert the gendered hierarchy while also disarticulating the codpiece from it. As a result, he implies that materializing masculinity through this part threatens to destabilize patriarchal gendered relations on account of its transferability.

By now, it should be clear that one of the primary strategies used to disarticulate the codpiece from masculine identity in the seventeenth century was emphasizing the item's prosthetic nature. It is important to recognize, however, that despite the prevalence of this strategy in texts from the period, it does not follow that detachable/transferable parts were *necessarily* less essential than other parts in early modern England. The handkerchief, as I suggested in the last chapter, was both integral and detachable. Moreover, the codpiece had itself been an essential component of masculinity for over a century before its decline.

Thus, instead of seeing the codpiece's prosthetic nature as an indication of the item's inevitable dispensability or superfluity, I would propose seeing it as a chance to witness the process of construction at work. That is to say, the various manipulations of the codpiece are particularly evident because the item itself is prosthetic, and we are therefore able to see it being attached, detached, or transferred. This is true at both an individual and a cultural level. But if we remember that these manipulations are also acts of intervention with regard to the dominant ideologies of the time – since these ideologies are constantly reiterating themselves (or failing to do so) through the item – then the item's prosthetic nature might be seen as an indication of its participation in the ongoing process of ideological construction, and an indication of the "instability" of the ideology itself.

Although this is especially true with a prosthetic item like the codpiece, it is worth saying that it is true of all items that materialize gendered identity including "biological" features like the private parts. Indeed, in this very chapter, I have discussed the changing forms of the male genitalia in early modern England. While morphological features like the penis and the testicles obviously don't appear and disappear in quite the same way as the codpiece or the beard, they do, as we have seen, matter and fail to matter at different moments in time.

I now want to turn to what might seem a paradox regarding the codpiece, and that is that even though both forms of this accessory eventually disappeared around the beginning of the seventeenth century, the emergent ideology of masculinity did not disappear along with them. This emergent ideology is what Phyllis Rackin and Jean Howard call "performative masculinity" or what Gary Taylor calls "the regime of the penis," and it was becoming dominant around the turn of the century. And, if, as I've suggested, the phallic codpieces helped to instantiate this ideology, then why did they disappear along with their more scrotal counterparts?

Although my answer to this question must remain somewhat speculative, I believe that it has something to do with the emergent ideology of masculinity itself. Indeed, throughout this chapter, I have tried to suggest that the various changes and developments regarding the codpiece need to be studied in relation to the ideologies of gender from the period. The texts that I have been studying in this chapter provide some indication of the rationale for the renunciation of the codpiece. They suggest that the newly emergent ideology of masculinity began to be materialized through the penis itself, as opposed to the codpiece.[64] John Marston, for instance, claims that it is only the "substance" and not the "shadow" which can really remove doubts about "what sex" an individual is. Similarly, the messenger in Middleton and Dekker's *The Honest Whore* suggests that the messenger is not a man if he has only a codpiece without a "pin" to put in it. We might therefore say that the cultural investment in the penis arises out of, and in conjunction with, the decline of the codpiece. It may, moreover, also have been at least partially an attempt to disavow transferability and detachability of masculinity and masculine/patriarchal power.[65]

3   "His majesty the beard": beards and masculinity

In August of 1605, James I paid a visit to Oxford as part of his royal progress.[1] While he was there, some of the students from the university staged a production of the play *Alba* in his honor. In order to try to make a good impression on the king, the students hired all of their costumes and props from suppliers in London. The resulting performance does not appear to have been particularly remarkable (in fact, James apparently fell asleep in the middle of it), but it is nevertheless of interest to theater historians because the inventories and receipts documenting the students' rental have survived to this day. When taken together, these records provide a fairly precise indication of what costumes and props were used to stage this play.[2]

One of the most startling things that the inventories reveal is that the students hired over twenty prosthetic beards. They include:

> 1 blewe hayre and beard for neptune.
> 1 black smooth hayre and beard for à magitian.
> 1 white hayre and beard for nestor. . .
> 2 hermeits beards the on graye th'other white. . .
> 3 beards one Red one blacke th'other flexen.
> 10. satyers heads and berds.[3]

Another "4 berds" were also sent along at a later date. A duplicate inventory states that these were "for Heremits." In total, then, twenty-two false beards were rented for this production.

If this seems remarkable, it is worth saying that there is other evidence that suggests that it may not have been completely anomalous. Indeed, when we begin to trace the provenance of the beards used by the students, it becomes clear that there was a brisk traffic in these theatrical props. The Oxford inventories indicate that all of the costumes were supplied by two men – Edward Kirkham and Thomas Kendall – both of whom were involved in the management of the boys' company at Blackfriars which was variously known as the Chapel Children, the Children of Blackfriars and Children of the Queen's Revels. It is therefore possible that the twenty-two beards sent to Oxford were supplied directly from the stocks of the Blackfriars troupe.[4] It is also possible, however, that these props were taken from the stocks of the Revels Office since Edward Kirkham was the Revels Yeoman at the time and one of the perquisites of his post was that he was entitled to rent out the costumes and other goods in his care. One of Kirkham's predecessors – John Arnold – had engaged in just such a practice and was so successful that in 1572 a London haberdasher named Thomas Giles filed a complaint against him. In his testimony, Giles explains that Arnold "havynge allone the costo-dye of the garmentes / dothe lend the same at hys plesure" and, consequently, Giles' own business was being undermined: as he puts it, he was "hynderyde of hys lyvyge herbye [because] . . . havynge aparell to lett . . . [he could not] so cheplye lett the same as hyr hyghnes maskes be lett."[5]

If Kirkham drew the properties for the Oxford performance from those owned by the Revels Office, he would undoubtedly have had enough false beards on hand to fill the order since beards were frequently purchased for the production of plays and masks at court. Although the Revels Office inventor-ies for 1605 do not survive, inventories from the late sixteenth century indicate that these props were purchased in large numbers. In 1572–3, for instance, the Revels Office purchased twenty-nine beards:

viij long white Beard*es* at xx^d the peece – xiij^s iiij^d/ Aberne Berd*es* ij & j black-fyzicians bearde – xiiij^s viij^d / Berds White & Black vj –viij^s/ Heares for plam*ers* ij – ij^s vij^d Berdes for fyshers vj – ix^s . . .Redd Berd*es* vj – ix^s.

Another twenty-two were bought the following season:

vij Long Aberne beard*es* at xvj^d the peece – ix^s iiij^d/ vij other berd*es* ottett at xiiij^d the peece for the haun*ces* Mask at xvj^d the peece – viij^s ij^d/ xij beard*es* Black & Redd for the fforesters Mask at like rate – xvj^s/ Heare for the wylde Men at xvjd the lb iij lb – iiij^s/ One Long white Bearde – ijs viijd.[6]

As with the Oxford inventory, the variety of colors and shapes here is remarkable.[7] If the acquisitions by the Revels office in the 1570s were in any way typical, Kirkham would have had a large stock of prosthetic beards to choose from.

According to the receipts from the Oxford rental, however, it was not Edward Kirkham, but Thomas Kendall who actually sent the beards, wigs, and vizards to the students. This may simply indicate who filled the request on that day and not where the props themselves came from, but it is also possible that Kendall filled the order from his own stocks, since he too appears to have trafficked in costumes and properties either on his own, or through connection to the Children of the Queen's Revels, or both. Kendall was a haberdasher like the complainant Thomas Giles who, thirty years earlier, had insisted that the Revels Yeoman was hurting his business by renting out the stocks from the Revels Office. In fact, records indicate that it was not uncommon for at least some haberdashers to rent theatrical properties and costumes including beards. For example, the haberdasher Harry Bennet supplied false beards in Coventry throughout the early 1570s.[8] Similarly, there was a London haberdasher named John Ogle who made all of the beards and wigs acquired by the Revels Office during the 1570s and 80s, including the fifty-six prosthetic beards delivered in 1572–4 that I listed above. Although these were sales, it is likely that Ogle both rented and sold beards as Bennet did. In fact, in preparation for the play-within-the-play in *The Book of Sir Thomas More*, one of the players goes to borrow a "long beard" from "Ogles," only to find that "Owgle was not with in, and his wife would not let [him] have the beard."[9] If these late sixteenth-century haberdashers were thus in the habit of supplying false beards for theatrical performances, it is certainly possible that Thomas Kendall had a similar business in the early seventeenth century.

Although it is ultimately impossible to tell exactly where the beards used in the Oxford performance came from, it would not be surprising to find that more than one of these avenues were involved, or, put differently, it would not be surprising to find that there was not a rigid distinction between the stocks of the Blackfriars company, the Revels Office, and Kendall's own personal property. But whatever the exact source, the crucial point for my purposes is that there appears to have been a fairly brisk trade in false beards. Moreover, it is worth pointing out that there are documents which indicate that only a few months after the Oxford performance, Kendall and Kirkham supplied beards for yet another student production. This time it was the Christmas play at Westminster School. An inventory indicates that the students rented "Crownes, hayres, and beards" for their performance. Although the inventory does not indicate exactly where these particular items came from, the only people it mentions are Kendall and Kirkham (both of whom are said to have supplied costumes). Kendall is paid "for the Lone of the Apparrell" and another payment is made to "Mr Kerkeham Man for his paynes for bringing a dublet (and) breeches."[10] It therefore seems likely that they supplied all the items, especially given their involvement with the Oxford rentals.

When all of this evidence is considered together, it suggests that false beards may have been a fairly common stage prop in student productions and in plays performed by the children's companies. There is a seventeenth-century poem which comments on the players' reliance upon these props in a humorous manner. The poem describes a donkey who decides to bequeath his hair to a group of players after his death so that it can be made into theatrical beards because "his Master did delight in Playes." According to the poem, "He wil'd that of his mane should beards be made, / And of his tayle, a head-tire for a Devill."[11] There is also other, more serious, evidence that indicates the importance of false beards as props. First of all, there are numerous references to beards in the plays themselves, particularly in the plays performed by the boys' companies. In fact, facial hair is mentioned in fully half of the extant boys' company texts.[12] In most cases, this means that some sort of comment is made about a character's beard, indicating that he should be played with a beard. This does not, of course, definitively prove that false beards were used. It is certainly possible that these passages were simply left out of the performance or that the boy actor who played the character had "real" facial hair. Nevertheless, it does strongly suggest the prevalence of these props. Moreover, it is important to bear in mind that false beards may have been used as part of the *mise en scène* without the script explicitly making reference to this.

Contemporary scholars have been slow to acknowledge the extent to which boy actors, in particular, relied upon prosthetic beards. W. Reavley Gair maintains in *The Children of Paul's* that the boys at Paul's "did not . . . use false beards or moustaches" at all, at least for the period from 1599 to 1602.[13] The evidence from the plays performed by these actors, however, contradicts this claim. First of all, at least five of the plays performed during those years explicitly call for prosthetic beards – either in the stage directions, or by having the character appear at one point in the play with a beard and another without it.[14] Moreover, there are another nine plays performed by Paul's boys that feature characters who are said to be bearded. While it is again possible that some of these characters might have been played by actors who had real facial hair, it is more likely that false beards were used. This is especially true since the color of the character's beard is often specified.[15]

Gair does acknowledge that false beards were used in some of these plays since they are mentioned in the stage directions, but he dismisses these cases as anomalies because he claims that the items were only used for comic purposes. At one point, Gair explicitly states that facial hair "on a fourteen-year-old" is "obviously comic."[16] While false beards could certainly be used for comic purposes, there is no reason to assume that these props were *only* used in that way. It seems just as likely that the comic scenes involving these props were playing ironically with a dramatic convention. Gair's resistance to acknowledging that the boys regularly used prosthetic beards may derive from the fact that he is trying to prove that the boys were serious thespians, and he seems to think that if they wore false beards, then the seriousness of their performances would have been compromised. The problem with this logic is that it assumes that false beards have no place in a serious dramatic performance, and that using them would necessarily compromise the artistic integrity of a production. I see no reason for these assumptions. We know that boys routinely wore dresses and wigs in order to play the parts of women, and no one assumes that these feminine props were "obvious[ly] comic" or that they necessarily compromised the artistic integrity of a production.[17]

Moreover, there is even some evidence that suggests that the spectacle of boy actors in beards might have been part of the appeal of children's company performances. In Robert Wild's seventeenth-century text *The Benefice*, one of the characters defends the play-going public, stating that they do not gather "for Mutiny," but rather "to see Children play Men, and Boys wear Beards."[18]

If "Boys wear[ing] Beards" was in fact a common occurrence then the next question is what dramatic function they served. Or, how were prosthetic beards used in actual productions? While it is difficult to answer this question with regard to the student performance at Oxford because the text of *Alba* does not survive, I believe that, generally speaking, prosthetic beards provided a means of constructing masculinity on the stage. This is suggested by the lines from Wild's *The Benefice* that I mentioned above. When the character says that people come "to see Children play Men, and Boys wear Beards": Wild implicitly links "play[ing] Men" and "wear[ing] Beards." If this is what prosthetic beards were generally used for, then they would have been particularly useful in performances where adult male actors were not present. In fact, it is my contention that boy actors needed false beards to stage masculinity in much the same way as they needed dresses and wigs to stage femininity.

Although I have thus far been describing the role of beards in the theaters, I eventually want to broaden my analysis and examine the "production" of masculinity in the culture at large. As the chapter progresses, I will try to suggest that the theater was only one of the cultural institutions or sites where the ideology of bearded masculinity was staged. But the aim of this chapter is not simply to demonstrate how the ideology of bearded masculinity was constituted, or to demonstrate the extent to which having a beard worked to make an individual into a man. In addition, I hope that focusing on the beard and its relationship to masculinity will lead to two important insights about gender identity itself. First, I hope it will help us to see that masculinity was not only constructed in contrast to femininity, but also in contrast to boyhood; as a result, we can say that men and boys were quite literally two distinct genders. Secondly, I hope it will help to demonstrate that early modern masculinity was in crucial ways prosthetic.

The first of these insights may sound somewhat strange today. While we certainly distinguish between men and boys, we do not usually consider men to be a distinct gender from boys in the same way as we consider men to be a distinct gender from women. For us, the difference between men and boys is a matter of degree whereas the difference between men and women is a matter of kind. In early modern England, however, sexual differences between men and women were, as Thomas Laqueur has shown, often conceptualized in terms of degree. Consequently, the distinction between men and boys would have been much more similar to that between men and women.[19]

In making this point, I hope to contribute to the growing body of research about the social category of "the boy" in early modern England. Much of the recent work on this subject has concentrated specifically on boy actors. Stephen Orgel's *Impersonations*, for instance, examines "why . . . the English stage [took] boys for women."[20] Similarly, Lisa Jardine has looked at the erotic interchangeability of boys and women in sexual encounters, arguing that it was not so much the gender of the "submissive" partner that mattered, but the expectation of that very submissiveness.[21] Whereas both of these studies focus primarily on the eroticization of boys, or on their sexuality, what I am interested in here is their place within the gendered hierarchy, or how the gendered category of "boy" was constituted. I believe that the distinction between boys and men was ultimately materialized through a range of attributes or parts. One of these was facial hair, but there were certainly others as well such as the voice, swords, armor, and daggers. There is one seventeenth-century text, however, that uses beard growth alone to separate the men from the boys. Randal Holme's *Academy of Armory* describes the different stages of masculine development beginning with the "child" who he says is "smooth and [has] little hair." Then, Holme defines a "youth" as having "hair on the head, but none on the face," and a "Man" as "having a beard."[22] Shakespeare seems to employ a similar schema in Jacques' "seven ages of man speech" in *As You Like It*: he speaks, for example, of the transition from "schoolboy" with a "shining morning face" to the "soldier" who is "bearded like the pard" (2.7.144–9).[23]

If "boys" were thus in an important sense "outside" the ideology of masculinity, they also functioned as actors who were called upon to stage it.[24] As I suggested earlier, one way in which they did this was through using false beards in theatrical productions. The main character in Nicholas Udall's *Thersites* provides an excellent example of this. The play was probably performed by a group of students at Oxford much like the production of *Alba*. It opens with the character Mulciber making a set of arms for Thersites, and at one point, he notes that Thersites is already outfitted with a "blacke and rustye grym berde." He asks "Would not thy blacke and rustye grym berde, / Nowe thou art so armed, make anye man aferde?"[25] Mulciber's comment here is meant to draw attention to Thersites' masculinity (albeit in an ironic way). Thersites' "masculinity" is characterized by the "fear" his beard supposedly inspires in other men, and by the martial analogy that Mulciber uses to describe it – he says Thersites is "armed" with his facial hair. In other plays performed by children's companies, facial hair is similarly associated with masculinity. For example, in Lording Barry's *Ram Alley* (a play performed by The Children of the King's Revels), there is a character who is actually named Lieutenant Beard. This moniker again links the beard with the military context and with manly activities.[26] Finally, the theatrical importance of false beards is dramatized, or rather satirized, in *The Book of Sir Thomas More*. There, as I noted earlier, the players are forced to postpone their performance while one of them goes to borrow "a long beard" from Ogle.[27]

Thomas Middleton's *A Mad World My Masters* follows this pattern, but it is different in that it does not simply utilize the false beard as a part of its *mise en scène*; instead, it incorporates this prop into the plot itself. The dramatic action centers around a boy who puts on a prosthetic beard in order to disguise himself as a man. The play might therefore be said to be a self-reflexive look at the theatrical use of false beards by boy actors. *A Mad World My Masters* is, in many ways, a typical crossdressing narrative. In this case, however, we are presented with boy/man transvestism as opposed to the more common boy/woman transvestism.[28] Middleton's play tells the story of Follywit, a "youth" and heir who dresses himself as a man (Lord Owemuch), infiltrates the house of his grandfather (Sir Bounteous Progress), and tries to repair their strained relations. As I noted above, Follywit's costume includes a "thin" beard. The exchanges in the play between "Lord Owemuch" and Sir Bounteous Progress often center on Follywit. They humorously draw attention to the differences between the "two" characters. For example, when Lord Owemuch asks Sir Bounteous to describe Follywit, Sir Bounteous reports that he is "*Imberbis juvenis* [a beardless youth]" and that his "chin has no more prickles than a mid-wife" (2.1.126–7). In statements such as this, Sir Bounteous not only calls attention to the contrast between "Lord Owemuch" and Follywit, he also questions the masculinity of the latter: first, Sir Bounteous makes the obvious pun about Follywit's lack of "prickles," and he also compares him to a "mid-wife" (possibly meaning "half-woman"). Given this comment, it is worth noting that later in the play, Follywit actually takes on the role of a woman: he dresses himself as a courtesan to deceive and rob his grand-father. While disguising himself, Follywit tells the other characters on stage (and, of course, the audience) that they shall "see a woman quickly made up here" (3.3.88). He uses "the lower part of a gentlewoman's gown," a "mask," a "chin-clout," a "couple of locks" (3.3.77–107) hanging out the back of his hat. The "chin-clout" and "mask" are particularly interesting because they would have been used to cover Follywit's facial hair.[29] And if the metadramatic aspects of these crossdressing scenes weren't clear enough, in the last scene, Follywit quite literally becomes an actor in the play within the play.

A Mad World My Masters thus illustrates how false beards might have been used by boy actors to stage masculinity. What I wish to emphasize here is that whenever the boy actors used beards in this way, they would have been as much "in drag" as when they used dresses and wigs to stage femininity. The children's company plays seem to be at least somewhat self-conscious about this. Indeed, they often ironically call attention to their staging of masculinity and to the fact that the boy actors use supplements in order to play the parts of men. Consider Nicholas Udall's *Thersites* which I mentioned earlier. When Mulciber asks Thersites "Would not thy blacke and rustye grym berde, / Nowe thou art so armed, make anye man aferde?,"[30] he highlights the temporary nature of Thersites' beard by pointing out that he is so armed "*Nowe.*" There are two possible explanations for this comment. First, it may be that the actor who played Thersites put on a beard in the midst of the performance and that he had not worn it earlier. Another possibility is that the comment "Nowe thou art so armed" is meant to be an aside that draws attention to the boy actor wearing the beard in the theatrical setting. In either case, the end result is more or less the same: the comment draws attention to the artificiality – and detachability – of Thersites' beard. Thersites' beard seems to be yet another "superfluous" part of his ensemble: it goes along with the club, sword, and "sallet" [helmet] that Mulciber outfits him with, but which he is afraid to use.[31] For my purposes, the crucial thing to note is that when boy actors made comments such as this, they called attention to the supplementation their bodies required in order to play the roles of men, and hence to the gendered difference between boys and men.

While the cultural work performed by Middleton's *A Mad World My Masters* is similar to that performed by *Thersites*, it is in some ways more complex. As I noted earlier, the play self-reflexively depicts the boy Folly-wit wearing a false beard in order to play the role of a man. It must be said, however, that the beard that Follywit dons is a "thin" one, and the rest of his disguise consists of "a French ruff . . . and strong perfume" (1.1.78).[32] These items are the hallmarks of an effeminate courtier. So even though Follywit fashions himself into a man, he nevertheless only seems to be able to become an effeminate one. The play thus implicitly questions Follywit's ability to inhabit fully the masculine role, and by extension questions whether boys can fully transform themselves into men. Masculinity here seems to be arrayed along a continuum rather than in a simply polar fashion. Indeed, the male characters in the play all seem to fall at different spots on such a continuum: at the one end, we have the beardless boy Follywit; in the middle, the effeminate but bearded courtier Owemuch; and finally, the fully masculine Sir Bounteous. Thus, prosthetic facial hair may have been used, not only to materialize polarized differences between men and boys, but also, more subtly, to materialize differences of degree between all sorts of males.

The boy actors in the children's companies were not the only ones who staged the gendered distinctions between boys and men. The actors in the adult companies did so as well, though in a slightly different way. This is most obvious when one of the characters in a scene simply distinguishes between the men and the boys on the stage. For example, in Robert Wilson's

The Three Lordes and Three Ladies of London, one of the men in the play calls several of the other characters "boys" and then goes on to justify himself, saying "be not angry that I call you boies, for ye are no men yet, ye have no beardes."[33] Although there are similar statements in the plays performed by the boys' companies, lines like this would have been particularly resonant in the adult companies, where both "adult" actors and "boy" actors were present.

Indeed, I believe that the adult companies' institutional structure was extremely significant in this context, and would have helped to reinforce the more general gendered distinction between men and boys. It is a well-known fact that the actors in these troupes were categorized as either "adults" or "boys" and that the roles that they performed were predicated upon their place in this hierarchy: it is generally assumed that "boy" actors played the parts of women.[34] In and of itself, this practice seems to imply that boys and women are to some extent homologous – that they are both alike in not being men. As Rosalind puts it in Shakespeare's *As You Like It*, "boys and women are for the most part cattle of this color" (3.2.371). But in addition, beard growth was often said to be one of the things that distinguished "boy" actors from their "adult" counterparts. One instance where this occurs is in the metadramatic scene in *A Midsummer Night's Dream*. As the rude mechanicals prepare to stage their production of "Pyramus and Thisby," the actor Flute is assigned the part of the female lead. He protests, however, saying "Nay faith let me not play a woman, I have a beard coming" (1.2.39–40). Flute thus implies that because he has a "beard coming" it would be inappropriate for him to play a woman and, by extension, that it would be inappropriate for him to be considered a "boy" actor. Statements like this are fairly common. In Shakespeare's *Coriolanus*, Cominius says that the beardless Coriolanus, with his "Amazonian chin," could "act the woman in the scene" (2.2.87–92). These passages seem to suggest that an actor's facial hair determined the roles that he would play. I do not mean to claim, however, that this was actually the case.[35] Instead, what I am suggesting is that to the extent that the professional distinction between adult and boy actors *was imagined* to be determined by beard growth (and therefore *imagined* in the same terms as the more general distinction between men and boys), the very structure of the theatrical companies would have been mapped onto the gendered categories of the culture at large.

But if the children's companies and the adult companies both contributed in their own ways to the project of constructing the gendered distinction between men and boys, we should note that in the process, they also frequently highlighted the prosthetic nature of the beard. We have already seen several instances of this in boys' company plays (such as *Thersites* and *A Mad World My Masters*).[36] Something similar occurs in the metadramatic performance in Shakespeare's *A Midsummer Night's Dream*. When Bottom is assigned the role of Pyramus, he asks Peter Quince: "What beard were I best to play it in? . . . your straw-color beard, your orange tawny beard, your purple-in grain beard, or your French-crown color beard, your perfit yellow" (1.2.73–8). The actor who played Bottom may well have held up each of these items for inspection by the audience while giving his speech. At the very least, his verbal inventory of these outlandishly colored props would have called attention to the artificiality of the beards, and provided yet another instance of Bottom's penchant for the hypertheatrical.

Much of the humor in the scenes featuring the rude mechanicals derives from the ineptitude of their theatrical practice. With regard to the beard, the humor focuses on them putting this prop on the "wrong" person. Peter Quince bungles all of his casting decisions and gets them completely backwards. Quince reverses the conventions of the adult companies by forcing Flute – the hairy boy-man – to remove his beard in order to play the "feminine" Thisby. He also makes Bottom wear a false beard in order to play the "masculine" Pyramus. This inversion would have been even more extreme if the character who played Bottom was smooth-faced as I believe he was meant to be.[37] There is some evidence in the play that indicates that this is how the part was supposed to be played. For instance, once Bottom has been "translated" into an ass, he notes that he "must to the barber's . . . for methinks I am marvelous hairy about the face" (3.3.22–3). This line suggests that Bottom may have developed the beard as part of his transformation and that he is not accustomed to having it. Bottom's beardlessness is also subtly suggested by his name. There was a long tradition (going back at least as far as Chaucer's "Miller's Tale") of comparing/contrasting the cheeks of the face with the body's other cheeks in precisely this way. One popular sixteenth-century woodcut depicts a young man bending over, exposing his buttocks to the viewer, with a caption that reads: "To drink with me, be not afferde, for here ye see groweth never a berde."[38] Furthermore, if Bottom was initially beardless, it would give an added twist to his transformation: his cross-species metamorphosis would have been compounded by his gender change from boy to man.

But regardless of whether the actor who played Bottom was beardless, it is clear that in the rude mechanicals' production, facial hair is constantly "put on" in the "wrong" way. Moreover, in their performance, Flute's smooth chin is ultimately just as "artificial" as Bottom's multi-colored beards. When Flute goes to play the part of Thisby, he does not remove the beard he has "coming"; rather, he plays it "in a mask" (1.2.41). This may strike modern readers or theatergoers as being somewhat strange: while we are at least somewhat accustomed to prosthetic beards, we are much less accustomed to prosthetic chins or faces. This may not have been the case in early modern England where facial hair was much more common. Indeed, we have already seen that a "mask" and a "chinclout" were used by Follywit to cover his beard and play the role of a smooth-faced woman in Middleton's *A Mad World My Masters*. The masks used in both of these performances may have been similar to the "eggshell vizards" listed in the inventories of the Revels Office.[39] But even if masks weren't common, it is clear that the use of a mask in this particular scene in *A Midsummer Night's Dream* does interesting cultural work with regard to gender. In short, it completely denaturalizes the distinction between bearded masculinity and beardless femininity. The contrast between the two is presented as the difference between two prostheses.

If I have thus far been exploring the use of false beards on the stage, I ultimately want to suggest that this theatrical production of masculinity can help us to understand the more general production of masculinity in early modern English culture. Put simply, I believe that the beard helped to make the man outside of the playhouses as well as inside them. This is not to say that there were no differences between the two domains. Indeed, it seems likely that false beards would have been much less prevalent outside the theatrical context.[40] Nevertheless, it is important to recognize that even "real" facial hair was to some extent "theatrical": that is to say, it had to be "put on" (or grown) by certain people in order for them to play the roles of men, and by contrast, it had to be "taken off" (or removed) by others in order for those people to "play" the roles of women or boys. In what follows, I will discuss some of the cultural discourses and practices that helped to insure that facial hair was "staged" in the "right" way in early modern English culture.

But before moving on, I want to acknowledge that this chapter may seem to be something of a departure from the previous two chapters: whereas both of them concentrated on accessories of dress, this one concentrates on a part of the body. Although we tend to distinguish radically between cultural artifacts and "natural" parts of the body, I want to suggest that the items I have included here are in some ways analogous, and that they actually have much in common with one another. If handkerchiefs and codpieces are, as we have seen, objects that can be "incorporated" into the body and that remake it in the process, I will be arguing that beards and hair are parts of the body that can be removed or "excorporated" and which likewise remake the body in the process. So the trajectory of the chapters of this book is from objects that become parts of the subject, to parts of the subject that are in some ways like objects. In the Derridian terms that I mentioned in my introduction, the movement is from *supplements* to *parergons*. The theatrical false beards with which I began this chapter provide a bridge between the two since they are accessories of dress that are meant to replicate "real" parts of the body. As I tried to suggest above, however, the conceptual distance between a false beard and a biological one is not as great as we might expect. In fact, I will be arguing that while the modern division between subject and object – or nature and culture – encourages us to distinguish sharply between things like hand-kerchiefs/codpieces and beards/hair, these prosthetic parts not only occupied a similar conceptual space in early modern England, but they also performed similar types of cultural work. In the end, I believe all of these things were instruments through which gender and the gendered body were materialized.

Returning to my discussion of the beard, I now want to move beyond the theatrical context and point out that there were many different cultural discourses and practices that helped to create and reinforce what I have called the ideology of bearded masculinity. Some of the prominent "texts" that contributed to this project are sermons, anatomy and physiognomy books, and literature. But perhaps the most striking is portraiture. Virtually all of the portraits of men from sixteenth- and seventeenth-century England portray the sitter wearing a beard. Take, for instance, the paintings from a recent exhib-ition at the Tate Gallery, *Dynasties: Painting in Tudor and Jacobean Eng-land*. This show included some sixty portraits of men painted between the years 1530 and 1630, and of those sixty, fifty-five had some sort of facial hair: usually this was a full moustache and beard.[41] That means that well over ninety percent of the men represented in these paintings were bearded.

The ubiquity of facial hair in these particular portraits is by no means atypical. In fact, Roy Strong has assembled approximately three hundred and fifty portraits of men in his encyclopedic *Tudor and Jacobean Portraits*, and of those, there are over three hundred and twenty in which the sitter is depicted with facial hair.[42] Thus, for every portrait of a man without a beard, there are almost ten portraits of men with beards. Again this is well over ninety percent. The prevalence of beards in these paintings is suggested in an encapsulated form by the Somerset Treaty Portrait (figure 10) where eleven different men are represented sitting together at a table, and all of them have some sort of facial hair.

It is my sense that many modern viewers simply fail to "see" the beards in these paintings, in much the same way as we previously failed to "see" the prominence of Christ's genitals in some early modern religious painting (as Leo Steinberg has demonstrated).[43] But once we acknowledge these beards, we also need to acknowledge that there are, in fact, many different styles of them. Charles I, for example, is shown wearing a "stiletto," John Knox a "cathedral," and an unknown sitter a "swallowtail" (figures 11–13).[44] The poet John Taylor catalogs some of the most popular facial hair styles in his satiric account of the beards seen at the court of James I:

> Now a few lines to paper I will put,
> Of men's beards strange and variable cut . . .
> Some like a spade, some like a fork, some square,

Figure 10. Unknown Artist, *The Somerset House Conference* (1604), with
ten bearded sitters.

Some round, some mow'd like stubble, some starke bare,
Some sharpe, stiletto fashion, dagger-like,
That may with whispering a man's eyes outpike:
Some with hammer cut, or Romane T,
Their beards extravagant reformed must be.[45]

Although Taylor's list may itself seem "extravagant," it is by no means
exhaustive. There were at least fifteen distinct and recognizable beard styles
worn during the period.[46] In addition to those I have already mentioned, there
were styles like the bodkin, the needle, the fantail, the pisa, and the marquisotte.

Each of these beards was supposedly worn by a specific group of people
and therefore came to have a specific set of social meanings. Some of these
are delineated in a text known as *The Ballad of the Beard*. It maintains, for
instance, that "The soldier's beard doth march in sheare'd, / In figure like a
spade, / With which he'll make his enemies quake and think their graves are
made." Here, soldiers are said to wear the "spade beard," and consequently
these beards are said to evoke fear. It is possible that the character Thersites, in
the play by Nicholas Udal that I mentioned above, is meant to wear this
particular style of prosthetic beard since he is a soldier/"adventurer" and

Figure 11. Daniel Mytens, *King Charles I* (1631), wearing a stiletto beard.

IOANNES CNOXVS.

Figure 12. Wood engraving of John Knox (1580), wearing a cathedral beard.

Mulciber claims that his beard would "make anye man aferde." *The Ballad of the Beard* also describes the "cathedral" cut, which was supposedly worn by churchmen and was understood to indicate piety. In the end, it would appear that the different styles of facial hair formed a complex semiotic system. While

Figure 13. John Bettes the Elder, *An Unknown Man in a Black Cap* (1545), wearing a swallowtail beard.

the semiotic significance of any particular beard was always shifting and contested, it was also crudely "fixed" by texts like *The Ballad of the Beard*.

Although it would probably be possible to "decode" the various social meanings attributed to the different cuts of facial hair, that is not my aim here. My project is more materialist in its aims. I want to suggest that all facial hair (whatever the particular style) was constitutive of masculine identity. This is not exactly the same as saying that facial hair was a "sign" of masculinity.

This latter formulation implies that the beard simply "signaled" a gendered essence that actually resided elsewhere. What I am trying to suggest here, by contrast, is that facial hair was itself a component of manhood – that it was a means through which manhood was materialized.

But if the beard was constitutive and essential, it was also something that had to be culturally produced. This is not to deny that people "naturally" grow hair on their faces and that some people grow more of it than others. Nevertheless, because of hair's malleability, these "natural" differences are in practice always subject to transformation. Moreover, the "natural" differences between individuals with regard to facial hair do not correspond exactly with the social categories of "men" and "women" (or "men" and "boys") since some "men" will "naturally" lack facial hair, and some "women" will "naturally" develop it. When seen from this perspective, it becomes apparent that the early modern writing on beards is often as much prescriptive as descriptive. That is to say, when early modern authors claim (as many did) that "a beard" appears "in each man's face" and that "every female beardless doth remaine,"[47] they are not so much describing a morphological reality as fashioning one. An analogous point can be made about the portraits that I have been discussing here. They were not simply transparent mirrors of historical reality; instead, they were also mechanisms of idealization.[48]

If portraiture was one medium through which cultural norms regarding beard growth were produced and reinforced, religious discourse was another. Indeed, the fact that beards first start to appear regularly in portraits during the 1530s and 1540s should alert us to the link between the gendered ideology that I have been sketching in this chapter and the Protestant Reformation. Interestingly, Protestant preachers often explicitly promoted bearded masculinity. One sermon insists, for example, that "God would have his people to preserve their beards" because "a decent growth of the Bearde is a signe of Manhood, and given by God to distinguish the Male from the Female sex."[49] Other pastors referred to the injunction in Leviticus 19:27 – "Ye shall not round the corners of your heads, neither shalt thou mar the corners of thy beard."

Protestant preachers didn't simply exhort others to wear beards, they also wore them themselves. They did so, in part, in order to distinguish themselves from their Catholic counterparts who, at least traditionally, were clean-shaven. Indeed, one religious historian notes that "virtually all of the continental clerical reformers had deliberately grown beards as a mark of their rejection of the old Church" and consequently, in mid-Tudor England, "the significance of clerical beards as an aggressive anti-Catholic gesture was well-recognized."[50] This is certainly the case in John Foxe's *Book of Martyrs*. The title page presents "The image of the persecuted Church" on the left-hand side of the page and "The image of the persecutying Church" on the right-hand side of the page, and virtually all of the Protestant figures have beards, whereas virtually all of the Catholic figures are beardless (figure 14). The contrast is particularly conspicuous in the two juxtaposed images at the center of the page. One image depicts seven Protestant martyrs being burned at the stake and all of them have large fully-developed beards. Across the page, the corresponding Catholics have no facial hair and have traditional tonsure. This imagery is reinforced by the woodcuts scattered throughout the book since many of the martyrs have sizable, flowing beards. One of the most striking images is that of Archbishop Thomas Cranmer being pulled down from his pulpit by his beard. The offender is, unsurprisingly, a beardless, tonsured monk.[51]

The distinction between bearded Protestant divines and clean-shaven Catholic priests and monks had a gendered subtext. Protestant clergymen adopted the beard as an indication of their masculinity, or more specifically, as an indication of their marriageability and reproductive capacity. They thereby attempted to distinguish themselves from their "effeminate" Catholic counterparts who did not marry or reproduce, and who were sometimes even called "eunuchs for God."[52]

But there were also some tensions *within* the Catholic Church about the issue of facial hair. Canon laws prohibiting beards had been in place since at least the eleventh century,[53] though these rules were sometimes disregarded. When Pope Clement VII threatened to enforce the canon law in the early sixteenth century, it provoked Pierio Valeriano to write a treatise entitled *Pro Sacerdotum Barbis* (1531)[54] in which he insists that Catholic priests ought to wear beards because the "beard is a token of manly nature" – "a garment for manly cheeks." This text was translated into English in 1533, just as facial hair was starting to become the norm in England.[55] The translator claims that he decided to publish the text because there is "no realm" where beards have been "been less accepted." He ultimately hopes, moreover, that "if it be proved no unmeet thing for a priest to wear a beard . . . it may seem so much the more sufferable in a lay man" (2). He contends that it "beseemeth menne to have longe beardes, for [it is] chiefly by that token . . . [that] the vigorous strength of manhode is decerned from the tenderness of women."[56] In these passages, the beard is fully transmuted into a component of gender identity. Facial hair moves from being "token" of "manhode" to being an indication of the "vigorous strength" of men (which is here contrasted with the "tenderness of women"). But if this treatise therefore clearly promotes the ideology of bearded masculinity, it must be said that the English translator's decision to appropriate a voice of dissent from within the Catholic Church was a particularly shrewd one given the shifting sands of religious belief in England in the 1530s.[57] The pro-beard discourse of this particular text could thus be seen either as coming from within the Catholic Church, or as a critique of it.

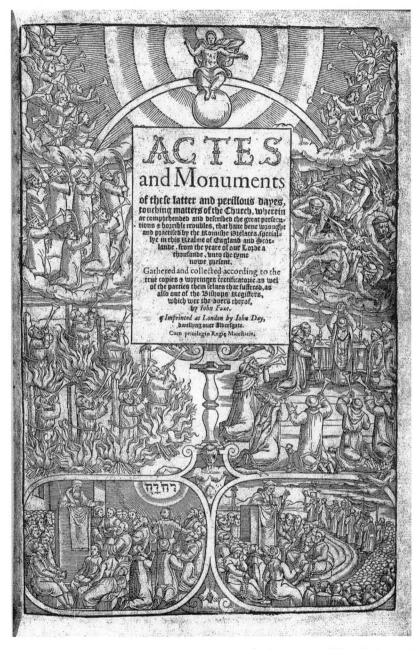

Figure 14. Title page of John Foxe's *Book of Martyrs* (1563), with bearded Protestants on the left and beardless Catholics on the right.

Another set of texts that helped to establish the beard as a fundamental feature of masculine identity were anatomy and physiognomy books. They, too, often present an idealized portrait of facial hair. The mid-seventeenth-century anatomist Daniel Sennert, for example, states categorically that "Men have beards, Women have none."[58] Nicholas Culpepper's *Bartholinus Anatomy* (1668) is equally categorical, asserting that hairs appear "On the Chins of men, but not of women."[59] Physiognomers make similar claims. The section on beards in Thomas Hill's *The Contemplation of Mankinde* (1571) sets out to explain why it is that "men are lone bearded, & not women."[60] And finally, Helkiah Crooke, the most prominent English physician of the day, writes in his *Microcosmographia: Description of the Body of Man* (1615) that "it is a venerable sight to see a man . . . his face compassed about with thicke and comely hair."[61] Women, however, "never" grow hair "in the chinne" (67) for "the smoothnesse of their face is their proper ornament; they needed no ensigne of majesty because they were born to subjection. And Nature hath given them such a form of body as is answerable to the disposition of their minde" (70).

These anatomical claims were even more thoroughly articulated in the book-length studies of facial hair published during the seventeenth century. The most exhaustive of these, at well over three hundred pages, is Marcus Antonius Ulmus' *Physiologia Barbae Humanae* (1603). Others include Joannes Barbatiu's *Barbae Maiestas, Hoc est de Barbis Elegans, Brevis et Accurata descriptio* (1614), Christian Beckmann and Valentius Hartungus' *Disceptatio de Barbigenio Hominus mere maris* (1608), and Georg Caspar Kirchmaier's *De Majestate Juribusque Barbae* (1698).[62] Although these books were all published on the continent, it is clear that at least Ulmus' book circulated in England. The mid seventeenth-century proto-anthropological writer, John Bulwer, for instance, discusses Ulmus' *Physiologia Barbae Humanae* at some length, explaining that for Ulmus the beard is "the signe of man, by which he appears a man" and that it is "an Index, in the face, of the Masculine generative faculty."[63] Sir Thomas Browne also mentions *Physiologia Barbae Humanae* in *A Letter to a Friend*. He asserts that Ulmus' book makes the beard into "a distinction of sex" and a "sign of masculine Heat."[64]

If the anatomy books helped to create a specific morphological ideal with regard to beard growth, that same ideal was also reiterated in other, less scientific, forms of writing. The poet Hugh Crompton, for example, asserts in *The Glory of Women* (1652) that "in each man's face appears / A beard extending upward to his ears . . . But every female beardless doth remaine, both old and young her face is still the same."[65] Nicholas Billingsley's short poem "On a Beard" is more openly prescriptive. Billingsley explicitly advocates the wearing of beards, concluding with the exclamation: "O what a grace . . . is a well-thatch'd face."[66]

It must be said, however, that these ideals were not uncontested. In the first half of the sixteenth century, when the ideology of bearded masculinity was still becoming hegemonic, the physician Andrew Boorde wrote an entire book attacking facial hair on men. Boorde is better known today for treating Henry VIII and other members of the aristocracy, and for his *The First Booke of the Introduction of Knowledge* (1547) and *A Compendyous Regyment or a Dyetary of Helth* (1542). This is, in part, because his book on beards has not survived. We only know of its existence through a satirical response to it entitled *The Treatyse Answerynge the Boke of Berdes*. The first page of the response announces it to be "a treatyse, made, answerynge *the treatyse of doctor Borde upon Berdes*." The author is identified as "Barnes."[67] From the comments in this text, we can extrapolate some of Boorde's "reproaches gyven unto berdes": he apparently argued, for example, that "there come . . . no gaines" from wearing facial hair, and that it was a catalyst to vanity since it "breed[s] much care."

The counterarguments of the *Treatyse* are often addressed directly to Boorde, as when the author states:

> But, syr, I praye you, yf you tell can,
> Declare to me, when God made man,
> (I meane by our forefather Adam)
> Whyther that he had a berde than;
> And yf he had, who dyd him shave,
> Syth that a barber he coulde not have.
> Well, then, ye proue hym there a knave,
> Bycause his berde he dyd so save.
>
> (314)

These verses imply that Adam must have been bearded since there was no "barber" available in the Garden of Eden. Therefore, in the terms that Boorde apparently set out, he must have been a "knave." While the lines are hardly polished, they are of interest because the argumentative strategy they adopt is a common one: simply put, they attempt to establish a normative corporeal ideal through reference to Adam's "natural" state in the Garden of Eden.

Boorde's book is significant because it demonstrates that the ideology of bearded masculinity was not uncontested. In fact, the contestation was performatively enacted in Antoine Hotman's *De barba dialogus* (1586), where Hotman stages a debate about beards between the interlocutors "Pogonias" and "Misopogon."[68] If Boorde and Hotman thus make the faultlines in the ideology of bearded masculinity apparent, it would, I believe, be somewhat misleading to downplay the extent of that ideology's hegemony. In fact, there does not appear to be another writer in all of sixteenth and seventeenth-century Europe that advocated the "Reformacyon of berdes" (308) as forcefully as Boorde did. Moreover, Boorde's ideas about beard growth were themselves somewhat equivocal, or perhaps changed over time, since in Boorde's chapter on "Manne's face" in the *Breviary of Healthe* (1552), he points out that although "The face may have many impediments," "The fyrst impedyment is to se a man having no berde, and a woman to have a berde."[69]

If most early modern anatomists and physiognomers thus describe the growth of facial hair in rigidly dichotomous terms (maintaining, for example, that "Men have beards, Women have none"), then one of the things we need to do in order to make the ideological work that these texts perform more visible is to recognize that facial hair is not, as I noted earlier, actually distributed bipolarly between males and females as these formulations consistently imply. Instead, it is distributed bimodally.[70] But if these descriptions of facial hair may thus appear somewhat distorted, this situation is complicated by the fact that the presence or absence of facial hair is also effected by cultural practices such as depilation. These practices can accentuate the dichotomy between males and females, and make statements like this appear more "true." In fact, we might even say that these anatomical "descriptions" were self-fulfilling prophecies, at least insofar as they would have helped to establish a morphological ideal which would, in turn, have governed the way in which facial hair was actually "put on" or "taken off."

The point that I am making here about the cultural production of facial hair in early modern England resonates powerfully with the central thesis of Judith Butler's *Bodies that Matter*. As I noted in my introduction, Butler's book is essentially an intervention in the current theoretical debate between essentialists and constructivists. She attempts to reconceptualize "the body" and gender in a way that will circumvent the current impasse, and help us to rethink the very terms of the discussion. Taking a strong constructivist position, Butler argues that the social and the somatic are inextricably intertwined, and, as the pun in her title implies, that it is only when corporeal differences between the sexes "matter" socially speaking, that those differences "matter" physically speaking (that physical differences are quite literally brought into being through this process). While this may sound radical, I believe that the developments regarding beard growth in sixteenth- and seventeenth-century English culture forcefully illustrate her point. There, the dichotomized differences regarding facial hair were made to "matter" socially through a wide range of texts and practices, and simultaneously, those dichotomized differences were often materialized – or made "matter" physically. But this chapter doesn't simply illustrate Butler's thesis, it also provides a kind of historical supplement to it. Indeed, another thing that I am suggesting is that the sexual differences that "mattered" in early modern England were not necessarily the same as those that "matter" today.

Returning to the descriptions in the anatomy and physiognomy books, we are now in a position to recognize that they are as much descriptions of a social body or reality as of a biological one. This might seem to be a problem from a modern perspective, but, as I noted in my introduction, early modern anatomists and physiognomers do not seem to be anxious about separating nature from culture, or the body from its socially constructed materializations. Indeed, they often veer from anatomical description to social commentary on the same page. In the descriptions of beard growth, for example, almost all of the writers make a point of connecting the purported differences in men's and women's facial hair with the differences in their social standing. The logic they use in these instances is not exactly what modern readers might expect. They do not point to the supposed physical differences between men and women as a means of justifying the uneven distribution of power in society (as is common in modern patriarchal discourse and thinking). Instead, they often do the opposite. Helkiah Crooke, as we have seen, says that "the smoothnesse of [women's] face is their proper ornament; they needed no ensigne of majesty *because* they were born to subjection."[71] In this formulation, Crooke assumes that the social status of women is given or fundamental. He then goes on to say that the "smoothnesse" of their faces is *an indication of* that social status, not *the basis for* it. As he puts it, it is "because" women were "born to subjection" that they do not have beards, not vice versa. The comments in Nicholas Culpepper's edition of *Bartholinus Anatomy* follow the same logic. He stipulates that "the Beard . . . adorns a man, and makes him venerable, especially if the hairs be spred all about. But in women there was no need of so venerable an appearance."[72] This passage again moves from the social to the physiological: it states that it is because women do not need to be venerated that they do not have facial hair. The modern version of this argument would almost certainly run in the opposite direction: it would suggest that because women do not have beards, they therefore do not need to be venerated.

These texts thus corroborate an important idea articulated by Thomas Laqueur in *Making Sex*. According to Laqueur,

in . . . pre-Enlightenment texts, and even some later ones, sex, or the body, must be understood as the epiphenomenon, while gender, what we would take to be a cultural category, was primary or "real." Gender – man and woman – mattered a great deal and was part of the order of things; sex was conventional, though modern terminology makes such a reordering nonsensical. At the very least, what we call sex and gender were . . . explicitly bound up in a circle of meanings from which escape to a supposed biological substrate – the strategy of the Enlightenment – was impossible.[73]

But if Laqueur thus suggests that before the Enlightenment, the relationship between nature and culture (or sex and gender) was understood very differently from the way it is understood in the post-Enlightenment world, what I want to add here is that these differing perspectives are rooted in the differing ontologies of the two historical periods. Put simply, early modern anatomists and physiognomers still have a powerful religious world view as well as a more modern, scientific one. Consequently, for them, religion and religious truth are often the basis for social reality, rather than nature. This will become clearer if we pay close attention to the verb tenses that these writers use. Note that both of the anatomists above shift into the past tense in the passages I quoted. In Culpepper's *Bartholinus Anatomy*, he claims that for women "there *was* no need of so venerable an appearance." The past tense here is presumably used to refer to the moment of creation. So he is suggesting that at that moment, there was no need for women to be given facial hair. This point might be compared to the one that Barnes makes in *The Treatyse Answerynge the Boke of Berdes*. In that text, we saw that Barnes insisted that Adam must have been bearded in the garden of Eden.

There is a comparable moment in Helkiah Crooke's *Microcosmographia*. He says that women "*needed* no ensigne of Majesty because they were born to subjection." He goes on to say that "Nature hath given them such a form of body as is answerable to the disposition of their minde." Again, it would appear that Crooke is talking about an originary moment of creation here: at that moment, women "*needed* no ensigne of Majesty." In this instance, however, Crooke is speaking about the way in which "Nature" hath made women, rather than the way in which God hath made them. While this is an interesting and important shift (and might be seen as the influence of a more scientific perspective), it is also clear that even though the creating agent has changed, the conceptual model of genesis remains the same. Crooke still seems to assume that there was a single moment when "Nature" gave women a specific "form of body."

In the end, all of these different texts (from portraiture to literature) helped to create or reinforce what I have called the ideology of bearded masculinity. It is worth saying, however, that early modern masculinity was not simply conceptualized as a bodily state; it was also associated with certain activities or social roles – for example, soldier and father. For my purposes, the crucial thing to note is that the physical aspects of masculinity were thoroughly imbricated with these more performative ones. As we shall see, beard growth was consistently linked with both fighting in battle and begetting children.

The connection between the beard and military combat was established by the constant use of martial language and metaphors to describe facial hair. For example, the anatomist Helkiah Crooke calls the beard an "ensigne of majesty."[74] Other seventeenth-century writers use the same term: one calls facial hair the "natural Ensigne of Manhood."[75] According to the *OED*, an "ensigne" is "a military or naval standard." Thus the beard is figuratively imagined in these passages as a "standard" that announces the wearer's masculinity in much the same way as an "ensign" announces the military identity of a group of soldiers. While other writers use slightly different terminology, they too link the beard with martial activity. Indeed, it is worth pointing out that many of the descriptions of beards that I have already cited use this type of language. In Jacques' seven ages of man speech in Shakespeare's *As You Like It*, for instance, the first stage of full-blown masculinity is that of the "soldier" who is "bearded like the pard" (2.7.145–50). Similarly, in Udall's *Thersites*, the eponymous character is a soldier/"adventurer" who is said to be "armed with a beard" along with a number of different weapons. Finally, in *Ram Alley*, the character is called Lieutenant Beard, rather than simply Mister Beard.

The pamphlet *Haec Vir* (1620) is particularly interesting in this regard, not only because of the way in which facial hair is described in the text, but also because the text itself was explicitly concerned with the production and regulation of sexual difference. The narrator claims that the womanish men of the day:

curl, frizzle and powder [their] hairs, bestowing more hours and time in dividing lock from lock, and hair from hair . . . than ever Caesar did in Marshalling his Army. [And what's more, they have] so greedily engrossed [the Art of face painting] that were it not for that little fantastical sharp-pointed dagger that hangs at [their] chins, and the cross-hilt which guards [their] upper lip, hardly would there be any difference between the fair Mistress and the foolish Servant.[76]

According to the passage, "curling," "frizzling," and "powdering" the hair have replaced "properly" masculine activities like "Marshalling an Army." Given this juxtaposition, it is hardly surprising to find that the beard is subsequently figured as a weapon. It is described as a "sharp-pointed dagger" with the mustache as a "cross-hilt." Here, the beard is imagined as a vestige of the older, properly masculine activity of combat. It is quite literally the last line of "defense" against effeminization – the only thing that separates the "fair Mistress and the foolish Servant."

The conceptual link between the beard and reproductive capacity was also forged through a range of different cultural discourses. Even the religious debates and practices that I mentioned earlier would have contributed to establishing this association, at least insofar as the facial hair of Protestant divines was figured as an indication of their ability to procreate and marry. But the link between the two was not simply a rhetorical one. In anatomy and physiognomy books, facial hair is quite literally described as an outgrowth of the production of semen. This "explanation" is most exhaustively articulated in Marcus Ulmus' *Physiologia Barbae Humanae* (1603). This book argues not only that the beard is an element of masculinity, but more specifically, that it is "an Index in the Face, of the *Masculine generative faculty*."[77] The physiognomer Thomas Hill elaborates on this idea. He contends:

The bearde in man . . . beginnith to appeare in the nether jawe . . . through the heate and moysture, carried unto the same, drawn from the genitours: which draw to them especially, the sperme from those places.[78]

In this section of his book, Hill figures the beard as a kind of seminal excrement. He maintains that facial hair arises as a result of the "heat and moysture" caused by the production of semen in the testicles. This is fitting, for all hair was thought to be an "excremental" residue left by the "fumosities" as they passed out of the pores of the body. According to Helkiah Crooke,

the immediate matter of Haires . . . is a sootie, thicke and earthy vapour which . . . passeth through the Pores of the Skin. For the vapor being thicke, in his passage leaveth some part of itself . . . where it is impacted by a succeeding vapor arising whence the former did, [and] is protruded or thrust forward.

The model used for understanding the growth of hair is that of soot building up in a chimney. As the smoke passes out of the chimney, soot builds up and is eventually pushed out by the uprising fumosities: "we see by the continual ascent of Soot, long strings of it are gathered as it were into a chaine." If hair was thus thought to be a kind of excrement that was produced by the "fumosities" in general, then the beard was considered to be a specifically seminal type of excrement, produced by the "sootie" excrement that is given off during the production of semen. As Hill explains: "Other Haires . . . [are bred] in Boyes when they begin to breed seed . . . come out in . . . the Chin and Cheekes."[79] Moreover, the language that Hill uses throughout his account works to further associate facial hair with procreative potential. For example, he calls the testicles "genitours" and thereby calls attention to their role in generation.

The link between facial hair and the production of semen is presented in a more socially accessible form in Shakespeare's plays through the common pun on "hairs" and "heirs." In *Troilus and Cressida*, Pandarus describes how Helen had spied a white hair on Troilus' chin and said: "Here's but two and fifty hairs on your chin – and one of them is white." To which Troilus replies "That white hair is my father, and all the rest are his sons" (1.2.146–51). In Troilus' response, he likens the hairs on his chin to his father (Priam) and his fifty sons. He thus associates his own production of facial hairs with his father's production of heirs (i.e. his fifty sons), in order to emphasize his own procreative potential. As in the medical texts, Troilus creates a direct link between the growth of his facial hair and his virility.

By now it should be clear that the beard was commonly connected to the masculine social roles of soldier and father. In fact, these sources demonstrate the extent to which the somatic and the social contours of "manhood" were articulated through one another. The connection between facial hair and reproduction is particularly important for understanding the gendered distinction between men and boys that I discussed earlier, since men were differentiated from boys not only on the basis of their beards but also on the basis of their ability to procreate. Francis Bacon, for instance, remarks in his preface to *The Great Instauration* (1620) that "the characteristic property of boys" is that they "cannot generate."[80] These two attributes are used interchangeably in a quip in William Cartwright's *The Ordinary*. Simon Credulous reprimands Meanewell: "Leave off your flouting! You're a beardless Boy; I am a Father of Children" (5.4.2362–3).[81] Here, Simon Credulous attempts to distinguish himself from the "boy" Meanewell (and to create a hierarchical power relation between them) by contrasting his own generativity with the beardlessness of Meanewell. In doing so, he forges an equivalence between the terms man/bearded/generative and the terms boy/beardless/non-generative, constructing at the same time an over-arching opposition between them.

One discursive site where the division between men and boys was most conspicuously articulated was in discussions of marriage, or more specifically, in discussions about who would make a proper husband. Laevinus Lemnius' seventeenth-century treatise on the humoral body, for instance, suggests "that such as are smooth and want beards, are not so strong for *Venus*-sports and fit to get children," and consequently, "many men are unwilling to Marry their daughters to them."[82] In this passage, Lemnius contends that beardless males would be unable to "get children" and that consequently, they are not considered appropriate husbands.[83] This idea was virtually proverbial, and was repeated in various forms in plays from the period. In Dekker's *Shoemaker's Holiday*, for instance, Eyre counsels Rose that she should "marry not with a boy that has no more hair on his face than thou hast on thy cheeks."[84] Similarly, the character Otter in Jonson's *Epicoene* maintains that "a boy or child under years is not fit for marriage because he cannot *reddere debitum* [literally 'pay the debt']."[85] While Otter insists that "boys" or "children under years" would be inappropriate marriage partners because of their inability to procreate, he does not explicitly mention that they lack facial hair as in the passage from Lemnius. Nevertheless, when these texts are seen in relation to one another, the underlying logic begins to emerge. This logic may also help to elucidate a passage from Massinger's *The Guardian* (1658) where beardless males are said to be unfit for marriage: one character asserts that "to marry . . . [i]n a beardless chin / Tis ten times worse then wenching" (1.1.62–4).[86] The implication of this statement is that marriage to a beardless boy is even "worse" than heterosexual intercourse outside of marriage ("wenching"). Presumably, this is because wenching would at least offer the possibility of reproduction (though only of an illegitimate sort). By contrast, marriage with "a beardless chin" would not offer any chance of procreation and would therefore "degrade" the institution itself. Such a non-reproductive marriage might even be considered sodomitical.

If all of these writers insist that boys and beardless males would not be appropriate husbands, in doing so they helped to (re)produce the gendered division between boys and men. Shakespeare manipulates this received wisdom in *Much Ado About Nothing*. Early in the play, Beatrice complains that she "could not endure a husband with a beard on his face" – she says she would "rather lie in the woollen" (2.1.25–6). But when Leonato suggests that she might "light on a husband that hath no beard" (27), Beatrice dismisses the notion:

What should I do with him? dress him in my apparel and make him my waiting-gentle-woman? He that hath a beard is more than a youth; and he that is more than a youth is not for me, and he that is less than a man, I am not for him. (2.1.28–32).

Interestingly, it is the play's proto-feminist character, Beatrice, who reiterates the dominant ideology of masculinity in this exchange. She links beard growth with both masculinity and marriage potential. First, she imagines that having a beard makes an individual a "man" and not a "youth": she categorically states "he that hath a beard is more than a youth," and she also suggests that she considers a youth to be "less than a man." The schema that Beatrice employs here is similar to the one that Randal Holme proposes in his *Academy of Armory*, or perhaps more relevantly, the one that Jacques adumbrates in his seven ages of man speech. When Beatrice says that beardless males are "less than" men, she also echoes the work of other early modern writers who claimed, as we shall see later, that a man who shaves away his beard aims to become "less man." In fact, in Beatrice's speech, she virtually transforms the beardless youth into a woman by comparing him to a "waiting-gentle-woman." But Beatrice not only suggests that youths are both beardless and unmasculine, she also asserts that they would not make appropriate husbands. In her words, the only "duties" a beardless youth could fulfill would be those of a "waiting-gentle-woman." In short, Beatrice does not think a beardless boy capable of fulfilling the "proper" duty of a husband: namely, procreation.

Part of the humor of this scene comes from the fact that it is the "feminist" character Beatrice who parrots the dominant ideology of masculinity. Equally ironic is the fact that the play's patriarch, Leonato, acknowledges the faultlines within that ideology: he admits that Beatrice might "light on" a husband who does not have a beard. We need to recognize, however, that even though proto-feminist Beatrice reiterates the schema and terminology of the dominant discourse of gender, she does so for her own ends. She is able to resist assimilation into the patriarchal marriage system by first stating her aversion to beards and then repeating the assumption that males without beards are not men and would not make appropriate husbands. In doing so, she adeptly demonstrates that early modern marriage discourses – and indeed the ideology of masculinity itself – were always open to appropriation or rearticulation by subordinate groups for non-hegemonic ends.

Thus far, I have tried to show that facial hair was one of the ways in which masculinity was materialized and that it worked to materialize differences between men and women, and men and boys. I now want to explain this claim a little better. Although facial hair was, as I've been arguing, constitutive, it was only one of the building blocks of masculine identity. Thus, it did not determine a person's gendered identity in and of itself. "Putting on" or "taking off" a beard would have helped to make an individual into a "man," but it would not have been enough to do so on its own. Take the case of Marie/Germain as an example. As I stated in the opening pages of this book, the version of the story that has circulated in contemporary criticism omits a crucial element of Montaigne's narrative: namely, that before Marie's metamorphosis, she was "remarkable for having a little more hair about her chin than the other girls; they called her bearded Marie."[87] Moreover, Montaigne points out that after the transformation, Germain went on to develop "a big, very thick beard." What I want to suggest here is that these descriptions of Marie's beard are not simply inconsequential details (as the current retellings imply by omitting them). Marie's beard may well have played a part in her reclassification as the male Germain.

By extension, the larger point is that facial hair was not a superfluous (or unessential/secondary) part, but rather it was constitutive. To say this, however, is not to say the same as saying that the beard determined gendered identity in and of itself. As I noted in my introduction, the beard was not a switch that would completely transform an individual's identity. Instead, it – and the other gendered parts – were more like weights on a scale. Moreover, it seems clear that different parts "mattered" to different degrees, and they thus had to be weighed against one another. If enough of them were aligned in a particular way, then the balance could be tipped. That appears to be what happened in the case of Marie/Germain.

There were other types of "sexual transformation" that occurred in the culture as well. In fact, eunuchs are often discussed in precisely these terms. Bartholomeus Cocles claims in his physiognomy book, for example, that eunuchs "are very much chaunged from the nature of menne, into the nature of women."[88] Cocles implies that "gelded persons" can no longer be considered "men." For my purposes, the crucial thing to note is that the beard again figures prominently in the exchanges concerning the gendered identity of eunuchs. In fact, Bulwer suggests that their lack of a beard is just as important as their lack of testicles. He writes that eunuchs "are smooth and produce not a Beard, the signe of virility" and that they are "*therein not men.*"[89] But if Bulwer emphasizes the eunuch's beardlessness, we have also seen that this was not unrelated to the testicles and the production of semen.

In the end, we might therefore say that the eunuch is an individual whose gender is materialized in a contradictory way. There were other such individuals as well, such as "women" with beards, and "men" without them.[90] This doesn't mean that the beard was any less crucial or constitutive, it just means that in these particular instances, the individual's facial hair was outweighed by other parts or factors. These could be things such as the genitals or the clothes, or could even be things like the person's demeanor or actions. Banquo's comment about the witches in Shakespeare's *Macbeth* illustrates this point. He addresses the "weird/weyward sisters" directly and says: "You should be women, and yet your beards forbid me to interpret that you are so."[91] In this line, Banquo insists that because these figures have beards, they cannot be "women" (presumably, this is because having a beard makes them into "men"). But despite this statement, Banquo actually does "interpret" the witches to be "women": he calls them "sisters" and, at another point, he uses the feminine pronoun in reference to them. It therefore seems clear that there must have been some gendered parts that led him to address these individuals as women. Banquo's contradictory statements are thus the result of his being pulled in opposing "interpretive" directions. This is not to say that he is given over to uncertainty, but rather that he experiences multiple, irreconcilable, certainties.

John Evelyn's diary entry for September 15, 1657 records a similar encounter with a "hairy Maid." He notes that he had seen this individual some twenty years earlier when she was a child. He claims that "she had . . . a most prolix beard, & *mustachios*." He goes on to explain that "She was now married, & told me she had one Child, that was not hairy, [as] nor were any of her parents or relations: she was borne in *Augsburg* in *Germanie*, & for the rest very well shaped, plaied well on the Harpsichord &c."[92] Evelyn's description here is somewhat different from Banquo's speech in *Macbeth*. Whereas Banquo explicitly acknowledges the contradictory gendering of the weird sisters and therefore questions whether they are even "Inhabitants o'th'Earth," Evelyn seems eager to (re)inscribe the figure in his account within the bounds of normative femininity. Unlike Banquo, he does not hesitate to call her a "woman" and he also mentions a number of other "feminine" characteristics that she possesses. These implicitly work to offset her facial hair. He states, for example, that she is "very well shaped, and plaied well on the Harpsichord &c." He also points out that "she was married" and "had one Child." These latter observations establish her femininity by indicating that she performed the most common social roles assigned to women of the period: namely, those of wife and mother.

Eleven years later, on December 21, 1668, Samuel Pepys saw what was perhaps the same "hairy Maid" in London. He writes in his diary that he:

went into Hoborne and there saw the woman . . . with a Beard; she is a little plain woman . . . about forty years old, her voice like a little girl's, with a beard as much as any man I ever saw, as black almost, and grizzly. They offered [to] show my wife further satisfaction if she desired it . . . But there is no doubt but by her voice she is a woman; it begun to grow at about seven years old – and was shaved not above seven months ago, and is now so big as any man almost that I ever saw, I say, bushy and thick.[93]

Pepys' account is much more openly conflicted than Evelyn's. The fluctuations in the passage indicate the contradictions that the bearded woman evoked for him. On the one hand, Pepys begins by clearly stating that this is a "woman": in the space of the first sentence, he twice designates her as such. He also notes that she has a "voice like a little girl's." But then Pepys turns to her facial hair, and in doing so, he acknowledges the beard's power to constitute masculinity to a much greater extent than Evelyn. In fact, Pepys compares the woman's facial hair to the beards of "men," saying that she had "as much as any man." In doing this, he insists upon the beard's connection with men and masculinity. But as the description continues, Pepys shifts yet again and his account becomes much more like Evelyn's as he increasingly attempts to (re)assimilate this woman into the category of the feminine. He mentions the possibility of getting "further satisfaction[s]," but ultimately reassures himself that there can be "no doubt but by her voice she is a woman." Thus, the voice to some extent compensates for her facial hair. While Pepys is still struck by the woman's beard and returns to it in the last sentence and reiterates how "big" it is, this time he adds the qualifier that it is only as big as that of "almost" any man.

If Pepys thus seems to be pulled in different directions in his account, his fluctuations echo the visual rhetoric of José de Ribera's portrait of Magdalena Ventura from the 1640s (figure 15).[94] This is despite the fact that the painting comes from a very different national context. Ribera's portrait is nevertheless similar to "portraits" of bearded women painted by the two celebrated English diarists in that it actively works to define Magdalena as a "woman" and to locate her firmly within the bounds of the social. The Latin text on the column at right of the composition begins by categorizing Magdalena as a "woman." It also explains that she "has borne three sons by her husband, Felici de Amici, whom you see here." As in Evelyn's account, Ribera here indicates that Magdalena performs the normative social roles of wife and mother. In fact, he not only emphasizes her role in biological reproduction, but also her role in social reproduction: the plinth says, more specifically, that she has given birth to "three *sons*." Even if all of her children were simply males, by specifying this the text on the plinth emphasizes her production of heirs and hence the continuation of the family line. There are also several other

Figure 15. José de Ribera, *Magdalena Ventura* (1631). '*The Bearded Woman*' (1631).

elements that are included in the painting that establish Magdalena's femininity. The most obvious of these are her clothes, her baby, her husband, and, of course, her breast. In addition, the still life on the plinth contains a spindle and bobbin. These are "feminine" accessories associated with traditional forms of women's work – sewing and weaving. Furthermore, it is worth noting that both of these implements are covered with a type of hair (i.e. wool). Thus, we might say that the "feminine" wool of the still life may be meant to be a way of compensating for the woolly beard of the sitter.

But it is not as if the painting simply and unproblematically reassimilates Magdalena into the early modern category of "woman." In fact, the number and variety of compensatory elements included in the painting might ultimately be seen as a testament to the cultural power attributed to the beard – it is an indication of the "weight" which was needed to offset it. The inscription on the plinth both visually and verbally encodes the "contradictions" which Magdalena seems to embody. The text states that at age thirty-seven Magdalena

began to become hairy and grew a beard [which was] so long and thick [. . .] that it seems more like that of any bearded gentleman than [that] of a woman who had borne three children by her husband.

First of all, it is worth saying that this description replicates almost verbatim the description in Pepys' diary. But the painting contains another element in its composition that is also significant and that has no equivalent in Pepys' diary. In the middle of the plinth, there is a large fissure which runs across the face of the rock and creates a break in the text between the words "long and thick" and "that it seems." This crevice effectively divides the passage on the plinth into two sections: first there is the description of Magdalena's facial hair, and then there is a second section in which her beard is compared to that of "any bearded gentleman." The cleft thus attempts to create a physical (and conceptual) chasm between the description of Magdalena's "long" and "thick" beard on the top half of the column, and the normative ideals of masculinity and femininity on the bottom portion of the plinth: in the lower half, facial hair is imagined to be the property of "any . . . gentleman" and not of a "woman who had borne three children." When seen from this perspective, the fissure could be construed as an apt embodiment of the problem of the facial hair: that is to say the problem of attaching it securely to either man or woman.

And yet, the normative ideals presented on the bottom of the column are themselves somewhat conflicted insofar as the text seems to offer the possibility that women too might have facial hair. Magdalena is said to have a beard that is "*more* like that of any bearded gentleman *than that of a woman*." If we take this statement to its logical conclusion, it suggests that a woman could have a beard, but that *this particular beard* is more like that of a man. Envisioned in these terms, gender difference is laid out along a continuum. Thus, it is not the presence or absence of facial hair that distinguishes a man from a woman, but the relative type or amount of it. Furthermore, given this formulation, it is striking that Magdalena's husband (himself a "bearded gentleman") is not nearly as hirsute as his wife. If Magdalena's beard is like that of "any bearded gentleman," we might ask if Felici's beard is meant to be like that of "any bearded woman"?

Although there are important differences in the "portraits" of bearded women by Ribera, Pepys, and Evelyn, all of them indicate that these individuals could be accommodated within early modern gender schemas at least to some extent. Nevertheless, the bearded woman obviously posed something of a challenge to the ideology of bearded masculinity. This becomes even clearer when we look at other "texts" from the period. Pierio Valeriano, for instance, claims in *Pro Sacerdotum Barbis* that "it hathe bene euer a monstrous thynge, to se[e] a woman with a beard, though it were very little" (10v). Similarly, John Bulwer maintains in *Anthropometamorphosis* that "Woman is by Nature smoothe and delicate; and if she have many haires she is a monster, as Epictetus saith, and the Proverbe abominates her, [A bearded woman must be greeted with stones from a distance]."[95] The hostility directed toward bearded women in these texts contrasts sharply with the treatment they received in the other sources I have examined. That hostility should be taken as an index of the threat that these individuals posed to normative gendered ideals. When seen from this perspective, it is not surprising to find that Valeriano and Bulwer were proponents of bearded masculinity. Tellingly, these writers do not claim that women with facial hair are manly. Instead, they say that they are "monsters." Valeriano contends that if woman has "many haires she is a monster," and Bulwer likewise maintains that it is a "monstrous" thing to see a woman with a beard. Though this may at first seem to be somewhat illogical, I believe that these writers consider bearded women to be "monstrous" because they combine supposedly antithetical or incommensurate parts in the same person much as a monster such as the monk-calf combines different species in the same person.[96] In addition, the fact that this particular appellation is used indicates quite clearly that sex/gender interpellation is such a fundamental part of the process of subjectification that when individuals are not "properly" gendered, it is not only their masculinity or femininity that comes into question, but rather their very humanity. Indeed, Valeriano and Bulwer seem anxious to exclude the bearded women from the realm of the social altogether, much as Ribera, Pepys, and especially Evelyn, had been anxious to reassimilate them. Finally, I want to return to the violence that Bulwer, in particular, aims at women with facial hair, for it is crucial not to lose sight of this. The menacing proverb that he mentions gives us an idea of the threats (and brutality) that could be used to establish and maintain the normative ideals surrounding facial hair.[97]

The cultural counterpart of the bearded woman was the beardless man. While representations of these figures are somewhat more scarce, they do exist and they would have done similarly complex cultural work. The protagonists in both Philip Sidney's *Arcadia* and William Shakespeare's *Coriolanus*, for example, are beardless, and yet in both cases they perform feats which are said to "demonstrate" that they are "men." In Philip Sidney's *Arcadia*, Pyrocles has "no hair of his face to witness him a man" and yet he performs martial exploits "beyond the degree of a man."[98] Similarly, in *Coriolanus*, Cominius describes Coriolanus' extraordinary feats of valor on the battlefield. He states that:

> [Coriolanus] fought beyond the mark of others . . .
> When with his Amazonian chin he drove
> The Bristled lips before him: he bestrid
> An o'er-pressed Roman and i' the consul's view
> Slew three opposers . . . in that days feats,
> When he might act the woman in the scene,
> He proved the best man i' the field . . .
> His pupil age Man-entered thus.
>
> (2.2.84–95)

In both of these instances, it is the individual's success in battle that establishes his masculinity, and although martial ability was usually correlated with the presence of the beard (as we have seen), in these cases the characters are still beardless. Cominius, for example, suggests that Coriolanus still has the appearance of a boy: he has an "Amazonian chin" and might "play the woman in the scene" (the latter is something that Pyrocles actually does in the *Arcadia*). Thus, we might say that these characters' martial feats serve as a kind of rite of passage and quite literally bring their masculinity into being. This is explicit in Coriolanus: by fighting "beyond the mark" of the "Bristled lips" and thus "prov[ing] the best man i' the field," Coriolanus is said to "Man-enter": meaning he shifts from being a pupil to being a man.

While both of these descriptions problematize the correlation between beard growth, the ability to fight in battle, and masculinity, they also to some extent reiterate those very connections by suggesting that these individuals are the exceptions that prove the rule. For example, when Sidney writes that Pyrocles has "no hair on his face to witness him a man," this formulation implies that it is normative for men who can fight "beyond the degree of man" to have hair on their faces. Similarly, Cominius implies that it is quite astounding that the beardless Coriolanus could defeat the "Bristled lips."[99]

Another way of putting this would be to say that Pyrocles and Coriolanus are essentially "boys" who are transformed into "men" by fighting successfully in battle, but who nevertheless remain beardless. Perhaps it is as a result of this that they are not demonized in the same way that other beardless men or bearded women were. Indeed, it is worth saying that "men" without facial hair were sometimes subject to hostility in much the same way as women with facial hair were. Bulwer, for example, maintains that shaving is a "monstrous . . . habit," and that men who "practice" it are "to be look'd upon with scoffs, and noted with infamy" (199). While these threats do not contain the same type of violence as those he hurled at bearded women, he does again use the language of "monstrosity" when speaking about these individuals, and again attempts to exile them from the realm of the social. Another example of a beardless man who is demonized is the "Lord" in Shakespeare's *Henry IV, Part 1* who goes to retrieve the prisoners from Hotspur after the battle of Holmedon. Hotspur claims that he refused to hand his captives over to this "man" with "his Chin new reap't" (1.3.33) because he did not think him an appropriate representative of the king. Hotspur insists that "He made me mad, to see him shine so Briske, and smell so sweet, and talk so like a waiting-gentlewoman, of guns, and drums, and wounds" (1.3.52–5). Hotspur's anger here is compounded by the fact that the beardless man appears on the battlefield. Indeed, the character's beardlessness and his inability or unwillingness to fight in combat are mapped on to one another in this scene in a way that is completely consistent with my earlier comments. Moreover, it is worth pointing out that the Lord is treated very differently from Pyrocles and Coriolanus. This is undoubtedly because those two were, prior to fighting in battle, still considered boys and not expected to participate in the conflict. By contrast, this "man" is expected to take part, and yet does not. According to Hotspur, the Lord claimed that "he would himself have been a soldier" (1.3.63), but "for these vile guns" (1.3.62). In the end, Hotspur does not threaten this figure with the same level of violence that Bulwer and Valeriano direct at the bearded woman, but the "Popinjay" does nevertheless evoke hostility and contempt.

These representations of "bearded women" and "beardless men" make it clear that although facial hair helped to make the man, it did not do so in and of itself. Shakespeare and Sidney both indicate, for instance, that an individual might be a "man" and yet might not have facial hair. Conversely, Evelyn in particular indicates that an individual might be a "woman" and yet still have a beard. Although writers like Evelyn describe "bearded women" (or "beardless men"), these labels are somewhat misleading for they imply that these individuals were really "men" or "women" despite the presence or absence of their beards. This label thus implicitly denies the constitutive power of facial hair. It might therefore be more accurate to say that these individuals have elements of both genders, or that their gender was materialized in a contradictory fashion. In all of these instances, the presence or absence of the beard is compensated for – or outweighed by – other factors, but this does not mean that it was therefore any less significant or fundamental.

Materializing masculinity through the beard had important ramifications for the way in which gendered identity itself was conceptualized. Crucially, it helped create the sense that masculinity itself was to some extent prosthetic. As I suggested earlier, theatrical performances drew attention to the detachability and transferability of masculinity, especially performances of plays such as *A Mad World My Masters* and *A Midsummer Night's Dream* where characters explicitly called attention to their use of false beards to make "men." There were other theatrical performances which likewise emphasized the prosthetic nature of facial hair, but in which it was not so obviously "artificial." Take Shakespeare's *Much Ado About Nothing* as an example. Earlier, I discussed how Beatrice repeats the normative rubrics of masculinity from discourses about marriage when she distinguishes between bearded men and beardless youths (and ironically claims that neither would be an appropriate husband for her). At that point in the play, these labels apply to the two most visible bachelors, Claudio and Benedick. On the one hand, Claudio is the play's beardless youth: he is called "lord Lackbeard" (5.1.182) and, at several other points, "boy."[100] On the other hand, Benedick is a prickly "man" whom Beatrice could not endure. During the course of the performance, however, Benedick is transformed and loses his beard. Claudio explains that "the old ornament of his cheek" was used to "stuff . . . tennis balls" (3.2.37–9). While Benedick's change is primarily meant to make him more compatible with Beatrice and her stated preferences, it also inevitably highlights the fact that facial hair is malleable and detachable. Thus, Shakespeare's *Much Ado* might be said to do some of the same cultural work as *A Midsummer Night's Dream*. It is worth saying, however, that it does it in a much more subtle (or one might even say "realistic") way. In this case, although the actor who played Benedick would almost certainly have worn a false beard or a smooth mask in order to enact the mid-performance shift, neither he nor any of the other characters calls attention to this fact in quite the same way as Bottom does.

Theatrical performances and texts were not the only cultural sites where the beard's prosthetic nature was "staged." Many of the writers that I have mentioned throughout this chapter call attention to this characteristic of the beard, even those who insist most vehemently that this part is essential for masculine identity. This may sound strange from a modern perspective since today many people assume that sexual characteristics such as facial hair (and especially "primary" sexual characteristics such as genital morphology or genetic make-up) are at least in some sense hard-wired. As Diana Fuss puts it in *Essentially Speaking*, we tend to assume "that nature and fixity go together."[101] If these "natural" physiological characteristics are seen as being fixed, they also then work to ground or to stabilize gendered identity, so that if a person has a certain set of characteristics, then that person is "really" either a man or a woman. These assumptions were much less prevalent in early modern English culture. In part, this is because the body and corporeal features such as the beard or genital morphology were not understood to be the basis for the patriarchal order. It was just as much God's word that provided the basis for this distinction and the body often only gave expression to the divinely ordained state of things. On account of this situation, there was less cultural pressure on the body to ground sexual difference. Consequently, people could openly acknowledge that it was possible for an individual's physical and sexual characteristics to change without calling the entire patriarchal edifice into question.[102] The controversy in early modern England was therefore not, for the most part, about whether corporeal features or characteristics *could* be remade,[103] but rather about how this *should* be done in order to bring bodies into accordance with God's will.

Thus, with regard to the beard, even the writers who argue that this feature is a necessary component of masculine identity readily acknowledge that it is alterable (though it might, of course, be "sinful" and "unnatural" to do so). John Bulwer explicitly states this at one point in his text. He says that "For men . . . to labour to extirpate so honest and necessary a work as the Beard is, is a practicall blasphemy most inexpiable against Nature, and God the Author of Nature, whose work the Beard is."[104] It is important to acknowledge that what Bulwer is repudiating here is not all reworking of the body, but rather this particular reworking: namely, "*men . . . labouring to extirpate . . . the beard.*"

Bulwer goes on to say that "the Beard is a singular gift of God, which who shaves away, he aimes at nothing than to become lesse man" (200). While this statement is partially rhetorical (and clearly meant as an attempt to deter men from shaving), I want to suggest that there is an element of truth to it as well. If the beard is considered to be constitutive of gendered identity, and if masculinity and femininity are arrayed along a continuum, then it makes sense to say that a man will become "lesse man" by removing his beard. This doesn't mean that he would be completely transformed into a woman on account of this act, but he would become "lesse man." The point I am trying to make here is related to the one I made in reference to Thomas Middleton's *A Mad World My Masters*. In that play, we were presented with a range of characters who had differing degrees of masculinity: from the effeminate

Follywit to the fully masculine Sir Bounteous Progress. In this case, instead of having different men arrayed along a gendered continuum, Bulwer presents us with the image of a single man moving from one point along that continuum to another. But if Bulwer indicates that it was possible for a man to shave and thereby become "lesse man," he also indicates that it was "blasphemous" to do so. Presumably, this is because it treated the patriarchal hierarchy (which was supposedly ordained by God) with irreverence.

Facial hair was not only thought to be prosthetic in the sense that it could be "taken off" by shaving or other means, it was also prosthetic in the sense that it could be "put on" or induced to grow. Laevinus Lemnius' treatise on the humoral body outlines several different techniques individuals could use to do this. He prescribes one "remedy" which is a "liniment" made of a variety of ingredients such as "Honey, fresh Butter without Salt, the juyce of a red Onion. . .Badgers grease." He insists that when the "chin" is "wet with these, [it] first brings forth a tender down, [and] after that a thick and long beard." In addition, he suggests – somewhat counterintuitively – that individuals who want to induce beard growth should "Rasour oft" using warm water, "For if the chin and upper lip be continually wet and soked with warm water, the heat and humour that flyes to those parts will be stirred up, and they will become hairy."[105] These passages clearly indicate that the beard was seen as something which could be "put on" as well as "taken off." It is worth saying, however, that in the text, Lemnius is careful to indicate that these methods of producing facial hair are for "young men that have no beard appearing, and look like boyes." Although Lemnius doesn't say it explicitly, he implies that these techniques should not be used by actual boys or by women. In other words, for him, the techniques are a way of bringing contradictory bodies ("young *men* . . . who look like *boys*") into alignment with gendered norms, not a means of undermining those norms. Lemnius' text is particularly interesting from my perspective because it demonstrates quite clearly that not all manipulation of the body and of gendered identity was considered to be sinful or blasphemous. Corporeal alteration was unproblematic if it made bodies agree with "God's holy order in nature."

But at the same time, the body could also be remade in non-normative ways. Indeed, the poet Hugh Crompton claims that shaving can cause hair to grow on women's faces. As we have seen, he writes in *The Glory of Women*:

> in each man's face appears
> A beard extending upward to his ears . . .
> But every female beardless doth remaine,
> Both old and young her face is still the same.

But Crompton then goes on to say:

Hence it was graven the Law Tables in
That women should not shave their tender skin
Lest that a hairy bush should chance to bud,
And spoyle the sanguine colors of their bloud.[106]

In these lines, Crompton suggests that women's shaving, instead of removing a "hairy bush," paradoxically causes one to "bud" on their supposedly beardless "face[s]" and thus disrupts gendered norms.[107] Crompton doesn't specify whether this hypothetical transgression is intentional or unintentional, but he does make it clear that it violates God's "Law." In fact, Crompton gives his prescription about shaving (and about facial hair more generally) an air of biblical authority by implying that it was "graven" in the "Law Tables" – implying that it was nothing less than one of the ten commandments. The reference to beards as "hairy bushes" also contributes to the biblical tone of the passage by conjuring up images of Moses and the Burning Bush. Crompton's obvious investment in establishing scriptural authority for the gendered norms is unsurprising, given that God's word or intent was, as we have seen, considered to be fundamental. Accordingly, in Crompton's poem, this religious "law" is imagined to be unequivocal (it is quite literally "graven" in stone) whereas the "tender" body is mutable and can be materialized in ways that do not accord with the divine law.

The crucial point from my perspective is that all of these texts call attention to the malleability of the beard and to the potential malleability of gendered identity materialized through it. The cultural work they do is in trying to regulate *how* individuals bring their bodies into being, not whether they do so in the first place.

The ambiguous materiality of the beard was further foregrounded by the medical debates about whether facial hair (and indeed all hair) was part of the body or not. Some early modern anatomists insisted that hair was merely an "excrement" and not fully corporeal. Helkiah Crooke, for instance, states that the hairs "are only excrements . . . utterly devoid of life, and therefore they are not to be reckoned among the parts of the Body" (82). Similarly, Nicholas Culpepper contends that "*Hairs* are indeed bodies, but not parts of the body" (127). On the other hand, anatomists like Daniel Sennert maintained that hairs were not "things merely excrementious"; he asserts that they "are (although ignoble, yet) parts of the body" (2611). What I want to suggest is that this debate, when viewed as a whole, would have served to emphasize the ambiguous corporeality of facial hair. It might therefore be compared to the religious debates about the resurrection of "the body" at the end of time. As Carolyn Bynum Walker has demonstrated, there were important theological discussions about what exactly it meant to say that "the body" would be "rejoined" at the end of time. Would all of the hair of the head or the fingernails that had been removed from the body, for instance, eventually return? These theological debates, like the anatomical ones after them, revolved around the question of what was properly part of "the body."

I believe that they may have had an impact on the way in which hair was understood and described. The Puritan preacher Thomas Hall compares facial hair to a whole range of other items, including the "Nailes" and also "Meate, Drink, [and] Cloaths."[108] Although this description is far removed from the anatomical and religious debates about hair, it likewise emphasizes the beard's ambiguous relationship to the body. Hall begins with another "excremental" part of the body ("Nailes"), then moves to external objects that are brought into the body ("Meate" and "Drink"), before ending with one which is attached to it ("Cloaths") but which, as I argued in my previous chapters, has the power to materialize the body in particular ways. Hall effectively creates a continuum between the body and the world, and locates facial hair in between the two poles.

In contrast to writers like Hall, there were other individuals who sought to disavow the beard's ambiguous materiality and to attach it more firmly to the body. John Bulwer is particularly interesting in this regard because he not only argues that hair is fully corporeal, but he also links this claim with the one about the beard constituting masculinity. Bulwer acknowledges that some "Superficiall Philosophers . . . say . . . that . . . haires [are] an excrement and not a part [of the body] . . . to which account the Beard must be reduced which is all haire." In response, however, he insists that "the beard is an existent part of the body" and also that it is "most necessary." Its necessity, he contends, arises from its role in constituting masculinity. As he puts it, "its necessity is from its use and office it hath in the body": namely, "its use and office" as "manly ornament."[109] This is particularly interesting because it implies that the beard must be part of the body in order to be an integral component of masculinity. It is thus somewhat similar to the modern fantasies about the prosthesis that I discussed in my introduction. There, we saw that writers like Freud suggested that to the extent that the prosthesis was absorbed into the body, it became part of the self.

There were certainly other early modern writers who made arguments like Bulwer's, but it is worth saying that this way of conceptualizing the detachable part and its relationship to identity was not necessarily the norm at this time. Indeed, we have seen that writers who claim that hair is an "excrement" could also maintain that it is an integral component of masculine or feminine identity. Helkiah Crooke, for instance, says both that the hairs "are only excrements" and that facial hair, in particular, is an "ensigne of majesty" for men, and that for women, "the smoothness of their Face is their proper Ornament."[110] In fact, virtually all of the anatomists that I mentioned above *on both sides of the debate* insist that hair is essential for gender identity. So the point I want to make here is that although the beard was sometimes attached firmly to the body in the process of constituting it as a crucial component of masculinity, this was not a necessary conceptual intervention.

The role that the beard played in forming identity, and the detachability and transferability of this part, is explored at some length in *The Book of Sir Thomas More*. As I noted earlier, the prosthetic beard in the play-within-the-play seems to be a crucial part of Wit's persona. In fact, the metadramatic performance is actually postponed while one of the characters goes to procure "a long beard for young Wit." But the prosthetic nature of facial hair is also subtly evoked throughout the rest of the performance as well, most notably through the eponymous character's on-again-off-again antics with regard to his beard. More grows a beard and then removes it several times during the course of the play. First, he describes himself as having a "thin" beard, but then after his alienation from the King, he receives what he (ironically) calls "a smooth court shaving" (4.2.56–7).[111] Subsequently, however, More's facial hair returns, and during his imprisonment in the tower, he contemplates having "a barber for his beard" (5.3.98), but then he decides not to cut it. Finally, he appears on the scaffold at the end of the play beardless, having removed the beard after all.

It is hardly surprising to find that the beard is so prominent in *The Book of Sir Thomas More* given that two of the best-known anecdotes about the life of the illustrious statesman and author involve his facial hair. Both of these incidents appear in somewhat attenuated form in the final scenes of the play. The first is described in many sixteenth-century sources, including John Harrington's *Metamorphosis of Ajax* (1596). Apparently, while More was imprisoned in the Tower, he told a courtier who was visiting him that he had had a change of heart. The courtier assumed that More had changed his mind about his refusal to subscribe to the Oath of Supremacy and Act of Succession, and he therefore ran to tell the King. When the courtier finally returned, he told More that he should put his recantation into writing. At that point, More explained:

I have not changed my mind in that matter, but only this; I thought to have sent for a Barber, to have bene shaven ere I had died, but now if it please the King, he shal cut off head, and beard, and all together.[112]

The second anecdote is an incident that took place on the scaffold itself before More's beheading. It is recorded by both Foxe and Holinshed. According to Foxe,

even when he [More] should lay down his head on the block, he having a great graie beard, stroked out his beard, and said to the hangman, I pray you let me lay my beard over the block, lest you should cut it.[113]

In the seventeenth century, More's biographers also included the quip: "My beard has done no offense to the King."[114]

If it is therefore historically appropriate that facial hair should feature prominently in *The Book of Sir Thomas More*, I want to suggest that it is also thematically appropriate, for one of the play's primary themes is the mutability or transferability of identity. This theme is again appropriate given that the main drama of Sir Thomas More's life is whether he would change his religious identity. Indeed, Jeffrey Masten has already begun to explore the importance of this theme in the play in his article "*More* or Less: Editing the Collaborative." Masten points out that many of the characters modify or transform their identities in the course of the performance, in part by identifying with, or as, others.[115] For example, in the opening scenes depicting the riots between the English and the "strangers," More quells the violence by asking all of the rioters to perform a kind of collective cross-identification: he asks the rioters to put themselves in the strangers' shoes. In the middle of the play, the servants Randall and Faulkner also go through important self-transformations. Finally, at the end of the play, More lives out, as Masten puts it, the kind of "estrangement or cross-identification" that he himself had conjured up in his speech to the rioters at the beginning of the drama: he goes from being a trusted advisor to a traitor and finally a martyr.[116]

If *The Book of Sir Thomas More* thus tends to figure identity as being both alterable and transferable, it also frequently links this with facial hair. For example, in the preparations for the metadramatic performance of *The Marriage of Wit and Wisdom*, the actors discuss whether the beard is a necessary part of Wit's persona. At first, an affirmative answer is implicitly given, since the performance of the play-within-the-play is postponed on account of it. This is reminiscent of the way in which Follywit and Bottom seemed to need their beards in order to play the parts of men. Later, however, it becomes clear that the beard does not completely determine Wit's identity. More intervenes and states that the actor "may be without a beard till he come to marriage, for wit goes not all by the hair" (3.2.143–4). Consequently, the actors do actually begin the performance without the beard. So the beard does not appear to be entirely necessary: as More puts it, Wit "goes not all by the hair." This statement implies that while facial hair might be an important part of Wit's identity, it does not constitute it in and of itself.[117] More further qualifies his statement about it being acceptable for Wit to be beardless by saying that this is only the case "till he come to marriage." This comment seems to reiterate the norms of the marriage discourse that I examined earlier. There, we saw that it was often said that a male must have a beard in order to be marriageable. While More is talking about the beard's relationship to Wit, both of his comments seem to echo aspects of the ideology of bearded masculinity that I have been exploring in this chapter.

Furthermore, it is worth saying that by addressing the question of whether facial hair is an integral part of Wit's identity, the metadramatic scene develops the ideas that had been presented in the scene immediately preceding it. There, More has a long discussion with the "ruffian" Faulkner in which he insists that Faulkner trim his long locks. When Faulkner refuses, More sends him to Newgate. This interaction suggests that for Faulkner his locks are a crucial part of his being and that he is willing to go to prison to preserve them. The foreshadowing of More's imprisonment in the final scenes of the play, and his efforts to preserve his religious identity, is unmistakable. More seems to acknowledge that Faulkner's hair is an integral part of his persona, and this is precisely why he wants him to remove it. When Faulkner and More first meet, and Faulkner identifies himself as the servant of a secretary, More states that "A fellow of your hair is very fit / To be a secretary's follower" (3.1.83–4). In this comment, More quibbles on the meaning of "hair" as "nature, or character," and thus virtually equates the two.[118] But Faulkner's hair, like More's beard, is detachable, and Faulkner does eventually decide to remove it, just as More decides to remove his beard in the final scenes of the play. When Faulkner does so, it brings about a total self-transformation. In fact, when More sees Faulkner again, he cannot believe he is still the same person: Faulkner says that he is "a new man my lord" and More responds "sure this is not he" (3.1.225–6).

If these scenes seem to call attention to the way in which hair materializes identity, they also call attention to its prosthetic nature and the consequent plasticity of identity. As we have seen, Faulkner's personal reformation is quite literally enacted by removing his hair. Similarly, in the metadramatic scene, More highlights the transferability of the beard by offering his own as a replacement for the one that the actor who is to play Wit is missing. He suggests that he'll "lend [Wit] mine" (3.2.167). More's offer here recalls the scene where he offers his clothes to his man Randall, asking him to play "Sir Thomas More." Randall is thus able to fool Erasmus into thinking that he is More. But if in the earlier scene More did successfully shift the markers of his identity, in this one this seems to be an impossibility. More jokes that he cannot loan his beard to the actor who will play Wit because it is "too thin." The jest here is that the impediment to the transfer is not the fact that it is More's "real" beard that is in question (as might be expected); rather, it is simply its size. Nevertheless, it is worth saying that More's proposal here is a classic instance of Freudian negation: he imaginatively enacts the transfer of his beard even as he denies it as a possibility. In addition, by invoking his beard's transferability, he implicitly equates it with the prosthetic beard that the player has gone to get. Indeed, even though More's beard is meant to be "real" in the scene, it is likely that it too was a theatrical property since the actor playing More had to go through a number of changes during the course of the play regarding his beard.[119]

The prosthetic nature of the beard and the malleability and transferability of identity established through it are all addressed again conspicuously in the final scenes of the play. In fact, an explicit dramatic link could be constructed between these two sections of the performance by having the actor who plays More wear Wit's prosthetic beard in the prison scenes. If this were done, it would visually underscore the parallels between the two characters – emphasizing the way in which More has been reduced to a Wit. Indeed, throughout the final scene, he banters in a jocular fashion. This costuming decision would also draw attention to the transformation of More's identity. Whereas earlier More himself had played Good Counsel and had "married" both wit and wisdom, here he can only play Wit because he is no longer considered a "wise" and respected statesman.

Moreover, having More wear a beard that was so conspicuously a part of a theatrical milieu would foreground the metatheatrical qualities of the final scenes – it would indicate that More is now being forced to perform a role in what is essentially the King's drama. He himself suggests as much when he says "my offense to his highness makes of a state pleader a stage player (though I am old, and have a bad voice) to act this last scene of my tragedy" (5.4.73–5). The image of More as a "stage player" already reverberates with the earlier play-within-the-play, where More joins the actors and plays Good Counsel, and where the players as a result are ready to convert him into one of them: "Would not my lord make a rare player? O, he would uphold a company beyond all ho, better than Mason among the King's players" (3.2.295–7). For his part, More, like Bottom, seems ready to play all the parts.

But even if Wit's false beard was not used to foreground the link between these two sections of the play, they would still echo one another thematically insofar as they both explore the beard's relationship to identity. The final scenes of the play describe More's imprisonment and eventual execution. The dramatic tension in them arises from the uncertainty about whether he will change his religious identity in order to save his life. More's constant references to his beard in these same scenes may, at first, seem to be comic relief: the gravity of the dilemma concerning his religious conversion is offset by the triviality of the dilemma concerning whether he should shave or not. But, as I tried to suggest earlier in this chapter, religious affiliation and beard growth were not completely unrelated concerns. Indeed, we saw that the religious differences between Catholic and Protestant clergy were often produced through facial hair. Understanding the beard's role in forming religious identity can help deepen our understanding of the final scenes of *The Book of Sir Thomas More*. In the Tower, for example, the main joke is that More changes his mind about his beard rather than about his religious affiliation. Although we initially see these two decisions as antithetical, we also need to recognize that they were often linked. Moreover, the scene gains part of its resonance from the contrast with the earlier scene with Faulkner. Whereas More has a change of heart about trimming his beard instead of about his conversion, Faulkner's haircut is his conversion.

What is odd about *Sir Thomas More* from my perspective is that although the beard (and the hair more generally) is portrayed as being integral to identity, it is not, for the most part, linked to masculine identity. I therefore want to say that, while I have focused on the beard and masculinity in this chapter, I don't mean to deny that facial hair worked to materialize a wide range of other identities including religious identity, Royalist identity, and even a newly emergent sense of racial identity.[120] But if the play thus deviates from the concerns of this chapter in some ways, it also resonates deeply with other ideas that I have explored. In particular, the play powerfully highlights the prosthetic nature of facial hair and the malleability of identity materialized by it.

In the end, I have tried to demonstrate the extent to which the beard made the man in early modern England. Moreover, I have argued that bearded men were distinguished from both women and boys. But in addition, I have tried to suggest that since facial hair could be removed, grown, or even at times transferred, this meant that when masculinity was materialized through this part, it would have been understood as being prosthetic. This was particularly apparent on the stage – in plays like *The Book of Sir Thomas More* – where false beards were often used in order to enable actors, and especially boy actors, to play the roles of men, but it was highlighted by other discourses and practices as well. If bearded masculinity was prosthetic, this has important theoretical implications. Most obviously, it means that masculinity had to be constantly (re)produced, and by extension, that facial hair had to be constantly "put on" or "taken off" by the "right" people. Or, to return to Butler's formulation, we might say that both masculinity and the beard itself had to be constantly made (to) matter.

4   "The ornament of their sexe": hair and gender

> Sometimes you like to let the hair do the talking.
> James Brown, *James Brown: The Godfather of Soul*[1]

In the introduction to this book, I discussed the advice that the French physician Ambroise Paré gives to his fellow medical practitioners about how to determine whether a "hermaphrodite" should be classified as being of the "male or female sexe." Interestingly, Paré recommends considering a whole range of physical features or characteristics in making this decision. I now want to return to Paré's advice and point out that one of the features that he mentions is the hair of the head. He says that physicians should ascertain whether the individual's hair is "fine or coarse" – the implication being that if they have "fine" hair it will indicate they are female and if they have "coarse" hair it will indicate they are male. This advice was altered slightly when Paré's work was translated into English in the 1630s. The English text stipulates that physicians consider whether "the haire of the head bee long, slender and soft."[2] The translation thus recommends examining the length as well as the texture of the hair.

This small but significant change hints at the crucial role that hair length played in materializing gender identity in seventeenth-century English culture. We can get a sense of this feature's cultural import if we consider that during the period from 1590 to 1690, there were a number of books published in England that were devoted entirely to discussing hair and tonsure. Many of these books are, quite strikingly, hundreds of pages long: they include W. T.'s *A Godly Profitable Treatise* (1590), William Prynne's *The Unlovelinesse of Love-lockes* (1628), the anonymous tracts *A Looking-Glasse for Women* (1644) and *Seasonable Advice . . . to the Professors of this backsliding Age* (1650), Thomas Hall's *The Loathsomenesse of Longe Hair* (1653), and finally, Thomas Wall's *Spiritual Armour to Defend the Head from a Superfluity of Naughtiness* (1688) and his *God's Holy Order in Nature* (1690).[3] In addition to these English texts, there were also a number of "hair books" that were written in Latin and published on the Continent. Some of these were at least ostensibly medical tomes – such as Jean Tardin's *Disquisitio Physiologica de Pilis* (1609) and Adrianus Junius' *De coma commentarium* (1556) – but the majority were polemical in nature: they include two books by Claude de Saumaise, the *Epistola ad Andream Colvium* (1644) and *De Coma Dialogus* (1645), Rodolph Hospinien's *De Rasione Comae & Barbae* (1639), Johannes Polyandrus a Kerckhoven's *Judicium & Consilium de Comae & Vestium Usu & Abusu* (1644), and Jacobus Revius' *Libertas Christiana circa usum capillitii defensa qua Sex ejusdem Disputationes de Coma ab exceptionibus viri cujusdam docti vindicantur* (1647).[4]

I will discuss these Continental sources in more detail later in the chapter, but at this point, I simply want to establish that there was a well-developed discourse on hair in England during the seventeenth century. And this discourse primarily addressed hair's relationship to gender. In fact, most of the books published in England argue, more specifically, that women should have long locks and men should have short locks. According to the pamphlet *Seasonable Advice . . . for the Professors of this Backsliding Age*, "Long hair by God's appointment pertains to Women, and Short Hair to Men."[5] Other texts from the period also helped to produce and reinforce these tonsorial norms. The Puritan Anne Hempstall, for instance, is said to have preached a sermon in which "the chief matter her Text was. . .That woman's hair was an adorning to her, but for a man to have long haire, it was a shame unto him."[6] (She was one of the many female preachers that took the pulpit in the middle years of the seventeenth century.) Other sermons concentrated on men's hair and chastised them for nourishing long locks. In Edward Reynolds' *The Sinfulnesse of Sinne* (preached at Lincoln's Inn), he insists that "long hair" on men is "condemned by the dictate of Nature and right reason." He cites Saint Augustine as an authority on the subject, noting that he "hath written three whole chapters against this sinful custome of nourishing haire, whiche he saith is expressly against the precept of the Apostle."[7] Similar prescriptions about the "sinful" and "unnatural" hair worn by men from the period were expounded in satires and tracts about gender. There was, for instance, a humorous poem addressed to "the Long-hair'd Gallants of these times" that admonished them to "Go . . . to the Barbers, go" and "Bid them your hairy Bushes mow. / God in a Bush did once appear, / But there is nothing of him here."[8] Samuel Rowlands also upbraids long-haired men in his satirical pamphlet *Earth's Vanity*. He ironically asserts, "Your Gallant is no man unless his hair be of the woman's fashion, dangling and waving over his shoulders."[9] Also using humor to reinforce gendered norms, the narrator of Thomas Dekker's *Gulls Hornbook* compliments a "Gallant" for his "long hair" and states that it "will make thee look dreadfully to thine enemies, manly to thy friends. It is in peace an ornament; in war, a strong helmet – it blunts the edge of a sword and deads the leaden thump of a bullet."[10] Here, the Gallant's long hair is not only ironically said to make him "manly," it is also more specifically imagined as a kind of impervious armor that will help him in battle. This martial imagery resonates powerfully with my discussion in the last chapter of the ways in which the beard was consistently likened to various martial implements. Finally, the *Hic Mulier/Haec Vir* pamphlet castigates both men and women about their hair, stating that "The long hair of a woman is the ornament of her sex, and bashful shamefastness her chief honor; the long hair of a man, the vizard for a thievish or murderous disposition."[11]

If it would thus appear that discussions of hair and its relationship to gender were somewhat ubiquitous in seventeenth-century English culture, the examples I have cited here will, I hope, also begin to give readers a sense of the cultural work that these texts performed. At first glance, this may not seem particularly remarkable. The pronouncements of these writers may even sound reminiscent of those made by conservatives during the 1960s, another era when, as James Brown put it, people "liked to let hair do the talking." At that time, men challenged gender conventions by growing long hair and "mop tops" (popularized by the Beatles) and women did so by wearing short bobs and "boyish crops" (popularized by Twiggy). This, in turn, spurred attempts to reinforce traditional tonsorial norms. Hence a billboard from the period read: "Keep America Beautiful – Get a Haircut!"

But despite the apparent similarities between the discourses on hair from the two periods, I want to stress that there are also important differences in the way in which this physical feature was imagined to materialize gender. Most importantly, in the early modern period, short and long hair were often said to be "natural" attributes of masculinity and femininity. Indeed, we have already seen that Paré (or rather the English translator of his works) implies that the length of an individual's hair can help physicians determine if that individual is of the male or female sex. This may seem somewhat odd to modern readers because, while we tend to associate long hair with femininity and short hair with masculinity, we don't usually assume that this difference is rooted in nature, or that the length of an individual's hair tells us anything definitive about their sex. Instead, we tend to assume that both males and females can, at least potentially, have long hair, and that the length of an individual's hair is determined primarily by barbers rather than biology. By contrast, early modern writers frequently imagine long hair to be a "natural" characteristic of women, and short hair to be a "natural" characteristic of men. John Bulwer, for example, asserts in his *Anthropometamorphosis* that "[i]n all kinds of Creatures, and in every sexe, Nature hath placed some note of difference, the judgment of Nature is no way ambiguous." Therefore, "she hath granted [women] by a peculiar indulgence, as an Ornament and beauty, the increase of long Haire, even down unto the Feet."[12] Similarly, William Prynne maintains in *The Unlovelinesse of Love-lockes* that long hair is a "natural badge to distinguish [women] from men."[13]

Thomas Hall takes these statements to their logical conclusion. He maintains that "nature hath allotted shorter hair (in the generality) to men than women" and goes on to perform a kind of thought experiment to illustrate his point. He says that if men were to "suffer their haire to grow to its utmost length, and never poll [cut] it," it would nevertheless not "be so long as most women's hair is."[14] So in essence what Hall is saying here is that if both men and women allowed their hair to grow unchecked, most men's hair would not grow to be as long as most women's hair would. This does not preclude the possibility that some individual men might have longer hair than some individual women, but rather, it means that as a group, men's hair would be shorter. In modern terms, we might say that Hall is insisting that hair length is a sexual characteristic rather than a gendered one.

These ideas were rooted in humoral theory. The hairs of the head were thought to be bred out of moisture arising from the body, and especially from the brain. The renowned anatomist Helkiah Crooke, for instance, notes in his *Microcosmographia* that "the cause of the length and shortness of haires, is the abundance or scarcity of the humor wherewith they are fed. And hence it is that the haires of the head are the longest of all the bodie, because the Braine affoordeth a great deale of a clammy moysture."[15] If the length of the hair of the head was thus thought to be the result of the "abundance or scarcity" of "clammy moisture," it follows that women's hair would be longer than men's since women were generally considered to be the more "watery" sex.

The influence of humoralism thus helps explain why women's hair might have been thought to be "naturally" longer than men's hair. Modern readers should, however, be careful about assuming that these beliefs were simply unscientific or erroneous. As I noted in my introduction, hair scientists today actually believe that Thomas Hall's assertions are correct (though the experiments have not been done in order to prove this definitively).[16] But while this is quite interesting, I think it would be a mistake for us to focus too much on ascertaining the scientific validity of these claims. This would ultimately draw our attention away from exploring the relationship between these early modern ideas about hair and the gender ideologies of the period. By extension, we might also consider how our own ideas about the body and sexual difference reflect our own gender ideologies. Indeed, we might ask why it is that people today don't generally "know" about the physiological differences between men's and women's hair. It is certainly not because we as a culture do not care about biological distinctions between the sexes. On the contrary, the massive investment in other corporeal differences makes it all the more interesting that this particular difference does not "matter." I believe that one reason why this knowledge does not circulate – and indeed, why the knowledge itself has not been definitively produced – is because hair length does not materialize gender in the "proper" way. Let me explain. Most of the sexual distinctions that "matter" in the modern western world share two characteristics. First, they are usually imagined to be sharp and dichotomous. That is to say, all men are thought to have one trait, whereas all women have another.[17] Second, sexual differences are also generally imagined to be hard wired or immutable. But even if there is a biological difference in men's and women's hair, it would clearly not share either of these characteristics: the difference would not be sharp and dichotomous, nor would it be entirely fixed. Consequently, we might say that hair wouldn't materialize gender identity in the "right" way.

This would have been less of a "problem" in early modern England. First of all, sexual differences weren't generally assumed to be sharp and dichotomous because males and females were not always seen as two distinct types of individuals with two distinct morphologies. Instead, they were often viewed along a continuum. Moreover, as I argued in more detail in my introduction, differences between the sexes were not necessarily considered to be hardwired or unchanging. Instead, they were often understood to be malleable or prosthetic.

The historical distance of the modern schema from its early modern counterpart becomes even clearer if we look at hair and beards together. Today, these two physical features are distinguished sharply from one another by virtue of the fact that they fall on opposite sides of the sex/gender divide. Facial hair is classified as a secondary sexual characteristic and is therefore thought to be a natural marker of difference, whereas the length of a person's hair is usually considered to be a gendered characteristic and is therefore thought to be culturally determined. In order for this conceptual distinction to work, we not only have to ignore the biological differences regarding the hair on the head, but we also have to overemphasize the biological differences regarding facial hair. Indeed, the classification of facial hair as a secondary sexual characteristic implies that only males possess this attribute.

In early modern England, by contrast, these two features were not so radically differentiated. In fact, they were often seen as being commensurate. The anatomist Daniel Sennert implies as much when he writes that just as men have beards, women have long hair: he says that he intends to explain "wherefore men only should have beards, and . . . women should not likewise have them; whereas notwithstanding women have on their heads the longer hair."[18] This commensurability is even clearer in John Bulwer's *Anthropometamorphosis*. He maintains that women's long hair is a "compensation" for their beardlessness. As he puts it, "Nature" allotted women "prolix hair" in "recompense for their smoothnesse and want of a Beard."[19] The point here is not that these statements are more biologically correct than our current beliefs, but rather that in both instances the ideologies of gender influence the way in which the "natural" differences are seen, understood, and produced.

If the sources I have discussed so far begin to suggest that short and long hair were crucial components of masculinity and femininity respectively, there is an early modern account of a sexual metamorphosis that provides a powerful testament to this. This is the story of a girl who was spontaneously transformed into a boy, and whose hair supposedly grew shorter as a part of her transformation. The "story" I am referring to here is none other than Ovid's Iphis and Ianthe. During the Renaissance, this "literary" text was often taken as a "realistic" description and was frequently mentioned alongside "medical" cases of sexual metamorphosis. In George Sandys' seventeenth-century commentary on the story, for instance, he notes that it is not hard to "believe that women have beene changed into men." He then goes on to invoke the authority of writers like Pliny and to cite several "medical" accounts of sexual transformation such as the case of Marie/Germain.[20] Similarly, Montaigne treats Ovid's story as if it were a medical case history. He uses it to illustrate his point that the imagination has the power to modify the body and to "incorporate" a "masculine member in girls," and like Sandys, he mentions it along with the case of Marie/Germain.[21]

It is interesting that these writers couple Iphis' metamorphosis with that of Marie/Germain because in both instances the "sex change" is said to include the transformation of a non-genital feature. Just as the growth of Marie/Germain's beard was a part of her metamorphosis, the shortening of Iphis' hair was a part of hers. The English translations of Ovid's tale invariably include this detail. Golding's sixteenth-century version, for example, describes Iphis' metamorphosis as follows: he says her "strength encreased, hir looke more sharper was to sight. Hir heare grew shorter, and she had a much more livelie spright, / Than when she was a wench."[22] Sandys' seventeenth-century translation reads: "Her strength augments; her look more bold appears: / Her shortening curles scarce hang beneath her eares; / By farre more full of courage rapt with joy: / For thou, of late a wench, art now a Boy."[23] In both of these texts, the transformation of Iphis' hair is said to occur suddenly and naturally during the course of her metamorphosis. Golding's somewhat paradoxical formulation – that Iphis' hair "*grew* shorter" – implies that this is a natural phenomenon like the growth of hair itself, and Sandys' description of her "shortening curles" likewise implies spontaneity. In fact, in Sandys' version, it is as if we witness Iphis' "curles" shrinking before our very eyes until they no longer hang beneath her ears.

Once we recognize that a sex change was (at least sometimes) said to involve a change in the length of the individual's hair, then this may give us a slightly different perspective on the polemical writing from the period. William Prynne's *The Unlovelinesse of Love-lockes*, for instance, maintains that growing or cutting the hair can "transform" a woman into a man, or "metamorphose" a man into a woman. Prynne rails against "the sundry of our Mannish, Impudent, and Inconstant female sexe [who] are Hermaphrodited, and transformed into men" by "unnaturally . . . cutting their hair short."[24] At another point, he continues this complaint, saying that these "mannish Viragoes" have been "transformed, and transubstantiated into Males, by a stupendous metamorphosis." Prynne also castigates the members of the "masculine race [who] are wholly degenerated and metamorphosed into women; not in Manners, Gestures, Recreations, Diet and Apparrell only, but likewise in the Womanish, Sinful, and Unmanly, Crisping, Curling, Frouncing . . . of their Lockes and Hairie excrements" (35–6). In these passages, Prynne repeatedly suggests that a change in the length of an individual's hair will alter their identity. He does not claim that women who cut their hair short look like men; instead, he says that they are "transformed" or "transubstantiated" into men. Likewise, he says that men who "crisp," "curl," and "frounce" their "Hairie excrements" are "degenerated" and "metamorphosed" into women. The modifications, according to Prynne, cause people to *be* members of the opposite sex, not simply *seem* like them.

Other polemical writers describe tonsorial changes in similar terms. In Thomas Wall's *A Spiritual Armour to Defend the Head from a Superfluity of Naughtiness*, he warns that "Men should not change their Natures to become effeminate" by wearing "a womanish length of hair."[25] If they do, he says that they will become "hermaphrodites" with "the faces of men, and . . . the hair of women" (31). Wall's rhetoric here is much more restrained than Prynne's but the idea he expresses is somewhat similar: just as Prynne maintains that men can be "wholly degenerated and metamorphosed into women," Wall claims that they can "change their Natures to become effeminate" or even "hermaphrodites."

Although all of these statements are clearly hyperbolic and not meant to be taken at face value, I think that they nevertheless resonate somewhat differently once we recognize that people believed that there were natural differences between men's and women's hair and that they thought it was possible for a sex change to include the alteration of an individual's hair. When seen from this perspective, it becomes evident that Prynne's hyperbole lies in suggesting that a change in hair length *in and of itself* could move an individual from one sexual category to the other, not in suggesting that such a transformation was possible in the first place or that a change in hair length might help instantiate it. Wall's comments are particularly interesting in this regard. Instead of saying that men who grow long hair are completely transformed into women (as Prynne did), he says that they become "hermaphrodites." As he puts it, they have the "faces" of men and the "hair" of women. This formulation treats the hair of the head as if it were an integral element of gendered identity roughly equivalent to the face. Although the modern tendency to accord less cultural weight to the hair than to the body beneath makes it difficult to hear this comment as anything other than figurative, I hope that we are now in a place where we are at least able to recognize the logic at work here.

Once we recognize that the length of the hair on an individual's head was considered to be a crucial means of materializing their masculinity and femininity, it will be less surprising to find that discussions of this physical characteristic invariably link it to broader issues about the roles of men and women in society. Indeed, I would argue that it is almost impossible to discuss the biological differences between the sexes without either implicitly or explicitly making some sort of reference to the patriarchal social order.[26] So, for example, when people today mention men's supposedly superior physical strength, it is often as a means of rationalizing their social dominance. Or, to take a somewhat more sophisticated example, when people invoke women's "biological" propensity to nurture, it is sometimes a means of "explaining" the gap between their salaries and those of men: the argument being that since women are biologically programmed to give birth and nurture, they are therefore less invested in work and careers and therefore do not make as much money as men.

Similar connections are made in early modern writing on hair. Thomas Wall, for instance, says not only that "it was . . . the pleasure of God to give unto the Woman a sign in nature [i.e. long hair] differing from Man," but also that this "sign" is meant "to teach her subjection to Man whose Glory she is."[27] Similarly, Prynne claims that "Nature hath bequeathed [long hair] unto Women, for a speciall use; to wit, for a . . . naturall Couering . . . or Embleme of their subjection to their Husbands."[28] Finally, the book *Seasonable Advice . . . for the Professors of this Backsliding Age* (1650) claims that "The woman's hair is called Long, because it was for length ordained of God before her fall to cover her face . . . [and] to perform the sign of her subjection to her Husband."[29]

Comparable formulations occur in other texts from the period that do not focus primarily on hair. Phillip Stubbes's *Anatomy of Abuses*, for instance, states that a wife's long hair was her God-given "sign of subjection . . . as the Apostle proveth,"[30] and William Whately's well-known marriage manual, *A Bride-Bush* (1619), likewise insists that "the woman was made for man and not the man for the woman . . . and nature hath given her [her] hair for a covering, as a naturall badge of this her inferiority to the man."[31] Thus, for Whately and Stubbes (and indeed all of the other writers and moralists I have mentioned so far), hair length is a "natural badge" that not only distinguishes between the sexes, but also demonstrates women's "proper" subservience to men.

Hair was linked to the social hierarchy in other, more subtle, ways as well. In order to see this, we first need to take note of the fact that women's tresses are constantly described as a "covering." Prynne, for instance, says that women's long hair is "a . . . Naturall covering"; the author of *Seasonable Advice* says hair is "ordained" by God to "cover the face"; and Whately says that "nature hath given her [her] hair for a covering."[32] Why, we might ask, was women's hair consistently called a "covering" as opposed to, say, "a veil" or "a cloak"? And why was it only women's long hair that was figured in this way? The beard might just as easily be described as a kind of "covering" for the face, and yet it was not. Instead, it was represented primarily as an "ensigne for manly cheeks" and was thus linked to martial activities and a military context. The most obvious answer to this question is that the term "covering" derives from 1 Corinthians where Paul states that women's "hair was given to her for a covering." Another possible explanation has to do with the changes in women's hairstyles. Fashion historians note that over the course of the sixteenth and seventeenth centuries, women slowly abandoned the wimple and the other headdresses that they had worn throughout the middle ages. Thus, we might speculate that hair itself came to be figured as a kind of "covering" as a way of compensating for the fact that other types of "covering" were no longer being worn.

There is yet another possible reason why these early modern writers figured women's hair as a "covering." They may have used the term in order to link the norms regarding hair length with the legal concept of *coverture*, and the construction of married women as *feme covert*. In fact, hair is sometimes explicitly called an "outward couverture."[33] The *OED* explains the concept of coverture, and the term "feme covert" by saying that the latter is "a woman under the cover or protection of her husband."[34] This definition does not, however, do justice to the disenfranchisement enacted through this social and legal practice. Coverture was, in effect, a "legal fiction" whereby the identity of the wife was subsumed into that of her husband: in the eyes of the law, the husband and wife were conflated into a single entity – the husband. As a result, a wife had no right to own property, sue, or make contracts.

While the legal concept of coverture was longstanding in England (it is usually traced back to the Norman conquest), the term itself was not introduced until the early part of the sixteenth century. Its first recorded use is in a statute introduced by Henry VIII in 1542–3. The term "feme covert" also entered the English language at about the same time – in 1528. Interestingly, this was the very period when women were beginning to abandon the headdresses that they had worn to cover their tresses throughout the middle ages. By pointing this out, I don't mean to suggest that the term "coverture" was coined in order to link the legal concept to women's hair or to the biblical proclamations about it, but I do think that using similar terms to refer to both women's legal status (coverture) and their hair (covering) would have worked to establish an implicit connection between the two.

This would also help to explain the observation made by the fashion historian Richard Corson that it was primarily *married* women who continued to wear headdresses into the later parts of the sixteenth century.[35] Thus, there would appear to have been more pressure on "wives" to be "covered," even when "maids" no longer were. An analogous point can be made about long hair itself. In many of the texts I mentioned above, women's long locks are said to demonstrate, not only their subordination to men in general, but often, more specifically, their subordination to their *husbands*. Prynne, for example, says that long hair is an "Emblem of their [women's] subjection to their Husbands"[36] and the author of *Seasonable Advice* likewise states that it is "the sign of her subjection [to her Husband]."[37] It is also worth noting that Whately's *Bride-Bush* (which I mentioned earlier) was a marriage manual, though, interestingly, in that text, he himself does not speak simply of long hair as an indicator of a wife's subordination to her husband; instead, he says that it is a "naturall badge of this her inferiority to the man."[38] The slippage between discussing the subordination of wives to their husbands and discussing the subordination of all women to men is indicative, I would argue, of a more general slippage between the use of long hair as a means of re-emphasizing the practice of coverture, and its use as a means of legitimating the patriarchy itself.

If it is thus clear that women's long hair was linked to their place in the social hierarchy, and possibly with the legal concept of coverture, it is crucial to recognize that the "natural" differences in men's and women's hair length were not seen as *the basis for* the divergent social statuses of those individuals. From a modern perspective this may seem quite paradoxical. Even though some early modern writers believed that women's hair was longer than men's hair biologically, they did not use that fact to ground and legitimate the patriarchal social order. Instead of seeing the "natural" differences in hair length as a foundation for – or justification of – the uneven distribution of power between men and women in society, the arguments of patriarchal writers from the period tend to move in the opposite direction: from assertions about the social order to comments on hair. This logical progression is apparent if we look at a fuller version of the passage from Thomas Wall's *God's Holy Order in Nature* that I cited above. Wall writes

Woman God made for Man . . . She also was made in subjection to Man, her earthly Lord and Husband . . . This being that holy Order God created Man and Woman in . . . it was therefore the pleasure of God to give unto the Woman a sign in nature differing from Man, to teach her subjection to Man whose Glory she is, namely long hair.[39]

In this passage, Wall begins with the "fact" that woman "was made in subjection to Man" and then goes on to discuss the physical "sign[s] in nature" that God subsequently gave to women that were meant to signal their place in this hierarchy. Thus, it is clear that for Wall, it is the patriarchal order that is primary, and the differences in men's and women's bodies are meant to express that order, not be the basis for it. The logic here is essentially the same as that underlying the descriptions of beards. As we have seen, Helkiah Crooke states that it is "because" women "were born to subjection" that they "needed no ensigne of majesty."[40] Although the anatomist Crooke and the preacher Wall write in very different contexts, their arguments both seem to follow a similar logical trajectory.[41]

The discourses on hair can help to clarify one of the ideas that I began to explore in my last chapter: namely, that early modern writers have a different conception of nature and the natural world than the one that we, as post-scientific revolution readers, would expect. When they maintain, for instance, that beards and short hair are "natural" features of men, they don't necessarily mean that those characteristics are rooted in biology. Instead of basing their claims about "nature" on empirical observation and analysis, they often base them on biblical authority. So "nature" therefore refers to the world as God created it and as it is described in the Bible. Wall, for instance, claims that "the main end" of his book is to explain, as his title suggests, *God's Holy Order in Nature* and specifically "in what order God created Man in respect of his hair."[42] Consequently, Wall's comments on hair might be compared to some of the comments on Adam's facial hair that I mentioned in the last chapter: just as writers like Barnes maintained that God made Adam bearded, Wall argues that "Man was created with short hair, and not long hair" (17). Wall attempts to "prove" this by using biblical exegesis and analysis. He makes much, for instance, of the Pauline injunction "Doth not even nature itself teach you that if a man have long hair, it is a shame unto him? But if a woman have long hair it is a glory to her" – *1 Corinthians 11.14–15*.[43] The point here is therefore that when early modern writers insist upon the "natur-alness" of the distinction between men's and women's hair, they are often speaking about "nature" as God supposedly created it rather than some sort of physiological "truth."

This may help to explain why the term " nature" is used in such a surprising variety of ways in the discourses on hair.[44] Indeed, virtually all the definitions that are proffered are quite different from what modern readers might expect. For example, some writers maintain that "nature" simply means "custome." Hall complicates the issue even further when he says that "Nature . . . cannot" really mean "Custome, for we never finde through the whole Booke of God, that ever that word is used for Custome."[45] But he does not then go on to contrast "nature" and "custome" in the way that is common in modern thinking. Instead, he explains that

by Nature here is meant, the light and dictate of right reason in the understanding, informing men by its common notions and instinct, what is good, and to be done, or what is evill, and to be avoyded: 'Tis that order and natural inclination which God hath put in the Creature: And thus Nature it self is said to condemne long haire, as being contrary to that order, and natural principles of decency and honesty, which God hath implanted in man: And though many Heathens have worne and doe weare, long haire, yet that is their abuse and sinne against Nature . . . The sinfull customes of some barbarous ones, cannot be called the Law of Nature; But Customes, when they flow from the principles of right Reason, and are agreeable to its Dictates, then they binde. (28)

So, for Hall, "nature" still refers to "custome" but he refines the ideas of others by saying that "nature" really only refers to "customs" that are "good," "honest," "decent," and most importantly, *that God intended*. These legitimate or "natural" customs are opposed to the "sinful customes of some barbarous ones." So "nature," for Hall, is entirely inextricable from culture and morality.

In the end, what Hall does in his text is establish the God-given gendered norms for men's and women's hair through biblical exegesis, and having done this, he then insists that the tresses be materialized accordingly. The question of whether these norms arise spontaneously or whether they are produced through human intervention is secondary. As we have seen, Hall does hypothesize that women's hair is naturally longer than men's, but this does not provide the basis for the divergent social status of men and women. Most writers left the question about the cause of this difference unanswered. Hence, a the modern nature versus nurture debate seems largely irrelevant. For example, the anatomist Daniel Sennert says simply that "women have on their heads most usually the longer hair," sidestepping the issue of how this situation arises.[46] Similarly, Crooke, whom I mentioned earlier, never explicitly says that women have longer hair on account of their humoral constitution. He does, however, imply that male and female hairs are fundamentally different. In fact, he even gives them different anatomical names, stating that in men, the hairs of the head "are called *Caesaries a frequenti casione*, because they are often cut: and in Women *coma*, because they bestow great paines in combing and curling them."[47] If this passage indicates that Crooke sees men's and women's hair as essentially different (so much so that he gives their hair two distinct names), it also clearly demonstrates the extent to which anatomy/physiology was, for him, bound up with cultural practices like "cutting," "combing," and "curling." In the end, these writers do not need to claim that the differences they are discussing are rooted in biology. This may be because, for them, those differences (and the social hierarchy which they signal) are already firmly established by God's word.

Another reason why early modern writers didn't feel compelled to address questions about the genesis of sexual differences is because the features themselves were openly acknowledged to be malleable. So even though nature was conceptualized as a book written by God, it was one whose text could be rewritten by human intervention. As a result, the crucial thing was the particular way in which nature and the body were materialized, not the way in which that materialization was achieved. It was, of course, considered sinful to rewrite God's book of nature in a way that contravened God's will. Hence, one of the texts on hair claims that when men grow their tresses long "the order of nature is altered." The men who do so, "despite [sic] God by the same, in that we abuse that which he hath given for so excellent an ornament to . . . women."[48] The use of the term "we" here is particularly interesting because it implies that the sinful propensity to alter "nature" in a way that goes against God's will exists in all men. It was also thought to exist in all women. The same author claims that "wee daylie see that they [women] seeke to bring into forme and fashion, that which hee in his mercie. . .apoyneted and framed otherwise at the first . . . [T]hey . . . strive to go beyond the excellencie of God, as though they could proportion that which he hath not fashioned aright."[49] This description of women who "seek to bring into forme and fashion, that which hee . . . apoyneted and framed otherwise at the first" is reminiscent of the discussions of the codpiece that I analyzed in my second chapter. There, moralists claimed that men "unfashion" the "partes" that "God fayre fashion'd" by wearing the codpiece, and in the process they "both deforme those gratious parts, & him."[50] All of these sources indicate that it was considered sinful to refashion the body in ways that went against God's will, but it is worth saying that it was not always clear exactly what God's will was. In other words, there was often a question about exactly how God "in his mercie. . .[had] apoyneted and framed" individuals.

The emphasis in these texts on the malleability of "nature" may sound somewhat odd today, for we tend to assume, as Diana Fuss points out in *Essentially Speaking*, that "nature" is largely fixed.[51] In other words, we tend to assume that a person's "nature" is precisely what is constant and enduring about them. It is therefore somewhat oxymoronic to speak of someone changing their nature. Early modern writers, as we have begun to appreciate, do not generally share these views. Earlier in this chapter, I discussed how both William Prynne and Thomas Wall maintained that men and women could "change their natures" and become "hermaphrodites" by cutting or growing their hair. Similarly, John Bulwer declares that "for a Woman to be shorne . . . is cleerly against the intention of Nature," and that "for Men to nourish long Haire is quite contrary to the intention of Nature."[52] In all of these formulations, an individual's gender identity is clearly understood as something that is open to alteration.

This had important ramifications for gendered norms and ideologies. Most importantly, it meant that they too were understood to be at least potentially open to transformation and rearticulation. Wall acknowledges as much when he says that "if Man do wear on his head long hair, Womans glory, he thereby saith by that action, He is no longer the Womans head . . . he maketh himself equal with his Wife in power."[53] Here, transforming the length of the hair is a means of overturning the patriarchal order itself, and both of these things seem to be possible.

But why is it that hair came to "matter" so powerfully in seventeenth-century English culture? Why did it play such a crucial role in materializing gender identity? I can only begin to sketch the outlines of an answer to this question here, but I want to mention two historical developments that seem to be relevant. The first is something that I alluded to above: namely, the shift in hair fashions. As we have seen, women's hairstyles changed dramatically as they slowly abandoned the headdresses that they had worn throughout the middle ages. According to the fashion historian Richard Corson, this process did not really get underway in England until the middle of the sixteenth century, for in "the early years [of that century] . . . there was a continuation of the fifteenth-century style, the hair being frequently concealed, especially by married women."[54] And over the course of the next hundred years, women gradually came to wear their tresses uncovered. The question of why this change occurred at this particular historical moment still remains to be explored, but the timing suggests that it may have had something to do with the religious upheavals of the Reformation. I was able to demonstrate in the last chapter that the Reformation contributed to the increasing cultural invest-ments in facial hair, so it certainly seems possible that this religious event had a similar impact on tonsorial fashions. But whatever the reason for this shift in women's hairstyles, we should note that there was also a corresponding shift in men's hairstyles that took place at roughly the same time: men began to wear long locks in increasing numbers for the first time in several centuries. Corson points out in *Fashions in Hair* that the seventeenth century ushered in a period of nearly "two hundred years of long hair . . . for men" (160). One early modern commentator said that this change had come into effect during "the Reign of James the First" and that men in England had previously worn short hair "for near five hundred years" going back to the reign of Henry I.[55]

If the early modern period thus witnessed significant changes in both women's and men's preferred hairstyles, the second major development we need to acknowledge is the fact that hair became the principal way of distinguishing between the two political factions of the English Civil War. Parliamentarians, on the one hand, supposedly had closely-cropped hair and came to be called "roundheads" as a result. Royalists, on the other, were known for their long flowing tresses and were labeled "cavaliers." The production of political differences through hair length was not completely distinct from the production of gendered differences, but they stood in complex relationship to one another. Indeed, the norms regarding masculine and feminine hair were both reinforced and subverted during the civil war period. Nevertheless, it may well be that it was the *intersection* of these gendered and political ideologies that combined to make hair "matter" so powerfully at this particular historical moment.

The terms "Roundhead" and "Cavalier" are usually said to have been introduced during the disturbances in London at the end of 1641, when "crowds calling for the exclusion of the bishops and catholic peers from the House of Lords were nicknamed 'Roundheads' and the army officers supporting the King were tagged 'Cavaliers'."[56] A pamphlet from 1643 described the emergence of these appellations as follows:

In these . . . times, the shaggehead Cavaliers, wearing all long haire, and the Citizens of London cutting their haire short round about their heads, there being so great a controversie between Cavalliers and the Citizens, to the end that they might make the Citizens ominous, they branded them . . . Round-heads, and therefore spread an universall tearme and appellation on all that cut their hair short.[57]

But it was not just the "Round-heads" who were "branded" with "an universall tearme and appellation." The "shaggehead Cavaliers" were also identified by their tresses: for example, the illustrated title page of the pamphlet *An Exact Description of a Roundhead, and A Long-head Shag-poll* (1642) presents a "Man of Haire" who is described as follows: "This Man of haire whom you see marching here, Is that brave Ruffian Monsieur Cavalier."[58]

One pamphlet even went so far as to humorously reduce the entire Civil War conflict to a matter of hairstyles:

The Puritans in the Reign of the Royal Martyr, to distinguish themselves from their Neighbours, took on them an extraordinary short Cut, and their Neighbors in opposition to them espoused a long one, because they would not be reputed Round-heads; and in nothing outwardly were the two Parties so much differenc'd as in their Hair, and happy had it been that the quarrel had ended in the Barbers Scissars, which we all know brake out afterwards into the long Sword, and instead of plucking each other by the ears a little, they fell into stabbing one another in the Guts. So that the mischiefs which the Barber might have prevented at first, had he kept an even hand on both parties and steered them both to an equal Cut, all the wit of man could not prevent.[59]

In this passage, the difference between "the Puritans" and "their Neighbours" is comically reduced to a difference of hairstyles. Thus, the implication is that if only the barbers had been able to keep a more even hand on their customers, the bloody civil war might have been avoided. While the humor here comes from transforming the very "real" differences between the two factions of the war into a seemingly "superficial" difference in hairstyles, I would argue that the passage also indicates the centrality of hair as a means of materializing the differences between the two parties.

Interestingly, these civil war politics mediated the production of gender identity, though the connection between the two was not entirely straightforward. At times, civil war politics reinforced or reiterated gendered norms and ideologies regarding hair, while at other times they undermined or subverted them. Gendered norms were reinforced, for example, when "Roundheads" cast themselves as properly masculine and their "long-headed" opponents as feminine. Tamsyn Williams' recent article on "Polemical Prints of the English Revolution" points out that parliamentarian "[w]oodcuts of cavaliers with ridiculously long locks" were a common "mocking device," and that the long locks of the cavaliers were the basis for "accusations of . . . femininity."[60] Indeed, such accusations were routine in polemical literature from the period, as when the author of the pamphlet *A Medicine for Malignancy* (1644) describes the Cavaliers as "shag-pole Locusts that have haire like women."[61] For that matter, even more neutral observers questioned the masculinity of the Cavaliers on account of their tresses: one claims that "if those that are termed Rattle-heads [Royalists] . . . would take up a resolution to begin in moderation of hair to the just reproach of those that are called Puritans and Roundheads, I would honour their manlinesse as much as [I honour] the others godliness."[62] Here, the author claims that if only the Cavaliers would "moderate" their long hair, he would "honour their manliness" as much as the puritans so-called "godliness."

When seen from this perspective, it is crucial to note that all of the books and pamphlets on hair that I have been discussing so far in this chapter were written by parliamentarians, and often, more specifically, by Puritans. The majority of them were, moreover, published in the 1640s and 50s – in the middle of the conflict.[63] While these books are primarily about the gendering of hair, there are points where the political inflections of their arguments become evident, as when Thomas Hall insists, in *Loathsomenesse of Longe Hair* (1653), that the Bible not only prescribes short hair for men, but it also prescribes that

they shall round their heads: the word is doubled in the original for greater emphasis . . . you shall round your heads, or in plaine terms you shall be Round-heads. The Text is cleare for that tearm in the very letter, the greater is their sinn who jeere at Gods Ministers and People for their short hair, and for rounding their heads, since we have Gods command for it; and the very Philosopher can tell them, that the roundest form is best and beautifullest.[64]

Here, Hall puts an explicitly politicized spin on the gendered prescriptions that fill the pages of his book.[65] Once we have recognized this, it becomes apparent that even comments that appear to be only about gender would also have had an implicit political valence.

Thus, the point I want to make is not simply that the books on hair need to be read in relation to the political discourses of the epoch, but also that the discourses of gender and politics were inextricably related. Nevertheless, the two did not, as I noted earlier, always reinforce one another. Royalists, for example, often subverted the traditional gendered norms by maintaining that hair length was not important. They argued instead that both men and women could (indeed should) have long hair and that women's hair should be bound or adorned whereas men's hair should be unbound. Two books published in this vein are Jacobus Revius' *Libertas Christiana circa usum capillitii defensa qua Sex ejusdem Disputationes de Coma ab exceptionibus viri cujus-dam docti vindicantur* and Johannes Polyander a Kerckhoven's *Judicium & Consilium de Comae & Vestium Usu & Abusu*,[66] but the Royalist writer that I will be concentrating on here is Claude de Saumaise, or Salmasius.[67] Today, Salmasius is known primarily as the author of the *Defensio Regia*, an import-ant pamphlet written in support of the English monarchy. Milton's *Defence of the English People* (1651) was written in direct response to the *Defensio Regia*, and was a point by point rebuttal of its arguments. It is less commonly known that Salmasius wrote and published two book-length studies on hair during the 1640s: in 1644, he published a seven-hundred-and-fifty-page volume entitled *Epistola ad Andream Colvium: super Cap. XI. Primae ad Corinth. Epist. De Casarie Virorum et Mulierum Coma*, and a year later, a one-hundred-page dialog, *De Coma Dialogus, Primus. Caesarius et Curtius interlocutores*.

In the *Epistola*, Salmasius explains that he was approached by Andreas Colvius and informed of how "certain pastors" had begun to chide their congregations "severely and menacingly . . . saying they would not tolerate any men who could not bear to part with their hair nor any women who, because of their wickedness, could not be persuaded to abandon their accus-tomed hairstyles." In fact, these threats of punishment from scripture against males with long locks and females with "dressed hair" had apparently become so severe that the pastors had even said that the members of their congre-gation "should expect on the day of judgement nothing lighter than the loss of their eternal soul."[68] Salmasius claims that it is because of this situation that he has decided to see what the scripture has to say on the matter. As might be expected, he ends up refuting the claims of the "pastors" and concluding, on the basis of his readings in scripture, that "It is an indifferent thing how long we will weare our haire, and a part of our Christian liberty to doe as please our selves herein."[69] Salmasius does not, however, mean to say that hair is, or ought to be, ungendered. Instead, he suggests that hair binding or adornment ought to be the way in which gender was materialized. He asks rhetorically "whether it is proper that women's hair be unfastened and unarranged?" and ultimately answers by saying that "this same Nature, from which we learn that women must be unshorn so they can maintain their seemliness, imposes on them a law requiring that they bind their hair. Therefore, it is equally feminine

to have hair not only bound up, but also unshorn: one follows from the other"
(613–14).

Parliamentarians, of course, disputed these claims. In *The Loathsomenesse
of Longe Hair*, Hall attacks Salmasius for suggesting that both men and
women could wear long hair:

Salmasius then is out [wrong], who is so bold as to affirme *nunquam in Scriptura sacra
improbari aut damnari caesariem (i) capillum virilem promissum modo non more
modoque muliebrie comptus & Ornatus habeatur* . . . pitty . . . he had not pleaded so
bad a cause . . . with such grossly false mediums, as that Christ himself wore long Hair,
and his Apostles also, &c.[70]

If Hall thus insists that hair length is indeed crucial, other writers take issue
with Salmasius' second contention: namely, that women's hair should be
bound or adorned. This point is rebutted at length in a text which appeared
the same year as Salmasius' *Epistola* – the pamphlet *A Looking-Glasse for
Women . . . Shewing the unlawfulness of any outward adorning of any attire of
Haire* (1644). Salmasius is never mentioned in the text, but it focuses almost
exclusively on the issue of "adornment." Its main purpose, as the title begins
to suggest, is "to prove its [sic] utterly unlawful for any woman to go in any
outward adorning of attire of haire, in laying it forth in any fashion whatso-
ever, under that seeming pretence of a covering."[71]

This passage indicates that one of the interesting issues that the author of
this pamphlet has to negotiate is how to condemn hair binding without
condemning all types of "covering." This is why he stipulates that this is
done "under that seeming pretence of a covering." The author is, on the one
hand, clearly invested in coding certain types of hair binding as "adornment"
and thus placing them within the purview of the more general Protestant
condemnation of ornamentation, but he is also, on the other hand, at pains to
distinguish between "adornment" and "covering" so as not to appear to be
condemning the "covering" that was prescribed by 1 Corinthians. Consequently, s/he argues that "a woman cannot [really] be said to be covered,
when. . .[her hair] is broidered and plaited, or laid forth" (5). According to the
author, this is "but a seeming covering, and no real covering." In fact, s/he
says "it will appear that it is rather an uncovering as you use it, then a
covering, in that you take it out of its proper place, to hang it down in another
place" (6).[72]

When a text like *A Looking-Glasse for Women* is viewed in relation to the
writing of a royalist like Salmasius, we can begin to get a sense of some of the
specific ways in which the seventeenth-century discourses of gender and
politics were intertwined. There are two final things to say about this situation. First, it seems clear that the political investments in hair would have
worked, in the aggregate, to intensify the role that this part played in forming

gendered identity. Although the two sides in the conflict disagreed on the particular way in which hair ought to materialize gendered identity, they both insisted that it should do so, and this would ultimately have served to make hair "matter" more. But at the same time, it is important to recognize that the mediation of gender by politics would not necessarily have been an additive process: that is to say, the political investments in hair were not simply added onto, or subtracted from, the gendered investments. Instead, these two ideological projects may well have played off one another in multiple, even exponential, ways.

At this point, I want to turn to the work of John Milton. I do so in order to suggest the extent to which his writing – and particularly his *Samson Agonistes* – is engaged with the seventeenth-century discourses and practices regarding hair that I have mapped out so far in this chapter. It is not particularly surprising to find that Milton was interested in this corporeal feature given its importance for both gender and politics. Nevertheless, the ideological work that his texts perform in this regard has remained largely unexamined. Although I will be concentrating primarily on Milton's *Samson*, I want to begin with a brief analysis of his treatment of hair in *Paradise Lost*. In Book IV, Milton provides a detailed description of the tresses of both Adam and Eve. This tonsorial portrait is part of the larger discussion of the gendered hierarchy in Eden. Milton writes that Adam and Eve are

> Not equal, as their sex not equal seemed;. . .
> Hee for God only, shee for God in him:
> His fair large Front and Eye sublime declar'd
> Absolute rule; and Hyacinthin Locks
> Round from his parted forelock manly hung
> Clustring, but not beneath his shoulders broad:
> Shee as a vail down to the slender waist
> Her unadorned golden tresses wore
> Disshevelld, but in wanton ringlets wav'd,
> As the Vine curls her tendrils – which impli'd
> Subjection, but requir'd with gentle sway,
> And by her yielded, by him best receiv'd,
> Yielded with coy submission, modest pride,
> And sweet reluctant amorous delay.[73]

In this passage, Milton first clearly indicates that Adam's hair is an element of his masculinity: as Milton puts it, Adam is "manly hung" with regard to his hair. But Milton also suggests that Adam's tresses are one of the physical characteristics that "declare" his "Absolute rule." Indeed, masculinity and "Absolute rule" are here virtually equated. When Milton turns to Eve's tresses, he focuses primarily on their erotic power, though he also subtly genders them as well. He represents Eve's hair as "a vail down to the slender waist" and indicates that this establishes her "proper" feminine subordination: her long hair is said to imply "Subjection." Moreover, it is worth saying that the way in which Milton codes the erotic charge of Eve's locks is itself strongly gendered: Eve passively "yields" her locks "with coy submission."

Milton's tonsorial portrait of Adam and Eve in *Paradise Lost* resonates strongly with the discourses on hair that I have been analyzing in this chapter, especially insofar as it links the hair with what other writers from the period call "God's holy order in nature," and more specifically insofar as it suggests that Adam's hair "declares" his "Absolute rule" and Eve's hair, to return to the formulation of Philip Stubbes, is a "sign of her subjection." These echoes might be explained by the fact that Milton's text closely parallels 1 Corinthians 11. This chapter of the Bible was, as we have seen, a central referent for much of the writing on hair. The biblical text, like Milton's, begins with pronouncements about the "divine" hierarchy, stating that "the head of every man is Christ . . . and the head of the woman is the man" (1 Cor. 11:3) and that "Neither was the man created for the woman . . . but the woman for the man" (1 Cor. 11:9), and it then moves to pronouncements about hair, especially the verses that I mentioned earlier: "Doth not even nature itself teach you, that, if a man have long hair, it is a shame unto him? But if a woman have long hair, it is a glory to her" (1 Cor. 11:15–16). The passage from Milton's *Paradise Lost* follows a similar progression, moving from his description of the gender hierarchy ("Hee for God only") to his description of Adam and Eve's hair.

If this section of *Paradise Lost* thus echoes the dominant seventeenth-century tonsorial discourses, it also differs from them in important ways. Most notably, Milton depicts Adam's "Hyacinthin locks" as being relatively long: he says that they "cluster" down to his "shoulders broad." This precise designation appears to be significant for Milton since he uses it again to describe the hair of several other male characters in his writing. Earlier in *Paradise Lost*, for instance, Milton stipulates that Uriel's tresses "Illustrious on his Shoulders fledge" (3.627). Similarly, in *Samson Agonistes*, when Samson's locks have "returned," Manoa claims that they are "on his shoulders waving down," "Garrisoned round about him like a camp / Of faithful soldiery" (1493–8). In both of these instances, Milton carefully specifies the length of the character's hair. Moreover, in Samson's case in particular, this length of hair is explicitly coded as being masculine. Indeed, the martial imagery that Manoa uses to describe Samson's locks – comparing them to "a camp / Of faithful soldiery" – might be likened to that used in descriptions of beards. It certainly suggests that Samson has fully recovered from his brush with "foul effeminacy."

Milton's representation of men with shoulder-length hair could, I believe, be seen as an intervention in the tonsorial debates that I have been analyzing in this chapter. These texts often seek to specify exactly what counts as "long" and "short" hair. While some writers claim that men's "short" hair could only be a few inches long, others are more liberal. The author of *Seasonable Advice*, for instance, asserts that "Womanish long hair" is hair which "one may with comb or hand bring it forward to cover his Face."[74] Wall uses a somewhat similar standard, stating that "long" tresses cover the eyes. Finally, Thomas Hall's *Loathsomenesse of Longe Hair* allows that "short" hair can be even longer, claiming that it is only when men's hair "lie[s] on their backs, and shoulders" that it "is utterly disapproved of by the Word of God." As he explains, "God hath ordained clothes (not Ruffianly Haire) to cover their backs & shoulders."[75]

When seen in relation to these other writers, Milton seems to be taking a position somewhat similar to that of Hall. Milton describes both Adam and Uriel with locks down to – but not beneath – their shoulders. Milton's representation of Adam is particularly significant since many of the arguments about tonsure centered on the question of how God created Adam and Eve with respect to their hair. Wall, for instance, contends that Adam must have had "short" hair, because he "was created so perfect in nature, that there was not anything about him . . . whereof he might be asham'd."[76] For his part, Milton does not mean to imply that Adam's hair was "long"; rather, he is extending the limits of what counts as short, masculine hair. Adam's hair is still much shorter than Eve's since hers reaches "down to her slender waist." Thus, there is still a tonsorial difference between the sexes, it is just that Milton redefines its specific dimensions.

Milton's intervention may well have been motivated by his preference regarding his own hair since, as far as we can tell, he consistently allowed it to grow down to his shoulders.[77] There is only one portrait of Milton that *doesn't* portray him with this hairstyle – the Morgan image of him at ten years old. John Aubrey, Milton's seventeenth-century biographer, claims that the reason Milton has short hair in this portrait is because his "schoolmaster was a puritan in Essex, who cutt his haire short."[78] Leo Miller's book on Milton's portraits explains Aubrey's comments as follows: "Inquisitive Aubrey noticed [the short hair of the portrait], and (apparently) asked, and was told (by Milton's younger brother Christopher?) that the boy Milton's schoolmaster preferred the fashion."[79] Whatever the reason for Milton's short hair in this early image, he does not wear it in any of his subsequent portraits or engravings. As Milton's biographer, William Riley Parker, notes, the adult Milton "no longer cut his hair short in a Puritan fashion, but let it fall loosely to his collar, covering his ears, like a Cavalier."[80] Milton's locks eventually became one of his signature features. Hence, when Vertue visited Milton's daughter Deborah Clarke and showed her an engraving of her father (probably the original Faithorne sketch) in order to verify its authenticity, she is said to have recognized it immediately, exclaiming: "O Lord! That is a picture of my father! How came you by it? Just so my father wore his hair."[81]

If Milton's *Paradise Lost* thus seems to perform a fairly straightforward intervention with regard to the current discourses on hair, and if that intervention seems to have been partially motivated by Milton's own preferred hairstyle, it is significant that he returned to the topic of hair again in *Samson Agonistes*. In choosing to write about Samson, Milton selected a figure who was known, above all, for his tresses. The religious historian Andrew Smyth Palmer claims that

it would hardly be too much to say that the *motif* which actuates the entire [Samson] narrative is his extraordinary endowment in the matter of hair. It is the distinctive characteristic which marks off Samson from every other personage in the Biblical history and, indeed, in literature. There are many mighty men of valor celebrated for their doughty achievements in saga, romance, or story; but none who owes his peculiar gift of strength to the abundant and unchecked growth of his hair. On this the interest of the narrative turns and the *denouement* of his career depends.[82]

These comments about the centrality of hair in the Samson story may seem self-evident, but oddly, most Miltonists have ignored the topic. Roy Flannagan – the editor of the *Riverside Milton* – even goes so far as to state that for Milton, "Samson's hair . . . [is] not important."[83] Not everyone has concurred with this assessment. In recent years, scholars like John Rogers have begun to explore the meanings of hair in *Samson Agonistes*. Rogers brilliantly analyzes the theological issues surrounding Samson's tresses in his article "The Secret of *Samson Agonistes*."[84] He maintains that the "central riddle of the poem" (the problem of whether Samson's final action is "instigated by God, or by his own valor") finds its correlative in the question of whether Samson's locks are simply a "sign" of divinely derived power or a more literal container where his strength is "stor'd" (111). The theological significance of Samson's hair was much debated in the seventeenth century and, according to Rogers, although Milton's *Samson* begins by acceding to the dominant Protestant interpretation of the story (which insisted that Samson's locks were simply a "sign" of divine favor), he subsequently "undo[es] the authoritative voluntarism" of this position by reinvesting "the hero's body as a viable . . . origin of power" (117).

Like Rogers, I want to read Milton's *Samson Agonistes* in relation to the contemporary discourses on hair, but I hope to expand and deepen his work by focusing on the gendered significance of hair as opposed to its religious significance. At first glance, Milton's *Samson* seems to take the dominant gendered prescriptions about hair and turn them on their head. The long-haired Samson is portrayed as being entirely – even aggressively – masculine: when he has his hair, "No strength of man, or fiercest wild beast c[an] withstand [him]" (127). When his locks are cut short, moreover, he is unmanned and reduced to "foul effeminacy" (410). Milton clearly codes the loss of Samson's locks as a kind of effeminization by comparing the shorn Samson to a "tame Weather" who has lost "all [his] precious fleece" (538) and by noting that he is made "to sit idle on the household hearth, / A burdenous drone" (566–7).

The treatment of hair in *Samson Agonistes* would thus appear to be very different from that in *Paradise Lost*. In *Samson*, Milton seems to question the very norms that he had earlier promoted, and as a result, he ends up providing a much more complex treatment of hair and its relationship to gender. This too might be explained by reference to Milton's biography. He may well have been particularly aware of the *problems* of materializing identity through hair since his own hairstyle did not really correspond with what would have been expected of him despite his efforts to legitimate it. The tensions Milton may have experienced regarding his hair are suggested by the incongruity of Parker's comment that Milton wore his hair "like a Cavalier." His locks may have caused other types of dissonance as well. Indeed, his university nickname – "our Lady of Christ's" – may have been provoked, at least in part, by his chosen hairstyle.

Whatever the reason, Milton's *Samson* ultimately eschews the polemical voice in favor of a more interrogative one.[85] What is odd about this is that Milton's questioning of the normative pronouncements about hair at first seems to bring him in line with royalist writers like Salmasius. Indeed, royalists often held Samson up as an exemplar who showed that long hair was acceptable for men, and parliamentarians, for their part, often sought to discredit this potentially subversive example. The Puritan divine Richard Rogers, for instance, addresses the issue of Samson's hair in his *Commentary upon the Whole Booke of Judges* (1613), a text which Rogers also "preached . . . and delivered in sundry lectures." He claims that there are some men "who will defend themselves" for the "unnatural fashion" of wearing long hair by citing "the practice of the Nazarites," but he insists that in reality this practice is "furthest off from the strict worship of God, and sincere walking after his will."[86] Similar responses appear in virtually all of the books on hair that I have been examining in this chapter. Thomas Hall provides an even more specific counterargument than Richard Rogers. He acknowledges that the tonsorial practices of the Nazarites might seem to contradict his claims about how women and men ought to materialize their tresses. He acknowledges that some might argue *"The Nazarites wore long haire Numb. 6.7.19. Now had it been sinfull, unnaturall, or no ornament to them, God would never have commanded it &c."* He then refutes this point by stating that this "is manifest non-sequitur, because God commanded the Nazarites to nourish their haire; therefore that we may doe so still it doth not follow." As he puts it later, this "extraordinary case will not make an ordinary rule."[87]

If Milton's descriptions of Samson's hair appear to undermine the traditional Puritan orthodoxy on the subject and to align him with royalist writers, it is worth saying that Milton further follows the precedent of royalist writers by suggesting that gender identity might be materialized through ornament and adornment. In Milton's poem, femininity is consistently associated with "veils" and adornment, though not necessarily with tonsorial adornment. The chorus (the voice of normativity in the poem) speaks of women in general as having "outward ornament . . . lavished on their sex" (1025–6) and the femininity of the main female character, Dalila, is also explicitly character-ized in this way. When she is first introduced, she is presented as a virtual compendium of accessories – a kind of prosthetic god:

> But who is this, what thing of Sea or Land?
> Female of sex it seems,
> That so bedeckt, ornate, and gay,
> Comes this way sailing
> Like a stately Ship . . .
> With all her bravery on, and tackle trim,
> Sails fill'd, and streamers waving,
> Courted by all the winds that hold them play,
> An Amber scent of odorous perfume
> Her harbinger, a damsel train behind;
> Some rich *Philistian* Matron she may seem,
> And now at nearer view, no other certain
> Than *Dalila* thy wife.
>
> (710–23)

Although it may at first appear that Dalila's identity is masked or effaced by her accoutrements, it is actually more accurate to say that her identity, and especially her femininity, emerges through them. Indeed, even before it is clear who this figure is, it is clear that she is "female of sex" because of the fact that she is "so bedeckt, ornate, and gay." This is because "sex" in this passage is not so much signaled by a particular kind of ornamentation as it is by ornament itself. John Guillory makes a similar observation in "Dalila's House" when he remarks that the poem does not really "expose . . . [Dalila's] femininity as a mask"; rather, this is "what femininity [itself] had already been determined to mean in the opening scene."[88]

Masculinity, by contrast, is imagined as a natural state characterized by lack of ornament. Again, this seems to echo Salmasius' claim that men, and men's hair in particular, should not be "adorned" or "bound." Samson – as the poem's representative of masculinity – is repeatedly said to have repudiated all artificial "trimmings" and "trappings." He even rejects weaponry:

> Samson . . . whom unarm'd
> No strength of man, or fiercest wild beast could withstand;
> Who tore the Lion, as the Lion tears the Kid,
> Ran on embattell'd Armies clad in Iron,

And weaponless himself,
Made Arms ridiculous, useless the forgery
Of brazen shield and spear, the hammer'd Cuirass
Chalybean temper'd steel, and frock of mail
Adamantean Proof;
But safest he who stood aloof,
When insupportably his foot advanc't,
In scorn of thir proud arms and warlike tools,
Spurn'd them to death by Troops. The bold *Ascalonite*
Fled from his Lion ramp, old Warriors turn'd
Thir plated backs under his heel;
Or grovling soiled thir crested helmets in the dust.
Then with what trivial weapon came to hand,
The jaw of an ass, his sword of bone,
A thousand fore-skins fell, the flower of *Palestine*.

(126–44)

These lines insist that Samson is unfettered by any accoutrements: he is "unarmed," "weaponless," and "scorn[s] . . . proud arms." Moreover, it is significant that the only implement that Samson does use – the jawbone of an ass – is itself an organic object and not a synthetic artifact or "warlike tool."

Samson is set apart from the other characters not only on account of his locks, but also on account of his in-dividuality – his imagined independence from prostheses. As Guillory puts it, "it is Samson's fixity that constitutes his identity" (114). Similarly, Stanley Fish points out that the poem seeks to juxtapose "male firmness" with "female changeability."[89] Samson's masculinity is not only established through contrast with Dalila, it is also established through contrast with the adorned Harapha. The introduction of "the Giant *Harapha of Gath*" parallels the opening description of Dalila. Like her, he has a "look / Haughty as is his pile high-built and proud," and as a result, he is explicitly compared to her: "what wind has blown him hither / I less conjecture than when I first saw / The sumptuous *Dalila* floating this way" (1069–72). The reference to "the wind" blowing Harapha "hither" instantly calls to mind Dalila's figuration as a "stately ship . . . courted by all the winds." In addition, Harapha is said to take pride in his ornamentation: he is "pile high-built and proud."

Harapha's reliance upon prostheses becomes even more evident as his encounter with Samson proceeds. Harapha challenges Samson, and he replies:

. . .put on all thy gorgeous arms, thy Helmet
And Brigadine of brass, thy broad Habergon,
Vant-brass and Greves, and Gauntlet, add thy Spear
A Weaver's beam, and seven-times-folded shield,
I only with an Oak'n staff will meet thee,

> And raise such out-cries on thy clatter'd Iron,
> Which long shall not with-hold mee from thy head.
>
> (1119–125).

Samson's parody of all of Harapha's "gorgeous arms" is similar to the denigration of "trivial weapons" in the earlier depiction of Samson himself (again there is a mocking inventory of the "Brigadine," "Habergon," "Vant-brass," "Greves," and "Gauntlet"). Furthermore, as in the first passage, Samson's only weapon is an organic object – this time an "Oak'n staff."

The contrast between Samson and Harapha is deepened when Harapha responds by defending his use of armored "coverings":

> Thou durst not thus disparage glorious arms
> Which greatest Heroes have in battel worn,
> Thir ornament and safety, had not spells
> And black enchantments. . .
>
> (1130–3)

In this passage, Harapha distinguishes between his "glorious arms" and Samson's hair which he says has "spells and black enchantments"; but in doing so, he inevitably creates a correlation between them. Thus, Harapha's allusion to his arms as "ornament" not only furthers the comparison with Dalila, it also hints that Samson's locks might themselves be seen as "ornaments."

Harapha eventually goes on to articulate this connection openly. He maintains that Samson's locks are merely ornamental (or even excremental) and are not therefore even as dignified as his own "glorious arms":

> . . .some Magicians Art,
> Arm'd thee or charm'd thee strong, which thou from Heav'n,
> Feign'dst at birth was giv'n thee by thy hair,
> Where strength can least abide, though all thy hairs
> Were bristles rang'd like those that ridge the back
> Of chaf't wild Boars, or ruffl'd Porcupines.
>
> (1133–8)

Here, Harapha compares Samson's tresses to the "bristles. . .that ridge the back of . . . wild Boars or . . . Porcupines" and thus suggests that for Samson to claim that his locks are the source of his strength is for him to put himself in the same category as beasts. In this model, hair becomes a marker of feral barbarity and is implicitly opposed to the civilized acculturation of "glorious arms." Thus, Harapha contends that they are the site "Where strength can least abide." Samson's hair is thus even less of a container of strength than the hair of wild animals. Whereas the rigid "bristles" of "boars" or "porcupines" do indeed manifest a certain kind of strength and protection, Harapha insists that this is not true of Samson's tresses. Indeed, at another point he notes that Samson is "best subdued" by "the barber's razor" (1163–8).

In response to these allegations, Samson replies: "I know no Spells, use no forbidden Arts; / My trust is in the living God who gave me / At my Nativity this strength, diffus'd / No less through all my sinews, joints and bones" (1139–42). As John Rogers notes, this is the point where Samson most clearly articulates (and accedes to) the dominant Protestant interpretation which rejects "the over-whelming suggestion of the bodily source of Samson's power."[90] But even though Samson does clearly dramatize his strength by emphasizing that it is the result of his faith in God, his response seems to work in the other direction as well: he insistently internalizes or corporealizes power, claiming that his strength is "diffused . . . through all [his] sinews, joints, and bones." It is almost as if the hair were not corporeal enough. Crucially, the anatomical parts where he does eventually locate his strength are characterized by their inwardness and also their indivisibility – these are the parts of the body that hold it together and give it its form. It is significant that Samson makes these claims in reply to Harapha, for throughout their encounter Samson strives to define himself as in-dividual, whereas Harapha is happy to acknowledge his dependence upon his "gorgeous arms." Indeed, it is in the moment when the parallels between Harapha's prosthetic armor and Samson's "excremental" locks begin to surface that Samson downplays the importance of his tresses.

Milton's *Samson Agonistes* thus seems to reiterate one of the crucial tenets of the royalist tonsorial counter-discourse: namely, that masculinity should be characterized by a lack of ornamentation. The poem also, as we have seen, associates femininity with adornment. If Milton thus evokes the royalist taxonomies, he also problematizes them in important ways. For example, the text clearly condemns the link between femininity and adornment. In particular, Dalila's "trims" and "trappings" are seen as being corrupt, a testament to her duplicity. As Samson puts it, "these are thy wonted arts, / And arts of every woman false like thee" (748–9). This valuation stands in direct opposition to that put forward by Salmasius.

If Milton's depiction of Dalila acts as an implicit condemnation of "femi-nine" adornment, it might therefore swing back to the other side of the debate and be understood as part of the more general Protestant critique. In a sermon from 1607, Robert Wilkinson warns about feminine adornment in terms that are remarkably similar to those that Milton himself would eventually use. He maintains that

Of all qualities, a woman must not have one qualitie of a ship, and that is too much rigging. Oh, what a wonder it is to see a ship under saile, with her tacklings and her masts, and her tops and top-gallants; . . . Yea, but what a world of wonders it is to see a woman . . . so . . . deformed with . . . her foolish fashions, that he [that] made her, when he looks upon her, shall hardly know her.[91]

This passage resonates powerfully with Milton's depiction of Dalila, who enters "sailing / Like a stately Ship . . . with all her bravery on, and tackle trim, / Sails fill'd and streamers waving" (714–17). According to Wilkinson, this "rigging" may seem wonderful on a ship, but it is "foolish" and even "deforming" when worn by women. Milton makes an analogous point in *Samson Agonistes*, but interestingly he does not limit his criticism to women. Harapha is also condemned, at least in part, on account of his adornment or "rigging." Indeed, he too is compared to a ship.

This denigration of adornment is yet another point of connection between *Samson Agonistes* and the seventeenth-century discourses on hair. As we have seen, Puritans frequently denounced tonsorial binding and/or adornment. The primary argument of the pamphlet *A Looking-Glasse for Women* (1644) was that "any outward adorning of any attire of Haire" was completely "unlawful."[92] Although the critique implied by Milton's representation of Dalila and Harapha is more general and does not focus explicitly or exclusively on hair, this does not mean that it can be divorced from the texts that do. With this in mind, it is worth returning to Milton's *Paradise Lost* and noting that in that poem, Milton specifically indicates that Eve's locks are "unadorned" and even "dishevelled."[93] Eve's lack of adornment provides an important point of distinction between her (and the model of femininity she represents) and the demonized Dalila.

But if Milton thus rejects adornment for both men and women in *Samson Agonistes*, he eventually comes to question even this stipulation. After Samson has been shorn, he describes himself as "a foolish Pilot" who has "shipwrack't / My Vessel trusted to me from above, Gloriously rigg'd" (197–200). Samson here employs the very nautical terms that are used to describe both Dalila and Harapha, but in this case it is clear that Samson's "glorious rigg[ing]" is something that is not only acceptable, but valued: it is "trusted to [him] from above." At the same time, it is significant that Samson characterizes himself in this way *after* he has had his tresses clipped. So it is only after his hair is detached that its prosthetic nature becomes more apparent. We might say that, after he has fallen, Samson is reduced to a state that is not unlike that of Dalila and Harapha. The term "glorious rigg[ing]" is particularly evocative in that it seems to amalgamate both Dalila's "tackle trim" and Harapha's " glorious arms."

What I have ultimately tried to suggest here is that Milton's *Samson Agonistes* engages with the ideas and terms that were central to the seventeenth-century debates about hair and gendered identity, but as a whole, the poem does not accede to any of the competing ideologies. On the one hand, Milton questions the materialization of masculinity and femininity through short and long hair respectively, not only by choosing Samson as his central figure, but also by insistently masculinizing him when he has long hair and feminizing him when he has his locks cut short. But if Milton might thus be understood to question the use of hair length as a means of producing gendered distinctions, this does not mean that he simply concurs with the royalist writers who suggested that binding or ornamentation ought to be the way of producing those distinctions. In Milton's text, as we have seen, he consistently works to problematize the schematic association between femininity and adornment, and, to a lesser extent, the association between masculinity and lack-of-adornment.

In the end, we might therefore say that whereas in *Paradise Lost* Milton seemed to be making a specific intervention with regard to the ideological production of gender identity through hair length, in *Samson Agonistes* he seems to be more interested in examining or questioning that ideological production itself. This conclusion corroborates Joseph Wittreich's assessment of the poem in *Interpreting Samson Agonistes*. Wittreich insists that although Milton's text "relies" heavily on specific historical "contexts" (and thus needs to be situated firmly in relation to them), it does not ultimately "submit to, or become dominated by, this or that version of myth or archetype; this or that portion of some field of knowledge; by this, not that, ideology." Instead, "*Samson Agonistes* is a poem that pushes norms into abeyance and that, in the process, signals its own resistance to codified wisdom and consensual belief."[94]

In conclusion, I want to suggest that my analysis of hair and its relationship to gender may also be able to teach us a larger lesson about ideologies and how they change. It is now common to think of gendered norms or ideologies as things that are imposed upon individuals from the outside. As Judith Butler puts it in *The Psychic Life of Power*, "We are used to thinking of power as what presses the subject from the outside, as what subordinates, sets underneath, and regulates."[95] By extension, I would add that we are also used to thinking of resistance as something that emanates from within individuals. In other words, we imagine people asserting their individual or collective wills against power and ideology in the name of emancipation. This model does not, however, adequately account for the social processes that I have been describing in this chapter. Here, we have seen that the dominant gendered ideology (which insisted that masculinity be materialized through short hair and femininity through long hair) came to be contested during the middle years of the seventeenth century, and we have also seen that both Salmasius and Milton worked, in their own ways, to disarticulate the normative ideals that were part of this ideology. But this resistance did not simply emanate from within these individuals; instead, it was at least to some extent socially produced. While it is possible to understand Milton's intervention in more personal terms,[96] Salmasius' attempts to rearticulate the dominant gendered norms and ideologies were clearly spurred by his political investments.

Moreover, Salmasius' project was by no means liberatory: he was not attempting to do away with gendered distinctions and hierarchies altogether, he was simply trying to (re)materialize them in a different way. What we therefore see here is not an instance of subversion or rearticulation in the name of emancipation, but subversion or rearticulation in the name of another ideological project. And finally, the conflict here is not so much between an individual and an ideology as it is between two competing ideologies.

5   Conclusion: detachable parts and the individual

If the preceding chapters have demonstrated that detachable parts such as handkerchiefs, codpieces, beards, and hair played an integral role in materializing gender identity in the early modern period, I now want to address how these "prostheses" eventually came to be relegated to the realm of the secondary or the superfluous. This will entail expanding my discussion of detachable parts and gender identity to larger ideas about identity and subjectivity from the period.

At least since Burckhardt articulated his influential thesis about the "Renaissance," it has been commonplace to say that, in England, the sixteenth and seventeenth centuries witnessed the birth of the modern individual.[1] And it is true that the term "individual" first started to be used as a noun to refer to "single human beings" at that time;[2] but nevertheless Burckhardt's thesis has frequently been contested in the hundred and fifty years since it was first put forward. Some scholars have sought to place the genesis of modern individualism at an earlier moment in time, while others have sought to place it later. What interests me here, however, is not the precise point at which this figure emerged,[3] but rather the characteristics that are attributed to it. What is the modern individual? How is it conceptualized? There are several traits that have traditionally been associated with it: interiority, social autonomy, agency, and self-reflexivity.[4] There is, however, another feature which is equally important but which has yet to be adequately acknowledged: namely, indivisibility. That is to say, the modern individual is often understood as an entity that is "whole," "unified," and quite literally "in-dividual" in its etymological sense of "indivisible" or "undividable." Paul Smith alludes to this characteristic in *Discerning the Subject* when he suggests that the "individual" is frequently characterized as being "undivided and whole" and, as such, is "the source and agent of conscious action or meaning."[5]

This suggestion resonates with the work that has been done on "the individual" by Raymond Williams and Peter Stallybrass. Both of these writers have explored the history of the concept, and especially the theoretical connotations that are encoded in the word itself. In *Keywords*, Raymond Williams points out that the English word "individual" was first used as an adjective which meant "indivisible." He suggests that this may at first sound somewhat paradoxical since the concept of an individual person now tends to evoke "distinction" or autonomy from others, whereas this alternate meaning of "'indivisible' [stresses] a necessary connection."[6] Peter Stallybrass builds upon Williams' research, emphasizing that before the seventeenth century "individual" was often used to indicate precisely this sense of social cohesion or connectedness. According to the *Oxford English Dictionary*, the first use of the term is in reference to the "indyvyduall Trynyte."[7] In this context, the three members of the Trinity are seen as three "people" that are not "individual" in the sense of being distinct, but rather "individual" in the sense of being necessarily connected. As Stallybrass puts it, "indyvyduall" here "suggests . . . indivisibility among what one would normally assume, outside a theological context, to be different elements" (594).

If both Williams and Stallybrass attempt to offset the dominant ways of thinking about the "individual" by insisting on what Williams calls the "necessary connection[s]" between people in society, the point I want to make here is somewhat different. I believe that the fact that the word "in-dividual" can mean "indivisible" does not simply contradict the now-dominant Burckhardtian sense of the term as Williams and Stallybrass suggest; instead, it also reinforces it.[8] This is because there is yet another twist to the complex semantic history of the word. As the term "individual" came to be used to connote social autonomy and distinction from others during the course of the seventeenth century, the other "paradoxical" usage – to connote "indivisibility" or connectedness – was subtly transmuted and incorporated into the newer meaning. The Burckhardtian "individual" is indeed "indivisible" but its indivisibility is personal or even corporeal rather than social. In other words, the modern individual is not imagined to be "indivisible" from other people and society, but it is imagined to be "indivisible" in and of itself – that is, whole and without detachable parts. When the individual's "indivisibility" is understood in this second way, it works to reinforce rather than to undermine the sense of the individual's autonomy from society.

In order to understand how and why this might have come about, we need to look at the link between the concept of the individual and that of the atom. As historians of science have noted, it was also during the seventeenth century that atomic theories of matter were popularized. This is not to say that the concept of "the atom" was invented at this time. Indeed, the notion that there were tiny, indivisible building blocks that made up all matter in the universe had been proposed by classical philosophers like Leucippus and Democritus. Nevertheless, the seventeenth century "occupies a very special place" with regard to the development of this idea since, according to Andrew G. Van Melsen's *From Atomos to Atom: A History of the Concept of the Atom*, this period witnessed not only a major "revival of philosophical atomism" derived from these ancient thinkers, but also the beginnings of a more *"scientific atomic theory."*[9]

The increasing cultural currency of the notion of the atom is relevant here because these indivisible particles served as models for individual people. Just as atoms were imagined to be the building blocks of matter, individuals were imagined to be the building blocks of society. Scholars have previously noted this link.[10] John Rogers, for instance, points out in *The Matter of Revolution* that "The lifeless and inert atoms of matter provided for many [in the seventeenth century] . . . tempting analogues for individual human beings."[11]

This conceptual connection is powerfully demonstrated by the linguistic overlap between atoms and individuals. As I noted earlier, the noun "individual" first came to be used in its modern sense – referring to "single human beings" – in the early seventeenth century, and interestingly, the particles that we today call "atoms" were, up until that time, known in English as "individuums" as well as "atoms." The term "atom" is derived from the Greek "atomos," whereas "individuum" is derived from Latin: it is the neuter form of the adjective *individu-us* used as a substantive. By the beginning of the eighteenth century, however, "individuums" was no longer used as an alternative term for "atoms." It was not simply supplanted by the term "atom"; it was also supplanted by another noun – "indivisibles" – which was introduced in the mid-seventeenth century. Thus, in 1647, one writer referred to "Indivisibles or Atomes." Although the term "indivisibles" eventually became archaic like the term "individuum," it is of interest here because it seems to have been introduced to take its place. This may have been necessary because the term "individuum" was, at the time, beginning to take on a new range of meanings: by the 1650s, it had become more or less synonymous with "individual" and was used, according to the *OED*, to refer to "individual person[s] or thing[s]." But if "individuum" thus shifted its meaning – from a term used to refer to the atom to one that was more or less synonymous with "individual" – it is worth noting that it was employed in its newer sense in preference to the more common word "individual" in order to emphasize the indivisibility of the "individual person or thing." Thus, in Bishop Walton's *Considerator Considered* (1659), for example, he asks rhetorically "Is not a man the same *individuum*, when his hair is cut or his nails pared, that he was before?"[12] So, to summarize, we might say that the term "individuum" slowly ceased to be used to refer to atoms, and was eventually subsumed into the word "individual." In the process, I would argue that it ended up reinforcing the idea that the "individual" was "indivisible," or, in other words, the idea that individuals had the same primary characteristic as individuums/atoms.[13]

If these overlapping terms suggest a conceptual link between atoms and individuals, this same link is articulated in the writings of two of the most important thinkers from the period: Thomas Hobbes and René Descartes. Hobbes is often acknowledged to be "one of the begetters" of modern individualism.[14] It is less often noted, however, that his notion of the individual is colored by his mechanistic view of the universe and, more specifically, by his ideas about atomic matter. Indeed, there seems to be "a conceptual affinity" between Hobbes's individualism and his atomism.[15] This affinity is particularly evident in the *Leviathan*. There, Hobbes meticulously describes the process whereby individuals come together to form the state. This process is implicitly analogous, for Hobbes, to the way in which mechanistic atoms come together to form an individual human being. In fact, he says at one point that the state is an "Artificial Man" created in imitation of "that Rationall and most excellent worke of *Nature*."[16] The celebrated image on the frontispiece of *Leviathan* powerfully illustrates this point, not only because the state takes a human form, but also because the figure is quite literally composed of a multitude of atom-like human beings. This image is quite striking because in most earlier analogies between the body and the state, the people of the realm were analogized to particular organs or limbs of the "Artificial man": the King usually served as the head (or sometimes the heart) and other individuals served as other parts of the body politic. In Hobbes, however, the subjects are imagined to be minute particles of matter out of which the entire figure is composed (figure 16).

In *Leviathan*, Hobbes maintains that these atomized individuals must come together to form a nation or they will live a miserable, anarchic existence. As he famously put it, life will be "solitary, poore, nasty, brutish, and shorte."[17] Hobbes thus seems to envision these individuals as atoms that will careen off one another in a chaotic and destructive way if there is not something to hold them together. And, according to Hobbes, the only way for them to be unified is for them to form a "pact" or "covenant" with "the sovereign" (the "sovereign" can be either a single person or an assembly). Hobbes insists that it is only through this "covenant" that "the Multitude" will be "united" and can therefore be "called a COMMON-WEALTH, in latin CIVITAS. This is the Generation of the great LEVIATHAN" (87). He also says that "Sovereignty" serves as an "Artificial *Soul*" for the state – it is that which gives "life and motion to the whole body" (1). Thus, we might say that the sovereign occupies the same place with regard to the state as the soul occupies with regard to the individual: the sovereign is the ghost in the machine that unifies all of the discordant parts and gives them cohesion, and even life. Quentin Skinner describes Hobbes's account of state formation as follows: he says that when "a sovereign is chosen, the commonwealth is duly instituted in the form of a single body united by virtue of having acquired a soul or *anima* to act on its behalf."[18]

Hobbes's vision of state formation has encoded within it a specific vision of the individual. As a matter of fact, his description of the formation of the

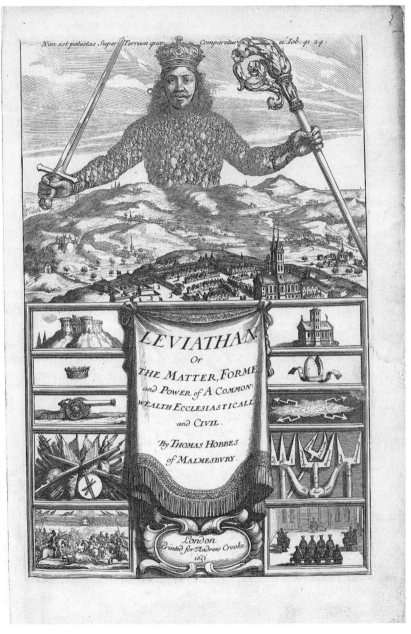

Figure 16. Title page of Hobbes, *Leviathan* (1651).

Leviathan clearly echoes the biblical account of the creation. Genesis states that "the LORD God formed man of the dust of the ground, and breathed into his nostrils the breath of life; and man became a living soul."[19] Hobbes evokes this creation myth by consistently using the term "covenant" to describe the "pact" between the sovereign and the people. He makes the comparison explicit when he writes that "the Pacts and Covenants by which the parts of this Body Politique were at first made, set together, and united, resemble that Fiat, or the Let us make man, pronounced by God in the Creation."[20] In this passage, Hobbes suggests that the "covenant" between the people and the sovereign brings the discrete individuals together to form the state in the same way as God brought the particles of dust together to "make man."

This comparison would also have worked to reinforce the conceptual link between individuals and atoms, because atoms, were frequently likened to particles of "dust." According to the *OED*, the "nearest popular conception" of the atom in the seventeenth century was a "particle . . . of dust . . . rendered visible by light." As one writer from the period put it, "Atoms signifie motes in the sunne."[21] When seen from this perspective, the analogy between the divine creation and state creation becomes even more readily apparent: just as God breathed life into the particles of dust – or atoms – in order to form them into a human being, the "covenant" with the sovereign breathes "life" into individuals in order to form them into a state.

Hobbes indicates, moreover, that when the state is formed, it becomes an entirely indivisible entity. In *De Cive*, he explains that the will of each individual is replaced by the will of the sovereign, thereby negating the possibility of internal self-division. He writes,

The *submission* of all of their wills to *the will of the one man* or of *one Assembly* comes about, when each of them obligates himself, by an Agreement with each of the rest, not to resist the *will* of the *man* or *Assembly* to which he has submitted himself.[22]

At another point, Hobbes repeats that the state can only be formed "if each man subjects his *will* to the *will*" (72) of the sovereign. Although Hobbes seems to imply that individuals actively choose to renounce their agency and submit themselves to the sovereign, this is not entirely accurate since this act of renunciation is in fact a formative precondition of the state. In other words, it is not that the individuals that make up the state come together first and form a union and then subsequently decide to relinquish their agency; rather, they come together to form the union in the act of relinquishing their agency.[23]

Consequently, when the state is formed, the will of the sovereign effectively becomes the will of the people. Hobbes claims that "whatever one [i.e. the sovereign] *wills* on matters essential to the common peace may be taken as the *will* of all and each."[24] It is important to recognize that the sovereign's will here does not *represent* the wills of the individuals who make up the state; instead, it simply *is* their will. As Hobbes puts it, the sovereign's will is "taken as" their will. This is crucial because whereas the notion of representation allows for a certain amount of internal dissent, Hobbes's notion of the state does not. We might therefore say that the individuals who have been united through the covenant with the sovereign are reduced to mechanistic atoms. As Nigel Smith succinctly puts it: "We have arrived at a self – the commonwealth – with an originating center [i.e. the will of the sovereign] that is a total expression of all the subjects, and which neatly dispels all the problems of inner dissent which arise in states, since only the sovereign is allowed to do [or will] anything."[25]

Interestingly, Hobbes's leviathan is "indivisible" in both of the senses that I discussed earlier in this chapter – it encodes both the social "indivisibility" emphasized by Williams and Stallybrass, as well as the more corporeal "indivisibility" that I have been emphasizing here. So when the leviathan is seen as a figure for the state, it is clear that the individuals that make it up are necessarily connected or united. But if the leviathan is also clearly an analogy for the individual human being, then this also suggests a more bodily kind of unity. Put simply, the individual's body is imagined as an entity that does not have any indivisible or discordant atoms or parts. This is because the being's will suffuses all of its members, and unifies them into an undivided whole.

Hobbes was not the only seventeenth-century thinker to conceptualize the "Modern subject" in these terms. Indeed, this characteristic is if anything even more readily apparent in René Descartes' writings. By pointing out this affinity between Hobbes and Descartes, I do not mean to obscure the important differences between them. Indeed, Hobbes unequivocally rejected many of Descartes' ideas, including the Cartesian mind/body dualism. Nevertheless, there is a striking point of convergence between the two with regard to their visions of the individual. Descartes writes,

There is a great difference between the mind and the body, inasmuch as the body is by its very nature always divisible, while the mind is wholly indivisible. For when I consider the mind, or myself . . . I understand myself to be something quite single and complete. Although the whole mind seems to be united to the whole body, I recognize that if a foot or arm or any other part of the body is cut off, nothing has thereby been taken away from the mind. As for the faculties of willing, of understanding, of sensory perception and so on, these cannot be termed parts of the mind since it is one and the same mind that wills, understands, and has sensory perceptions. By contrast, there is no corporeal or extended thing that I can think of which in my thought I cannot easily divide into parts; and this very fact makes me understand that it is divisible. This would be enough to show me the essential difference between mind and body, even if I did not sufficiently know this already.[26]

In this passage, Descartes claims that the essential characteristic of mind (and by extension subjectivity itself) is its indivisibility. Indeed, his dualism seems to arise out of this characterization. He suggests that the body cannot be essential to the subject because parts of the body can be detached without it having any effect on consciousness. He says, "if a foot or arm or any other part of the body is cut off, nothing has thereby been taken away from the mind." As a consequence, the dividual body cannot for Descartes be part of the in-dividual.[27]

We might say that Descartes' method here is deductive in the most literal sense of that word: he proceeds by stripping away all divisible parts – which are, on account of their divisibility, deemed to be inessential – until he reaches a core "self" that cannot be divided any further. That indivisible kernel is, of course, the cogito. As Jonathan Sawday puts it in *The Body Emblazoned*, it is "the susceptibility of the body (as opposed to the mind) to the process of division which confirm[s] the distinction between body and mind inherent within the Cartesian project."[28]

While Descartes' writing is generally acknowledged to be the starting point for modern thinking on subjectivity, it is worth saying that many of his propositions continue to be extremely controversial.[29] The controversy usually revolves around the question of whether Descartes is correct to have equated subjectivity with cognition and to have reduced the body to a mechanized object that has no effect on notions of the self. In response to Descartes, other thinkers have located the theoretical line between subject and object further and further "outward." Some include not only the body itself, but also external objects. They ask whether it might make sense to see items as diverse as coats, telescopes, and chairs as integral since "the imagination [consistently] works to distribute the facts and responsibilities of sentience out into the external world."[30] While the desire to extend the boundaries of subjectivity "outward" obviously bears a certain affinity with my own project, what I have been focusing on in this conclusion is not so much where the theoretical line in the sand between "subject" and "object" ought to be drawn, but on the *criterion* that has been used to draw such a line in the first place. And, in the case of Descartes, that criterion is clearly divisibility, or detachability.[31] If this is a crucial aspect of Descartes' theory of subjectivity, it is one which has, I believe, been obscured by the seemingly endless controversy about Cartesian mind–body dualism.

William Kerrigan's article "Atoms Again" maintains that there is a relationship between Descartes' notions of the self and the atomic theories of matter that I discussed earlier in this chapter. Kerrigan suggests that Cartesian subjectivity forfeits

mass and weight, which are transferred onto atoms. But in exchange he secures analytic mastery over *res extensa*. Atoms might be, as Descartes thought, subject to mechanical laws, or they might be, as others hoped, the vital and organic substrate of a universe dedicated to life. But [in both cases] some form of . . . dualism . . . appeared to guard the philosophical ego from any conceivable consequences of the new sciences. The atom had become, in effect, the ego's ally.[32]

In effect, what Kerrigan is proposing here is that the Cartesian dualism between subject and object (mind and matter) worked as a kind of prophylactic for the subject against "any conceivable consequences of the new sciences." He goes on to say, moreover, that despite the separation of mind from matter, Descartes paradoxically imagines the thinking subject as "A supreme atom, an inviolable atom of thought" (99). In other words, Kerrigan claims that even though Descartes excludes atoms (and by extension the mechanized body) from the realm of subjectivity, he ends up conceptualizing the latter in terms of the former. For my purposes, the crucial point to make here is that in the process he also endows the thinking subject with the same primary characteristic as the atom.

If it is thus clear that Descartes, Hobbes, and other seventeenth-century writers considered indivisibility to be a definitive characteristic of the individual,[33] what I want to stress is that figuring the individual in this way inevitably worked to render detachable parts superfluous. This is evident in the passage from Bishop Walton's *Considerator Considered* (1659) that I mentioned earlier, where Walton implies that removable elements of the body cannot have any real bearing on an "individuum's" identity or subjectivity. He asks rhetorically, "Is not a man the same *individuum*, when his hair is cut or his nails pared, that he was before, nay though his skin be scratched or some blood drawn?" Descartes' assertions are in a sense simply a more radical version of this argument. He essentially maintains that "man" is still "the same individuum" when he loses a "foot" or an "arm" and not simply when he has his hair cut, his nails pared, or his blood drawn.

If the vision of the individual articulated by Bishop Walton and Descartes became dominant over the course of the seventeenth century and persists to this day, it was not firmly instantiated throughout much of the early modern period; instead, it stood in tension with the vision of the self as a kind of prosthetic god. The cultural tension between these opposing viewpoints is manifest – albeit in a somewhat transmuted form – in the books on hair that I analyzed in the last chapter. One of the issues that is debated in these books is whether the hair of the head should be considered to be part of the body (and, by extension, whether it is an integral part of an individual's identity). Some of the early modern writers on tonsure would have agreed with Bishop Walton's assessment that a person is still "the same individuum" after having their "hair cut." The anatomist Helkiah Crooke, for example, insists that hairs "are only excrements . . . and therefore not to be reckoned among the parts of the body."[34] Other writers, however, strongly disputed this contention. John Bulwer, for instance, argues that the tresses most certainly are a part of the body in his *Anthropometamorphosis* (1654). He acknowledges that some "Superficiall Philosophers do much please themselves . . . saying, that . . . haires [are] an excrement and not a part," but he insists that this cannot be true because "[i]f the Haire were an excrement, it should be shut quite out of the Body, but this remains in."[35]

This debate about the status of hair, and the more general debate about the status of dividual parts in relation to the individual, resonates profoundly with the theological controversies surrounding the resurrection that had been an important part of English culture since the middle ages. Carolyn Walker Bynum has brilliantly analyzed this controversy in *Fragmentation and Redemption* and *The Resurrection of the Body in Western Christianity, 200–1336*. She points out that "Christian preachers and theologians from Tertullian to the seventeenth-century divines asserted that God would reassemble the decayed and fragmented corpses of human beings at the end of time."[36] But if it was clear that the bodies of all true believers would be resurrected, there were differences of opinion about exactly what this meant. Did, for example, all of one's discarded fingernails rise again? What about the hair on one's head? In Luke 21.18 it states that "Not a hair on your head shall perish," but does this mean that all of the hairs that had ever grown on one's head would return? This was not simply an arcane theological debate. It had important practical ramifications for burial practices (should all the parts of "the body" be buried together to await the final trumpet?) and the validity of relics (if all of the body was to be resurrected, then how could Christ's tooth or foreskin still be here on earth?).

This controversy continued in England well into the seventeenth century. In 1627, Thomas Goffe insisted in a sermon that "If dissected limbes lie torne assunder, in places as distant as one end of the Pole is from the other, yet will he [God] soader them together, and make them in every severall *individuum*, a perfect, entire, numericall body againe."[37] Although Goffe is discussing the resurrection here, he addresses many of the same issues that I have been exploring in this chapter. Most importantly, he implies that human beings are entities that are ultimately individual. He recognizes that a person's "limbes" might be "torne assunder" while here on earth, but he also says that they will eventually return and the body will be made "perfect," "entire," and an "individuum." In saying this, Goffe diverges sharply from thinkers like Descartes who maintained that such "dissected limbes" are not really part of the individual. By saying that they will most certainly be "soader[ed] . . . together" again at the last judgment, Goffe implies that those parts are indeed integral.

There were other early modern writers who disputed the claims of people like Goffe. In 1643, for example, Sir Kenelm Digby wrote:

Methinkes it is but a grosse conception to think that every *Atome* of the present individuall matter of a body; every graine of *Ashes* of a burned *Cadaver*, scattered by the wind throughout the world, and after numerous variations changed peradventure into the body of another man; should at the sounding of the last Trumpet be raked together againe from all corners of the earth, and be made up anew into the same *Body* it was before of the first man.[38]

Digby explains that the really important thing is the form that the body takes, not what particular particles of matter make up that body: as he puts it, "That which giveth the . . . individuation to a *Body* . . . is the substantial forme," and therefore "[a]s long as [the substantial forme] remaineth the same, though the matter be in a continuall flux and motion, yet the thing is still the same" (82). Digby goes on to compare the human body to the Thames, saying that although the river does not contain the same water that flowed through it in previous times, it is nevertheless the same river. At another point in his discussion, Sir Digby suggests that the "substantial forme" is more or less synonymous with the "Soule": he says that the resurrected body is still itself because "it hath the same distinguisher and individuator; to wit, the same forme, or *Soule*" (84). In this commentary, Digby disputes the claims of authors like Goffe, but in doing so, he also changes the terms of the argument somewhat. Whereas Goffe discusses the fate of the "dissected limbes," Digby speaks of the "*Atome[s]* of..a body." He presumably did this because focusing on minute particles made it easier for him to claim that they were not integral or necessary. But like Goffe, Digby engages many of the same questions addressed by Hobbes and Descartes. In fact, his account might be seen as a synthesis of these two philosophers' ideas. Like Hobbes, Digby imagines the body being made up of atoms, and claims that those material particles are given life, or individuation, by being infused with "forme" or the "Soule." But like Descartes, he doubts whether any particular "atoms" are really essential, or in this case whether they will actually return at the last judgment.

The religious debate about the resurrection thus feeds into broader questions about the nature and limits of the body and self. When seen in this light, it is crucial to recognize that the theologians who participated in this debate did not limit themselves to discussing hair, fingernails, and "dissected limbes." As Bynum notes, they also asked whether food that had passed through the body would be resurrected, and whether clothes would be worn in heaven. I hope that this will come as less of a surprise here at the end of this book than it might have at the beginning. In fact, Bynum notes that by the late thirteenth century, a "consensus had developed that digested food" was indeed "of the substance of human nature" and that it would therefore be resurrected with the individual at the end of time.[39] Cordelia Warr's research on "Clothing for the Afterlife" examines the garments that were worn in late-medieval representations of the final judgment, and suggests that a similar consensus may have been reached about dress.[40] In the end, the crucial thing for my purposes is not whether this consensus was actually reached and if so, how long it lasted, but rather simply the fact that these items were part of the debate in the first place. This indicates that they were, at least potentially, considered to be integral components of the body and the self.

In closing, I want to stress that we need to be careful about assuming that those who argued that things like hair, clothing, or food were not parts of the body necessarily felt that they were therefore inessential. This was certainly not the case with the debates on hair that I mentioned earlier. Although a writer like the anatomist Crooke might claim, as we have seen, that the hairs were "excrement[s]" and "not to be reckoned among the parts of the body," this did not stop him from suggesting that facial hair was a crucial means of materializing masculine identity: he insisted that "it is a venerable sight to see a man. . .his face compassed about with thicke and comely hair" and that "the smoothnesse of [women's] face is their proper ornament; they needed no ensigne of majesty because they were born to subjection."[41] Conversely, for someone like Descartes, things might be fully part of the body, and yet still not be integral to the self. I do not mean to deny that there is, at times, something of a tendency towards modern modes of thought. John Bulwer, for instance, seems to feel that he must argue that hairs are corporeal in order to argue that they are essential to gender identity: so he insists, for example, both that "the Beard is an existent part of the body and most necessary" and that "its necessity is from its use and office it hath in the body" – namely as "the forme of Man" or "the signe . . . by which he appeares a man" (208). But as I have tried to show throughout this book, early modern writers were quite comfortable imagining parts to be both detachable and essential, or with acknowledging that identity was in crucial ways prosthetic.

Notes

INTRODUCTION: PROSTHETIC GENDER IN EARLY MODERN ENGLAND

1 Sigmund Freud, *Civilization and its Discontents* in *The Standard Edition of the Complete Psychological Works of Sigmund Freud*, translated under the general editorship of James Strachey (London: Hogarth Press, 1961), 21: 90–1.

2 Neil Jordan, *The Crying Game*, in *A Neil Jordan Reader* (New York: Vintage International, 1993), 237.

3 Ambroise Paré, *On Monsters and Marvels*, translated with an introduction and notes by Janis L. Pallister (Chicago: University of Chicago Press, 1982), 27–9.

4 Some of the differences between these texts derive from the fact that the English translation is based on the Latin version of the workes. See Ambroise Paré, *The workes of that famous chirurgion Ambrose Parey translated out of Latine and compared with the French by Th. Johnson* (London, 1634), 973.

5 See Ruth Gilbert's *Early Modern Hermaphrodites: Sex and other Stories* (New York: Palgrave, 2002), 39–43, and Lorraine Daston and Katharine Park's "The Hermaphrodite and the Orders of Nature: Sexual Ambiguity in Early Modern France," *GLQ: A Journal of Lesbian and Gay Studies*, 1:4 (1995): 426.

6 Alice Domurat Dreger, *Hermaphrodites and the Medical Invention of Sex* (Cambridge: Harvard University Press, 1998), 182.

7 This argument owes much to Karen Newman's *Fashioning Femininity*; Patricia Fumerton's *Cultural Aesthetics: Renaissance Literature and the Practice of Social Ornament* (Chicago: University of Chicago Press, 1991); Stephen Orgel's *Impersonations: The Performance of Gender in Shakespeare's England* (Cambridge: Cambridge University Press, 1996); and Ann Rosalind Jones and Peter Stallybrass' *Renaissance Clothing and the Materials of Memory* (Cambridge: Cambridge University Press, 2000). Although this book focuses largely on gender identity, it is worth saying that these detachable parts played important roles in forming other types of identity as well. There has been some fascinating research done, for example, on the construction of racial morphologies through hair and beard growth. See Elliott Horowitz, "The New World and the Changing Face of Europe," *Sixteenth Century Journal*, 28.4 (1997): 1181–201; and Londa Schiebinger, *Nature's Body: Gender in the Making of Modern Science* (Boston: Beacon Press, 1993). Karen Newman examines the racialization of the handkerchief in *Fashioning Femininity and English Renaissance Drama*, foreword by Catharine R. Stimpson (Chicago: University of Chicago Press, 1991), as does Natasha Korda in "The Tragedy of the

Handkerchief: female paraphernalia and the properties of jealousy in Othello," in *Shakespeare's Domestic Economies: Gender and Property in Early Modern England* (Philadelphia: University of Pennsylvania Press, 2002).

8 Allan Peterkin contends that this style of facial hair originated in gay culture as part of the "clone" look that was an exaggerated imitation of working-class masculinity. Later, this style went mainstream, as is exemplified by Tom Selleck's trademark moustache. See Peterkin's *One Thousand Beards: A Cultural History of Facial Hair* (Vancouver: Arsenal Pulp Press, 2001), 134–5.

9 Anne Hollander, *Sex and Suits: The Evolution of Modern Dress* (New York: Knopf, 1994) and Valerie Steele, *Fetish: Fashion, Sex, and Power* (Oxford: Oxford University Press, 1996). See also Diana Crane's *Fashion and its Social Agendas: Class, Gender, and Identity in Clothing* (Chicago: University of Chicago Press, 2000).

10 On "tertiary" characteristics, see Rom Harré, "Sex and Gender, Man and Woman," in *Body and Flesh: A Philosophical Reader*, edited by Donn Welton (London: Blackwell, 1998), 12–13. Technically, the relationship between the "primary" and "secondary" sexual characteristics is supposed to be temporal rather than hierarchical: that is to say, the term "primary sexual characteristics" is used to refer to those features that are present at birth and the term "secondary sexual characteristics" is used to refer to those that appear later in life. Nevertheless, it is clear that this is not the way these terms are often understood in their everyday usage.

11 Gail Kern Paster analyzes how gender was diffused throughout the body on account of humoral theory. See *The Body Embarrassed: Drama and the Disciplines of Shame in Early Modern England* (Ithaca: Cornell University Press, 1991), 82.

12 Diana Fuss describes these assumptions as follows: ". . . the natural provides the raw material and determinative starting point for the practices and laws of the social. For example, sexual difference (the division into 'male' and 'female') is taken as prior to social differences which are presumed to be mapped on to, *a posteriori*, the biological subject." See *Essentially Speaking: Feminism, Nature and Difference* (New York: Routledge, 1989), 3.

13 Daston and Park, "The Hermaphrodite," 431 and 427–8. I discuss some of the early modern meanings of the term "nature" in my chapter on hair.

14 Stephen J. Gould, *The Mismeasure of Man*, revised and expanded edition (New York: W.W. Norton, 1996), 33–4.

15 One recent text that works to reiterate the essentialist notion of gender identity is John Colapinto's *As Nature Made Him: The Boy who was Raised as a Girl* (New York: Harper Collins, 2000). Interestingly, the intersex movement has also rallied around this case as a way of resisting the sex assignment surgeries routinely performed on infants. Cheryl Chase, founder of the Intersex Society of North America, maintains that, ideally, individuals like David Reimer (and intersexed individuals more generally) would be allowed to elect which, if either, identity suited them. This view has also been defended by Anne Fausto-Sterling in *Sexing the Body: Gender Politics and the Construction of Sexuality* (New York: Basic Books, 2000). I believe that activists could find a valuable historical precedent in pre-Enlightenment ideas about gender. See also Judith Butler's article on the case of David Reimer: "Doing Justice to Someone: Sex Reassignment and Allegories of Transsexuality," *GLQ*, 7:4 (2001): 621–36.

16 Fuss, *Essentially Speaking*, 6.
17 This proverb is mentioned by Robert Burton in *The Anatomy of Melancholy* (London, 1621), 567. Tilley cites two slightly different versions that emphasize the role that clothing plays in this process: "God makes and apparel shapes but money makes the man" and "Meat makes and cloth shapes but manners make the man." See Morris Palmer Tilley, *A Dictionary of the Proverbs in England in the Sixteenth and Seventeenth Centuries* (Ann Arbor: University of Michigan Press, 1950), 261 and 454.
18 It was not, however, thought to be possible for men to be transformed into women.
19 Thomas Laqueur, *Making Sex: Body and Gender From the Greeks to Freud* (Cambridge: Harvard University Press, 1990). Michael C. Schoenfeldt also stresses that the early modern body was conceptualized as being much more interconnected with the environment and the outside world, and that it was therefore much more open to various types of alteration and change. See *Bodies and Selves in Early Modern England: Physiology and Inwardness in Spenser, Shakespeare, Herbert, and Milton* (Cambridge: Cambridge University Press, 1999), 11.

For overviews of early modern ideas about the body, see Anthony Fletcher's *Gender, Sex, and Subordination in England 1500–1800* (New Haven: Yale University Press, 1995) and Nancy G. Siraisi's *Medieval and Early Renaissance Medicine: An Introduction to Knowledge and Practice* (Chicago: University of Chicago Press, 1990). For the medieval perspective, see Joan Cadden, *Meanings of Sex Difference in the Middle Ages: Medicine, Science, Culture* (Cambridge: Cambridge University Press, 1993). There has also been a lot of work on humoral theory by literary critics. See especially Paster's *The Body Embarrassed* and Shoenfeldt's *Bodies and Selves*. I too will primarily be focusing on ideas derived from Galenic medicine, but I don't mean to imply that those ideas weren't contested.
20 Jordan, *The Crying Game*, 237.
21 Although this is the way that "sex changes" are understood in the dominant culture, transsexual writers and activists have been at the forefront of the movement to change these assumptions. They usually speak of "transitioning" rather than "sex change," and tend to view gender as much more of a continuum. Kate Bornstein, for instance, criticizes the dominance of phallocentric notions of gender and argues for instituting something much less dimorphic. See *Gender Outlaw: On Men, Women and the Rest of us* (Routledge, 1994), especially pp.27–52, and also *My Gender Workbook: How to Become a Real Man, a Real Woman, the Real You, or Something Else Entirely* (New York: Routledge, 1998). Other important works in transgender studies include *Blending Genders: Social Aspects of Cross-Dressing and Sex-Changing*, edited by Richard Ekins and David King (New York: Routledge, 1996); Leslie Feinberg, *Trans Liberation: Beyond Pink or Blue* (Boston: Beacon Press, 1998); Claudine Griggs, *S/he: Changing Sex, Changing Clothes* (New York: Berg, 1998); *Unseen Genders: Beyond the Binaries*, edited by Felicity Haynes and Tarquam McKenna (New York: Peter Lang, 2001); and Riki Anne Wilchins, *Read My Lips: Sexual Subversion and the End of Gender* (Ithaca: Firebrand, 1997).

22 Greenblatt, "Fiction and Friction," in *Shakespearean Negotiations* (Berkeley: University of California Press, 1988). For incisive critique of Greenblatt's argument, see Julia Epstein, "Either/Or – Neither/Both: Sexual Ambiguity and the Ideology of Gender," *Genders* 7 (1990): 99–142.

23 *The Diary of Montaigne's Journey to Italy in 1580 and 1581*, translated with introduction and notes by E. J. Trechmann (New York: Harcourt, Brace and Company, 1929), 6. Montaigne's comments about Marie having a beard before her transformation only appear in one of his accounts of this incident. Moreover, they do not appear in Paré's account. Laqueur's focus on Paré's account may help to explain his omission of the details about Marie/Germain's facial hair, though he does mention both of Montaigne's accounts. Nevertheless, his failure to mention Marie/Germain's beard is symptomatic of a larger issue in his book: namely, the fact that he virtually equates "sex" with "genital morphology." This tendency has been previously noted by Paster in *The Body Embarrassed*, 17 and 82. Harriette Andreadis' unpublished paper "Consolidating Early Modern Sexual Categories: Hermaphrodites and Other Deviants" discusses the similarities and differences in all of the early modern accounts of the case of Marie/Germain. This paper was presented as part of a seminar entitled "Early Modern Texts and the History of Sexuality" at the annual meeting of the Shakespeare Association of America in 2001.

24 Paré, *The Workes*, 974–5.

25 Francesco Maria Guazzo, *Compendium Maleficarum: The Montague Summers Edition*, translated by E. A. Ashwin (New York: Dover Publications, 1988), 59.

26 George Sandys, *Ovid's Metamorphosis Englished, Mythologiz'd, and Represented in Figures* (Oxford, 1632), 336.

27 Helkiah Crooke, *Microcosmographia* (London, 1615), 250. During the course of the seventeenth century, anatomists increasingly contested the possibility of spontaneous sexual transformation and Crooke is certainly skeptical. He says that these stories are "all of them monstrous, and some not credible." Thus, in the passage that I cite here, Crooke is actually describing beliefs that he takes to be erroneous, though he sees them as being typical of the Hippocratic tradition.

28 The "story" that I am describing here is none other than Ovid's "Iphis and Ianthe," but as I explain in some detail later in the book, this narrative was often taken to be a realistic description of a sexual metamorphosis, and was therefore often discussed in relation to other cases of spontaneous sex change like that of Marie/Germain. The version that I cite here is Sandys' seventeenth-century translation, *Ovid's Metamorphosis Englished*, 336.

29 This is Golding's sixteenth-century translation. Ovid, *The xv. Bookes of P. Ovidius Naso, entitled, Metamorphosis* (London, 1584), 129.

30 Guazzo, *Compendium Maleficarum*, 58.

31 Juan Huarte, *The Examination of Men's Wits*, facsimile reproduction with an introduction by Carmen Rogers (Gainesville: Scholars' Facsimiles and Reprints, 1959), 269–70.

32 Paré, *The Workes*, 974. This case is also described by Nathaniel Wanley in *Wonders of the Little World* (London, 1678), 53. He says that there was "a man (at *Rhenes* in an Inn which had a swan for the sign of it, *Anno Dom.* 1560) who was ever reputed a Female, to the fourteenth year of her age; at which time it fell out,

that wantoning in bed with a Maid that lay with her, the signs of a man brake out of her; which when her Parents were informed of, by interposition of Ecclesiastical Authority, her name was chang'd from *Joan* to *John*, and from thenceforth she wore the habit of a man."

33　Mary Beth Norton, *Founding Mothers and Fathers: Gendered Power and the Forming of American Society* (New York: Knopf, 1996), 187. See also Kathleen Brown's article on the same case: "'Changed . . . into the fashion of a man': The Politics of Sexual Difference in a Seventeenth-Century Anglo-American Settlement," *Journal of the History of Sexuality*, 6:2 (1995): 171–93.

34　This case is discussed by Ruth Gilbert in *Early Modern Hermaphrodites*, 1–2.

35　Jones and Stallybrass, *Renaissance Clothing*, 2.

36　"The Fetishism of Dress," in *The Norton Shakespeare* (New York: W.W. Norton, 1997), 57.

37　Jonas Barish, *The Antitheatrical Prejudice* (Berkeley: University of California Press, 1981), 92.

38　Dympna Callaghan, "'And all is semblative a woman's part': Body Politics and *Twelfth Night*," *Textual Practice*, 7 (1993): 433.

39　Orgel, *Impersonations*, 104.

40　Jean E. Howard, *The Stage and Social Struggle in Early Modern England* (New York: Routledge, 1994). See especially chapter 5, "Power and Eros: Crossdressing and Dramatic Representation and Theatrical Practice."

41　Wanley, *The Wonders*, 52.

42　Guazzo, *Compendium Maleficarum*, 58.

43　*Hic Mulier, or The Man-Woman* (London, 1620), B1v and B2r.

44　C. G., *The Minte of Deformities* (London, 1600), Bv.

45　See Mark Breitenberg, *Anxious Masculinity in Early Modern England* (Cambridge: Cambridge University Press, 1996), 151–2. Similarly, Jean Howard writes that "male – female difference was . . . less grounded in ideas of absolute bodily difference than is typical today" and that it was because of this that "much emphasis was placed on behavioral differences and on distinctions of dress" (*The Norton Shakespeare*, 1595). For an extended discussion of this issue, see *The Stage and Social Struggle*, 98. There, she contends that masculinity and femininity were not "built upon a self-evident notion of biological sexual difference," and as a result, "gender difference and hierarchy had to be produced and secured . . . on other grounds" – such as clothing or "by virtue of [women's] lack of masculine perfection (softer, weaker, less hot)." While Howard is making much the same point as Breitenberg, her formulations are preferable in that they do not suggest that "biological differences" weren't essential.

46　At another point, the editors say that "gender was unstable." See *Desire in the Renaissance: Psychoanalysis and Literature*, edited by Valeria Finucci and Regina Schwartz (Princeton: Princeton University Press, 1994), 6.

47　Laura Gowing writes that "In Renaissance culture we seem to be left with a world of flexible sex and no secure corporeal basis for gender roles," in *Common Bodies: Women, Touch and Power in Seventeenth-Century England* (New Haven: Yale University Press, 2003), 3. Similarly, Fletcher claims that "sex was . . . unstable and indeterminate" and therefore "Ideas about the body in early modern England provided shifting sands . . . for a system of gender order." See *Gender, Sex, and Subordination*, 83.

48 It seems likely that these misperceptions ultimately derive from the work of Laqueur, and particularly from his somewhat confusing claim that there was only "one sex" before the Enlightenment. This does not mean that male and female bodies were thought to be *identical* during the Renaissance, or that corporeal differences were not acknowledged; instead, it simply means that male and female bodies were thought to be *structurally homologous*. In Laqueur's defense, it should be noted that he is primarily interested in the shift in thinking that occurred over the *longue durée*. Thus, his description of the "one sex model" is meant primarily as a foil for the later "two sex model," and although his argument and terminology make sense when viewed diachronically, they become problematic when viewed synchronically.

49 Lorraine Daston, "Imagination and Self in Early Modern England." This paper was delivered as a plenary address at "Inhabiting the Body/Inhabiting the World: An Early Modern Cultural Studies Conference," held at The University of North Carolina, Chapel Hill, March 2004. "The Material Powers of the Imagination" was presented at "'Interior Temptations': Early Modern Imagination," held at Northwestern University, December 2003.

50 Quoted in Laqueur, *Making Sex*, 128–9.

51 Michel de Montaigne, *The Complete Works: Essays, Travel Journals, Letters*, translated by Donald M. Frame (London: Everyman Library, 2003), 83.

52 John Sutton, *Philosophy and Memory Traces: Descartes to Connectionism* (Cambridge: Cambridge University Press, 1998), 200–1.

53 Daston, "Imagination and Self."

54 Thomas Wall, *Spiritual Armour to Defend the Head from the Superfluity of Naughtiness* (London, 1688) 3.

55 Fletcher makes a similar observation. He says that "Patriarchy was . . . founded upon God's direction" and that gender was "not rooted in an understanding of the body." See *Gender, Sex, and Subordination*, xvi–xvii.

56 The point I am making here is a more religiously inflected version of one of Laqueur's observations. He says that before the Enlightenment "biological sex [did] not provide a solid foundation for the cultural category of gender." See *Making Sex*, 124.

57 *Hic Mulier*, B2v.

58 This dialogue is included in the *Haec Vir* pamphlet. *Haec Vir: or, The Womanish-Man* (London, 1620), B1r-v.

59 Ibid., B4v.

60 Donna J. Haraway, *Simians, Cyborgs, and Women: The Reinvention of Nature* (New York: Routledge, 1991), 133.

61 Fuss, *Essentially Speaking*, 6.

62 Judith Butler, *Bodies that Matter: On the Discursive Limits of "Sex"* (New York: Routledge, 1993), 66 and 9.

63 Butler, *Bodies that Matter*, 231.

64 Anne Hollander, *Seeing through Clothes* (New York: Viking Press, 1978), 131.

65 In effect, Hollander argues that clothes leave their imprint on the subject in much the same way as a person leaves his/her imprint on a favorite article of clothing.

For a poignant discussion of similar issues, see Peter Stallybrass's "Worn Worlds: Clothing, Mourning and the Life of Things," *Yale Review*, 81 (1993): 35–50.

66 This phenomenon might be compared to what Harry Berger calls "prosthetic backlash." Berger contends that after items are incorporated into the physical portrait, there is then a sense of deprivation that comes from having lost them. Consequently, we might say that the "natural" body comes to be perceived as incomplete or wanting. See Harry Berger, Jr., "Second-World Prosthetics: Supplying Deficiencies of Nature in Renaissance Italy," in *Early Modern Visual Culture: Representation, Race, and Empire in Renaissance England*, edited by Peter Erickson and Clark Hulse (Philadelphia: University of Pennsylvania Press, 2000), 98–147.

67 See Michel de Certeau, *The Practice of Everyday Life*, translated by Steven Rendall (Berkeley: University of California Press, 1984), 147.

68 Butler, *Bodies that Matter*, 231 and 230.

69 Laqueur, *Making Sex*, 125.

70 I will return to this point in more detail later in the introduction. This phrase comes from Fernand Braudel's *Afterthoughts on Material Civilization and Capitalism*, translated by Patricia M. Ranum (Baltimore: The Johns Hopkins University Press, 1977), 6–7.

71 Raymond Williams, *Keywords: A Vocabulary of Culture and Society* (New York: Oxford University Press, 1976), entry for "Personality," 195.

72 McLuhan, *Understanding Media: The Extensions of Man* (New York: McGraw-Hill, 1964), 45–6.

73 Woolf is quoted in Naomi Schor's *Reading in Detail: Aesthetics and the Feminine* (New York: Routledge, 1987).

74 *A History of Private Life*, edited by Philippe Ariès and Georges Duby (Cambridge, MA: Belknap Press of Harvard University Press, 1987). Fernand Braudel, *The Structures of Everyday Life: The Limits of the Possible*, translated by Siân Reynolds (Berkeley: University of California Press, 1992). *Renaissance Culture and the Everyday*, edited by Patricia Fumerton and Simon Hunt (Philadelphia: University of Pennsylvania Press, 1999). This new work on the history of everyday life is, according to Lynn Hunt and Victoria Bonnell, part of a much broader movement within the field of history away from traditional economic and political sources and perspectives, and toward more social and cultural ones. See *Beyond the Cultural Turn: New Directions in the Study of Society and Culture* edited by Victoria E. Bonnell and Lynn Hunt (Berkeley: University of California Press, 1999), 1–34. This shift is also addressed in *The New Cultural History*, edited by Lynn Hunt (Berkeley: University of California Press, 1989), 1–22. Hunt and Bonnell also note that the historical research on everyday life frequently overlaps with research on material culture. In this regard, see Daniel Roche's *A History of Everyday Things: The Birth of Consumption in France, 1600–1800*, translated by Brian Pearce (Cambridge: Cambridge University Press, 2000), which includes a useful, theoretically informed discussion of the relationship between "culture and material civilization."

75 Henri Lefebvre, *Everyday Life in the Modern World*, translated by Sacha Rabinovitch, with a new introduction by Philip Walker (New Brunswick, NJ: Transaction,

1999). Norbert Elias, *The Civilizing Process*, translated by Edmund Jephcott (Cambridge, MA: Blackwell, 1994).

76 Braudel, *Structures of Everyday Life*, 29.

77 Michel Foucault, *Discipline and Punish: The Birth of the Prison* (New York: Penguin, 1977), 139.

78 Margreta de Grazia has suggested that one of "the main function[s] of superfluous things" is to mark social distinctions. See "The Ideology of Superfluous Things: *King Lear* as Period Piece," in *Subject and Object in Early Modern Culture*, edited by Margreta de Grazia, Maureen Quilligan, and Peter Stallybrass (Cambridge: Cambridge University Press, 1996), 23.

79 Pierre Bourdieu, *Outline for a Theory of Practice*, translated by Richard Nice (Cambridge: Cambridge University Press, 1977), 94.

80 Braudel, *Afterthoughts on Material Civilization and Capitalism*, 6–7.

81 See Althusser's "Ideology and Ideological State Apparatuses," in *Lenin and Philosophy and Other Essays*, translated by Ben Brewer (New York: Monthly Review, 1971).

82 Interestingly, the term "prosthesis" first enters the English language in the sixteenth century, where it was used to refer to "artificial" body parts, and to a rhetorical figure. David Wills explores this fascinating conjunction in his *Prosthesis* (Stanford: Stanford University Press, 1995).

83 Allon White, "Prosthetic Gods in Atrocious Places: Gilles Deleuze/Francis Bacon," in *Carnival, Hysteria, and Writing: Collected Essays and Autobiography* (Oxford: Oxford University Press, 1993), 172–3.

84 Derrida develops this idea in many different places, but see especially *Of Grammatology*, translated by Gayatri Chakravorty Spivak (Baltimore: Johns Hopkins University Press, 1998).

85 This is one of the examples Jonathan Culler uses to illustrate this concept in *On Deconstruction: Theory and Criticism after Structuralism* (Ithaca: Cornell University Press, 1982), 102–3.

86 This concept is mapped out in "The Parergon," *The Truth in Painting*, translated by Geoff Bennington and Ian McLeod (Chicago: University of Chicago Press, 1987), especially 37–83.

87 *The Truth in Painting*, 63.

88 See the *OED*'s entry for "prosthesis."

89 Harry Berger discusses some of the current usages of the term "prosthesis," and especially the tendency to conflate "prostheses" with "technology" more generally. See "Second-World Prosthetics," 98–147.

90 Adrienne Rich makes the suggestion that "perhaps we need a moratorium on saying 'the body'." See her discussion of this issue in *Blood, Bread and Poetry: Selected Prose 1979–85* (New York: W.W. Norton, 1986), 215. My reservations about the notion of "the body" are historical as well as ideological. In my conclusion, I discuss the religious debates about what exactly should be considered part of "the body." These have been brilliantly analyzed by Caroline Walker Bynum in *Fragmentation and Redemption: Essays on Gender and the Human Body in Medieval Religion* (New York: Zone Books, 1991) and in *The Resurrection of the Body in Western Christianity, 200–1336* (New York: Columbia University Press, 1995).

91 See particularly *The Body and Physical Difference: Discourses of Disability*, edited by David T. Mitchell and Sharon L. Snyder (Ann Arbor: University of Michigan Press, 1997); Rosemarie Garland Thompson, *Extraordinary Bodies: Figuring Physical Disability in American Culture and Literature* (New York: Columbia University Press, 1997); and Thomas G. Couser, *Recovering Bodies: Illness, Disability, and Lifewriting* (Madison: University of Wisconsin Press, 1997). For other important works in the field of disability studies, see *The Disability Studies Reader*, edited by Lennard J. Davis (New York: Routledge, 1997) and *Disability Studies: Definitions and Diversity*, edited by Gary Kiger, Stephen C. Hey and J. Gary Linn (Salem, OR: Society for Disability Studies and Willamette University, 1994).

92 Edgar Allan Poe, "The Man that Was All Used Up," in *Collected Works of Edgar Allan Poe, Tales and Sketches, 1831–1842*, edited by Thomas Ollive Mabbott (Cambridge, MA: The Belknap Press, 1978), 376–92.

93 Richard Rambuss points out "that the depersonalization and loss of individual identity being critiqued by Poe is precisely the goal of the 'military machine' in any number of its incarnations. In *Full Metal Jacket*, this is the telos of boot camp, not the unfortunate result or after-effect of battlefield damage." See his "Machine-head," *Camera Obscura: A Journal of Feminism, Culture, and Media Studies*, 42 (1999): 97–122.

94 O'Connor also analyzes the use of the term prosthesis in modern theoretical writing, and argues that it has been cut off from its roots in Victorian medical discourses. See O'Connor's chapter "Fractions of Men: Engendering Amputation in Victorian Culture," in *Raw Material: Producing Pathology in Victorian Culture* (Durham: Duke University Press, 2000).

95 A. A. Marks, *A Treatise on Artificial Limbs with Rubber Hands and Feet* (New York: A. A. Marks, 1903), 397, 317, and iv. See Jennifer Davis McDaid's article which includes a discussion of Marks, "'How a One-Legged Rebel Lives': Confederate Veterans and Artificial Limbs in Virginia," in *Artificial Parts, Practical Lives: Modern Histories of Prosthetics*, edited by Katherine Ott, David Serlin, and Stephen Mihm (New York: New York University Press, 2002), 119–47. Erin O'Connor quotes many of the testimonials included in Marks's catalogs in her chapter on prostheses in *Raw Material*, 124 and 134.

96 Katherine Ott notes that "Many scholars use the term 'prosthesis' regularly, and often reductively, as a synonym for common forms of body-machine interface. This occurs most explicitly in discussions of the cyborg." She also points out that although "Voluntary bionics can be very desirable," "when the wearer has less of a choice, or when the technology references disability and not glamour, the attraction of engineered beauty fades. Rehabilitation technology is not worshipped in popular culture." See *Artificial Parts, Practical Lives*, 2 and 21.

   Similarly, Erin O'Connor argues that the compensatory fantasy surrounding prostheses is often taken up uncritically in current theoretical writing: "'Prosthesis' circulates in contemporary cultural studies as a metaphor for the particular intimacy between body and machine." Moreover, "machines" and "technology" are often imagined to be "fabulously capable supplements to a comparatively limited flesh," and thus the prosthesis itself is "deployed as model for a more or less idyllic materialism." See *Raw Material*, 146.

97 Haraway, "A Manifesto for Cyborgs," 65–108.

98 See *Artificial Parts, Practical Lives*, 3 and 5.

99 Marks, *A Treatise*, 254.

100 The anthropomorphizing of the false limb that we witness in this passage seems to be fairly common. Indeed, patients often describe "bonding" with their prostheses, and children are encouraged to sleep with their new limbs and to bestow doll-like names upon them.

101 As one of S. W. Mitchell's patients put it: "If . . . I should say, I am more sure of the leg which ain't than the one that are, I guess I should be about correct," in "Phantom Limbs," *Lippincott's Magazine of Popular Literature and Science*, 8 (1871): 566–7. This passage is cited by O'Connor, *Raw Material*, 114.

102 Oliver Sacks, *The Man who Mistook his Wife for a Hat, and Other Clinical Tales* (New York: Harper and Row, 1970), 69.

103 Marks, *A Treatise*, 232.

104 Ibid., 121.

105 William James, "The Consciousness of Lost Limbs," in *Essays on Psychology* (Cambridge: Harvard University Press, 1983). Cited in O'Connor, *Raw Material*, 122.

106 Greenblatt, "The Paradoxes of Identity," *The Norton Shakespeare*, 59. Howard offers a similarly two-sided appraisal, though she sees the two as more compatible. She claims that "increasingly . . . with the production of bourgeois interiority, the marks of gender difference were not to be inscribed solely on the outside of the body through apparel but to be worn inwardly and made manifest through a properly gendered subjectivity." See *The Stage and Social Struggle*, 99.

107 Jones and Stallybrass, *Renaissance Clothing*, 2.

1 THAT SHAKESPEAREAN RAG: HANDKERCHIEFS AND FEMININITY

1 This incident is described in several of Elizabeth's biographies, especially Elizabeth Jenkins, *Elizabeth and Leicester* (New York: Coward-McCann, Inc., 1961), 115–16. Neville Williams provides a direct quotation of this section of Randolph's letter in *All the Queen's Men: Elizabeth I and her Courtiers* (New York: Macmillan, 1972), 91.

2 Jacob Voorthuis, "Portraits of Leicester," *The Dutch in Crisis 1583–88: People and Politics in Leicester's Time* (Leiden, 1988), 58–9. Cited in *Dynasties: Painting in Tudor and Jacobean England 1530–1630*, edited by Karen Hearn (London: Tate Publishing, 1995), 96–7.

3 John Nichols, *The Progresses and Public Processions of Queen Elizabeth, among which are interspersed other solemnities, public expenditures, and remarkable events during the reign of the illustrious Princess* (London: John Nichols and Son, 1823), 1: 113 and 116.

4 O'Hara has written extensively on the handkerchief's role in marital negotiations, examining ecclesiastical court depositions in the diocese of Canterbury for the period 1542–1602. She finds that clothing comprised fully a third of all love tokens given, and that handkerchiefs were one of the most common types of clothes exchanged (along with gloves and purses). In general, these tokens were considered

tangible "proof" of a couple's conjugal relationship. Martin Ingram's *Church Courts, Sex, and Marriage* explains that the courts were forced to look to these tokens and other ritual actions as evidence because marriage at the time was somewhat nebulously defined (technically, a verbal declaration followed by sexual relations was all that was required to form a marriage). See Diana O'Hara, "The Language of Tokens and the Making of Marriage," *Rural History*, 1992, 1–40, especially 4, and Martin Ingram, *Church Courts, Sex, and Marriage in England, 1570–1640* (Cambridge: Cambridge University Press, 1987), 197.

5 Katherine Morris Lester and Bess Viola Ierke, *Accessories of Dress* (Peoria, IL: Manual Arts Press, 1940), 426.

6 M. Braun-Ronsdorf, *The History of the Handkerchief* (London: F. Lewis Publishers, Ltd., 1967), 18.

7 Quoted in Lester and Ierke, *Accessories of Dress*, 429–30.

8 Norbert Elias, *The Civilizing Process, The History of Manners*, translated by Edmund Jephcott (New York: Urizen Books, 1978), 148–51.

9 Pierre Bourdieu, *Outline of a Theory of Practice* (Cambridge: Cambridge University Press, 1977), 95.

10 On the gendering of "sweat" see Lorna Hutson's *The Usurer's Daughter: Male Friendship and Fictions of Women in Sixteenth-Century England* (New York: Routledge, 1994), 38.

11 Stephanie S. Dickey, "Women Holding Handkerchiefs in Seventeenth-Century Dutch Portraits," in *Beeld en zelfbeeld in de Nederlandse kunst, 1550–1750, = Image and Self-Image in Netherlandish Art, 1550–1750*, edited by Reindert Falkenburg, Jan de Jong, Herman Roodenburg, and Frits Scholten, *Kunsthistorisch Jaarboek*, 45 (Zwolle: Waanders Uitgevers, 1995), 340.

12 Juana Green, "The Semster's Wares: Merchandising and Marrying in *The Fair Maid of the Exchange* (1607)," *Renaissance Quarterly*, 53:4 (2000): 1087. I thank Juana for sharing her work with me prior to publication.

13 Gail Kern Paster, "Leaky Vessels: The Incontinent Women of City Comedy," in *The Body Embarrassed: Drama and the Disciplines of Shame in Early Modern England* (Ithaca: Cornell University Press, 1993), 25.

14 Douglas Bruster, *Drama and the Market in the Age of Shakespeare* (New York: Cambridge University Press, 1992), 69.

15 The *OED* lists "sweat" as one of the available meanings of "sauce" in the Renaissance.

16 There are, of course, countless plays that feature handkerchiefs, though none of them quite matches *Othello*. See, for instance, Jonson's *Volpone* (1616), Kyd's *The Spanish Tragedy* (1592), the anonymous *A Warning for Fair Women* (1599), and Lording Barry's *Ram-Alley* (1611).

17 "A Short View of Tragedy," in *The Critical Works of Thomas Rhymer*, edited by Curt A. Zimansky (New Haven: Yale University Press, 1956), 164.

18 Lynda Boose, "Othello's Handkerchief: 'The Recognizance and Pledge of Love'," *English Literary Renaissance*, 5 (1975): 360–74.

19 See Harry Berger's "Impertinent Trifling: Desdemona's Handkerchief," *Shakespeare Quarterly*, 47:3 (1996): 235–50. Douglas Bruster discusses *Othello* in a chapter entitled "The Farce of Objects: *Othello* to *Bartholomew Fair*," in *Drama and the Market in the age of Shakespeare*, 81–6. See also, Natasha Korda's "The

Tragedy of the Handkerchief: Female Paraphernalia and the Properties of Jealousy in Othello," in *Shakespeare's Domestic Economies: Gender and Property in Early Modern England* (Philadelphia: University of Pennsylvania Press, 2002); Karen Newman's *Fashioning Femininity and English Renaissance Drama*, foreword by Catharine R. Stimpson (Chicago: University of Chicago Press, 1991), 90–2; Edward A. Snow's "Sexual Anxiety and the Male Order of Things in *Othello*," *English Literary Renaissance*, 10 (1980): 384–412; Andrew Sofer, *The Stage Life of Props* (Ann Arbor: University of Michigan Press, 2003); and Peter Stallybrass's "Patriarchal Territories: The Body Enclosed," in *Rewriting the Renaissance*, edited by Margaret W. Ferguson et al. (Chicago: University of Chicago Press, 1986), 123–42.

20 Throughout this chapter, I will be using *The Norton Shakespeare*, edited by Stephen Greenblatt (New York: W.W. Norton and Co., 1997). The link between the handkerchief and the hand is also suggested in Dekker's *Shoemaker's Holiday*. There, when Hammon woos the shopkeeper Rose, he begins by asking, "How do you sell this handkercher?" When Rose says "Good cheap," he then asks: "How sell you then this hand?" (12.24–7). Part of what this scene explores is the potential commodification of women, and thus, it is important to note that Rose herself sharply rejects Hammon's advances and categorically states that her "hands are not to be sold" (28). The dialog nevertheless highlights the continuity between the organ and its auxiliary, in part by highlighting the role that both of these "parts" played in the courtship process. Indeed, before Hammon enters the shop, he notes: "Thrice have I courted her, Thrice hath my poor hand been moistened with her hand" (12.3–4). See Thomas Dekker, *The Shoemaker's Holiday*, edited by Anthony Parr (New York, W.W. Norton, 1990).

21 Michael Neill, "'Ampitheatres of the Body': Playing with Hands on the Shakespearean Stage," *Shakespeare Survey 48* (Cambridge: Cambridge University Press, 1995), 23 and 27.

22 Jonathan Goldberg, *Writing Matter: From the Hands of the English Renaissance* (Stanford: Stanford University Press, 1990) and Katherine Rowe, *Dead Hands: Fictions of Agency, Renaissance to Modern* (Stanford: Stanford University Press, 2000).

23 John Bulwer, *Chirologia, or the Natural Language of the Hand* (London, 1644), 87–8.

24 See Howard's note in *The Norton Shakespeare*, 2887.

25 Bulwer, *Chirologia*, 116.

26 Richard Saunders, *Palmistry, The Secrets thereof Disclosed* (London, 1664).

27 Ernest Adrian Mackenzie Colman, *The Dramatic Use of Bawdy in Shakespeare* (London: Longman, 1974), 197. Jean Howard, in her editorial comments on *The Winter's Tale* in *The Norton Shakespeare*, echoes Coleman's assertion, stating that "Early modern texts often represent hands as erotic body parts" (2887). In Thomas Carew's "The Complement," an erotically charged blazon, the speaker describes his beloved's "moist palme" and claims that "the dew" of it is "balme" (49–50). In the end, however, the speaker of the poem denies his attraction to these features in much the same way as the speaker in Shakespeare's "Sonnet 130": the full line reads "I love thee not for thy moist palme, / Though the dew thereof be balme."

See *The Poems of Thomas Carew*, edited by R. Dunlap (Oxford: Oxford University Press, 1949), 101.

28 Thomas Dekker, *Blurt Master-Constable* (London, 1602), c4v.

29 Bartholomeus Cocles, *Contemplation of mankinde, contayning a singuler discourse after the art of phisiognomie*, translated by Thomas Hill (London, 1571), 6. This was commonplace. Thomas Hill, for instance, says that "Those bodies naturally moyst" are "delighting to coeate often" in his *A Pleasant History: Declaring the whole Art of Physiognomy* (London, 1613).

30 "Watery and running" eyes were another supposed indicator of a "moyst compleccyon." See Hill, *A Pleasant History*, 6.

31 Dickey, "Women Holding Handkerchiefs," 336.

32 Othello's comments here about Desdemona's "crocodile tears" resonate with Donne's more general (and equally misogynistic) comments about women's tears in "Twicknam garden": the speaker of the poem says that with regard to "your mistresse Teares," "all are False . . . Alas, hearts do not in eyes shine, / Nor can you more judge a womans thoughts by teares, / Then by her shadow, what she weares" (lines 21–5). See *The Complete English Poems*, edited by C. A. Patrides, introduced and updated by Robin Hamilton (North Clarendon, VT: Dent, 1994), 26.

33 See 4.1.240–1 and 4.1.251, and the reference to her being "false as water" (5.2.143).

34 Throughout this section on the marital handclasp, I am deeply indebted to Dale B. J. Randall's excellent article "The Rank and Earthy Background of Certain Physical Symbols in *The Duchess of Malfi*," *Renaissance Drama*, 18 (1987): 171–203. He describes the performance of the handclasps in the Anglican ceremony in some detail. I have also drawn upon Katherine Rowe's "God's Handy Worke," in *The Body in Parts: Fantasies of Corporeality in Early Modern Europe*, edited by David Hillman and Carla Mazzio (New York: Routledge, 1997), 285–313.

35 *The Book of Common Prayer* (London, 1611), d2v.

36 See Randall's "The Rank and Earthy Background," 177.

37 Randall mentions this belief and gives many other examples of its dramatic representation. See "The Rank and Earthy Background," 178.

38 Rowe, *Dead Hands*.

39 Neill, "Ampitheatres of the Body," 38.

40 See Valerie Traub's "Jewels, Statues, and Corpses: Containment of Female Erotic Power in *Hamlet, Othello*, and *The Winter's Tale*," in *Desire and Anxiety: Circulations of Sexuality* (New York: Routledge, 1992), 25–49.

41 Lynda Boose, "Scolding Brides and Bridling Scolds," *Shakespeare Quarterly*, 42:2 (1991): 182.

42 Anne Hollander, *Seeing through Clothes* (New York: Viking Press, 1978).

43 Harry Berger, Jr., "Second-World Prosthetics: Supplying Deficiencies of Nature in Renaissance Italy," in *Early Modern Visual Culture: Representation, Race, and Empire in Renaissance England*, edited by Peter Erickson and Clark Hulse (Philadelphia: University of Pennsylvania Press, 2000), 98–147. At one point Berger describes this process. He says that "we [first] become dependent on our machines, when usage converts technological enhancements into necessities, they come to feel less like enhancements and more like compensatory or prosthetic supplements,

that is, things we can't seem to do without." Afterwards, there is a "backlash produced by the interplay of these factors, [and] a tendency to disparage residual cultural constructions of nature and human nature as well as of the body" (101).

44 Braun-Ronsdorf, *History of the Handkerchief*, 18.

45 John Taylor, *The Praise of Cleane Linnen* (London, 1624), B3v.

46 See Korda, "The Tragedy of the Handkerchief: female paraphernalia and the properties of jealousy in Othello," *Shakespeare's Domestic Economies: Gender and Property in Early Modern England*.

47 Juana Green, "The Semster's Wares: Merchandising and Marrying in *The Fair Maid of the Exchange* (1607)," *Renaissance Quarterly*, 53:4 (2000): 1084–118. Part of what I'm suggesting here is that we need to be somewhat cautious in our approach to these representations, for descriptions of women's agency were sometimes coopted for patriarchal ends. Indeed, in *Othello*, it is Iago who construes the handkerchief as a possible instrument of Desdemona's erotic agency: he imagines her bestowing the handkerchief on "any man" she chooses. In this case, however, his description of her agency is clearly meant to produce anxiety in Othello, and it ultimately serves to survey and control Desdemona's behavior.

2 "THAT CODPIECE AGO": CODPIECES AND MASCULINITY

1 For general information about the history of the codpiece, see Grace Q. Vicary, "Visual Art as Social Data: The Renaissance Codpiece," *Cultural Anthropology* (1989): 3–25; Jeffrey C. Persels' article "Bragueta Humanística, or Humanism's Codpiece," *Sixteenth Century Journal*, 28 (1997): 79–99; and W. L. McAtee, *On Codpieces* (Chapel Hill, 1954). There are also many studies in fashion history that include information about codpieces. See, for example, Michael Batterberry and Ariane Batterberry, *Mirror, Mirror: A Social History of Fashion* (New York: Holt, Rinehart and Winston, 1977); François Boucher, *20,000 Years of Fashion: The History of Costume and Personal Adornment*, 2nd edn. (New York: Harry N. Abrams, 1987); C. W. Cunnington, P. Cunnington, and C. Beard, *A Dictionary of English Costume* (Philadelphia: Doufour, 1960), and Milla Davenport, *The Book of Costume* (New York: Crown, 1976).

2 *Englands Vanity: or the Voice of God Against the Monstrous Sin of Pride, in Dress and Apparel* (London, 1683), 123. This is an almost verbatim repetition of a description from a much earlier source. See *The Treasurie of auncient and moderne Times* (London, 1613), 371.

3 Vicary analyzes representations of codpieces by approximately forty different Renaissance artists and maintains that "The crucial fact learned from studying visual art data is that between 1400 and 1600 there was more than one kind of codpiece. Codpiece number one was, as we have seen, a soft, triangular flap attached to the hose with laces made of the same material as the hose . . . Next came stiffened, padded, protruding codpieces worn as additions matching either the clothes or the clothing. The first were worn generally in the 15th century, the others in the 16th century." See Vicary, "Visual Art as Social Data," 8.

4 Aileen Ribeiro, *Dress and Morality* (New York: Holmes and Meier Publishers, Inc, 1986), 62.

5 John Bulwer, *Anthropometamorphosis* (London, 1654), 539.

6 Anne Hollander, *Seeing through Clothes* (New York: Viking Press, 1978).
7 Judith Butler, *Bodies that Matter: On the Discursive Limits of "Sex"* (New York: Routledge, 1993), 66.
8 Henry Medwall, *The Plays of Henry Medwall*, edited by Alan H. Nelson (Totowa, NJ: Rowman and Littlefield Inc, 1980), 49.
9 Anon., *Wiley Beguiled* (London, 1606), 48.
10 Richard Niccols, *The Furies with Vertues Encomium* (London, 1614), Epigram VII.
11 These lines appear in "Satire 2: Quedam sunt, et non videntur," from *The Metamorphosis of Pigmalions Image and Certaine Satyres* (London, 1598), 46.
12 Throughout this chapter, I will be using *The Norton Shakespeare*, edited by Stephen Greenblatt (New York: W.W. Norton and Co., 1997).
13 M. Jean Carmel Cavanaugh, *Techonogamia by Barten Holyday: A Critical Edition* (Washington, DC: The Catholic University of America Press, 1942), 1.4.460–3.
14 Bulwer, *Anthropometamorphosis*, 539.
15 Andreas Musculus, *Hosen Teuffel* (Frankfurt, 1555).
16 Lyndal Roper, *Oedipus and the Devil: Witchcraft, Sexuality and Religion in Early Modern Europe* (London: Routledge, 1994), 117.
17 See, for example, Batterberry and Batterberry, *Mirror, Mirror*; Pearl Binder, *The Peacock's Tail* (London: Harrap, 1954); and James Laver, *The Concise History of Costume and Fashion* (New York: Scribners, 1969).
18 Leo Steinberg, *The Sexuality of Christ in Renaissance Art and Modern Oblivion* (New York: Pantheon/October, 1983), 90.
19 Steinberg, *The Sexuality of Christ*, 183 and 90.
20 Marjorie Garber, *Vested Interest: Cross-Dressing and Cultural Anxiety* (New York: Routledge, 1992), 122.
21 Published by Nich. Culpeper Gent. And, Abdiah Cole, Doctor of Physick, *Bartholinus Anatomy; Made from the Precepts of his Father* (London, 1668), 55.
22 Thomas Gibson, *The Anatomy of Humane Bodies Epitomized* (London, 1688), 110.
23 Jean Howard and Phyllis Rackin, *Engendering a Nation: A Feminist Account of Shakespeare's English Histories* (New York: Routledge, 1997), 187.
24 Gary Taylor, *Castration: An Abbreviated History of Western Manhood* (New York: Routledge, 2000).
25 Rebecca Ann Bach, "Tennis Balls: *Henry V* and Testicular Masculinity; or, According to the *OED*, Shakespeare doesn't have any balls," *Renaissance Drama*, 30 (1999–2001): 5. Bach sees the shift that I have been discussing taking place at a slightly later historical moment, near the end of the seventeenth century.
26 Quoted in Helkiah Crooke, *Microcosmographia* (London, 1615), 45.
27 Quoted in Bach, "Tennis Balls," 6.
28 Thomas Vicary, *The Englishemans Treasure, or Treasor for Englishmen* (London, 1586), 58.
29 Crooke, *Microcosmographia*, 243.
30 Culpepper, *Bartholinus Anatomy*, 2.
31 *A Foreign View of England in the Reigns of George I & George II: The Letters of Monsieur César de Saussure to his Family*, translated and edited by Madame Van Muyden (London: John Murray, 1902), 87–8.
32 Thomas Boreman, *Curiosities in the Tower of London* (London: Thomas Boreman, 1741), 2: 55 and 60.

33 John Dunton, *Voyage Round the World* (London 1691), 134.

34 Ned Ward, *The London Spy Compleat in Eighteen Parts*, with an introduction by Ralph Straus (London: Casanova Society, 1924), 321.

35 From Freud's *On Dreams. The Freud Reader*, edited by Peter Gay (New York: W.W. Norton and Company, Inc., 1995), 171.

36 Ward, *London Spy*, 321.

37 *A Collection of Ballads originally formed by John Selden* (London, c. 1575–1703), 3: 178.

38 On the material history of pins in seventeenth-century England, see Joan Thirsk's *Economic Policy and Projects: The Development of a Consumer Society in Early Modern England* (Oxford: Oxford University Press, 1978).

39 Louis Montrose, "The Elizabethan Subject and the Spenserian Text," in *Literary Theory/Renaissance Texts*, edited by Patricia Parker and David Quint (Baltimore: Johns Hopkins University Press, 1986), 313–14.

40 *Dynasties: Painting in Tudor and Jacobean England, 1530–1630*, edited by Karen Hearn (New York: Rizzoli, 1996), 49.

41 A detailed analysis of the various representations of Henry VIII (in his own lifetime and afterward) and their relationship to the ideologies of masculinity lies outside the purview of this book. While there is an obvious biographical "explanation" for the changing perceptions of Henry and his codpiece, it would be a mistake to divorce the biography from a discussion of the historical shifts in the ideologies of masculinity. Indeed, the two were mutually constitutive.

42 Thomas Nash, *The Unfortunate Traveller*, edited by Philip Henderson, illustrated by Haydn Mackey (London: The Verona Society, 1930), 20.

43 C. G., *The Minte of Deformities* (London, 1600), 4. One of the characters in Samuel Rowlands' *The Knave of Harts* (1612) is said to be "as stale as Breech with Cod-piece fashion."

44 Robert Hayman, *Quodlibets, Lately Come over from New Britaniola* (London, 1628), 3.

45 Mary Poovey, *Uneven Developments: The Ideological Work of Gender in Mid-Victorian England* (Chicago: University of Chicago Press, 1988).

46 Marston, *The Metamorphosis of Pigmalions Image*, 46–7.

47 According to the *OED*, a "brisk" was "a gallant" or "fop."

48 *OED*.

49 C. G., *The Minte of Deformities*, Bv.

50 See my discussion of these issues in the introduction of this book.

51 François Rabelais, *Gargantua and Pantagruel, Book 1 English*, (London, 1653).

52 Thomas Middleton, *Your Five Gallants* (London, 1608), D3v.

53 Max von Boehn, *Modes and Manners: Sixteenth Century*, translated by J. Joshua (London: Harrap, 1932), 128.

54 Sigmund Freud, *Jokes and their Relation to the Unconscious*, translated by James Strachey (NY: Norton, 1963).

55 Thomas Middleton and Thomas Dekker, *The Roaring Girl*, edited by Paul A. Mulholland (Manchester: Manchester University Press, 1987), 2.2.93.

56 Thomas Middleton and Thomas Dekker, *The Honest Whore, Part I* (London, 1604), 1.10, G3v.

production of femininity in early modern England, in which case sexual distinctions would have been fourfold.

20 Stephen Orgel, *Impersonations: The Performance of Gender in Shakespeare's England* (Cambridge: Cambridge University Press, 1996).

21 Lisa Jardine, "Twins and Travesties: Gender, Dependency, and Sexual Availability in Twelfth Night," in *Erotic Politics: Desire on the Renaissance Stage*, edited by Susan Zimmerman (New York: Routledge, 1992), 27–38. See also her article "Boy Actors, Female Roles, Elizabethan Eroticism," in *Staging the Renaissance: Reinterpretations of Elizabethan and Jacobean Drama*, edited by David Scott Kastan and Peter Stallybrass (New York: Routledge, 1991), 57–67.

22 These definitions are part of Holme's description of the different stages of a man's life. See *The Academy of Armory* (Chester, 1688), 391.

23 Bruce Smith discusses the different stages of masculine development in *Shakespeare and Masculinity* (Oxford: Oxford University Press, 2000), 70–82.

24 I thank the anonymous reviewer at Cambridge University Press for this formulation.

25 Nicholas Udall, *Thersites* (London, 1537), 43.

26 Lording Barry, *Ram Alley* (London, 1607–8).

27 Scott McMillin argues that the play was performed by Strange's Men and then The Admiral's Men. See *The Elizabethan Theater and the Book of Sir Thomas More* (Ithaca: Cornell University Press, 1987).

28 Actually, the play includes the latter as well since Follywit dresses himself as a woman.

29 According to the *OED*, a "chin-clout" is an item like the chin-strap on a wimple: "a band or cloth passing under the chin formerly worn by women."

30 Udall, *Thersites*, 43.

31 Interestingly, Italian suits of armor often have beards sculpted directly onto the facemask. See *Heroic Armor of the Italian Renaissance: Filippo Negroli and his Contemporaries*, catalog by Stuart W. Pyhrr and José-A. Godoy (New York: Metropolitan Museum of Art, 1998).

32 *A Mad World, My Masters*, in *The Works of Thomas Middleton*, edited by A. H. Bullen (London: John C. Nimmo, 1885), 3: 256.

33 Robert Wilson, *The Three Lordes and Three Ladies of London* (London, 1590), B3v.

34 According to T. J. King, "evidence from eight Elizabethan playhouse documents shows that the boy actors in these companies do *not* play adult male roles, nor do adult actors play female roles." See *Casting in Shakespeare's Plays: London Actors and their Roles, 1590–1642* (Cambridge: Cambridge University Press, 1992), 6. James Forse disputes this received wisdom and has proposed that adult actors may indeed have played female roles, especially the large ones. See *Art Imitates Business: Commercial and Political Influences on the Elizabethan Theater* (Bowling Green, OH: Bowling Green State University Press, 1993). The chapter dealing with this question is entitled "Why Boys for (Wo)Men's Roles? or, Pardon the Delay, 'the Queen was shaving'." For my thoughts about this debate, see Fisher, "The Renaissance Beard," 182.

35 It is, however, certainly possible that beard growth played a part in the decision about what roles an actor would play. I discuss this issue at some length in "The Renaissance Beard," 183.

36 In John Marston's *Antonio's Revenge* (another boys' company play), Balduro enters a scene with his beard half on and half off. See *Antonio's Revenge* (London, 1602), c3v.

37 Jan Knott touches on a number of related topics in "Bottom and the Boys," *New Theater Quarterly*, 9:36 (1993): 307–15.

38 This woodcut is printed in the response to Boorde's *Book of Berdes*, which is now lost. *The Treatyse answerynge the boke of berdes* (London, 1541).

39 The account books list payments "for egges to trymme vyzerdes . . . iid." *Documents relating to the Office of the Revels in the time of Queen Elizabeth*, 236 and 263.

40 There is, however, some evidence to suggest that false beards were available to the public at large. See, for example, the satire *The Bourse of the Reformation*, in the Percy Society's *Poetry, Ballads, and Popular Literature of the Middle Ages* (London, 1849), 27: 194.

41 There are only five portraits of men who are clearly shaven, and interestingly, three of them are priests. See *Dynasties: Painting in Tudor and Jacobean England, 1530–1630*, edited by Karen Hearn (New York: Rizzoli, 1996).

42 These figures include only portraits painted between 1540 and 1630. It is my sense, however, that this phenomenon continued until at least 1640 and perhaps even until 1660. See Roy C. Strong, *Tudor & Jacobean Portraits* (London: HMSO, 1969).

43 See Leo Steinberg's *The Sexuality of Christ in Renaissance Art and Modern Oblivion* (New York: Pantheon Books, 1983).

44 For writing on hair and beards in the field of fashion history, see Richard Corson, *Fashions in Hair: The First Five Thousand Years* (New York: Hastings House, Publishers, 1965); Reginald Reynolds, *Beards: Their Social Standing, Religious Involvements, Decorative Possibilities and Value in Offense and Defense through the Ages* (London: Allen and Unwin Ltd, 1950); Bill Severn, *The Long and the Short of It: Five Thousand Years of Fun and Fury over Hair* (New York: David McKay Company, Inc., 1972); Augustin Fangé, *Mémoires pour servir a l'histoire de la barbe de l'homme* (Liège: Jean-François Broncart, 1774); and Jacques Antoine Dulaure's *Pogonologia, or a Philosophical and Historical Essay on Beards* (Exeter: R. Thorn, 1786). For an excellent, scholarly introduction to beards in the middle ages, see Giles Constable's essay in *Apologiae Duae: Gozechini Epistola Ad Walcherum; Burchardi, Ut Videtur, Abbatis Bellevallis Apologia De Barbis*, edited by R. B. C. Huygens and Giles Constable (Turnhout: Brepols, 1985). It accompanies an edition of *Apologia de Barbis*, a twelfth-century manuscript written by Burchardus, Abbot of Bellevaux.

45 John Taylor, *Superbiae Flagellum, or, the whip of pride* (London, 1621), c7r–c8v. For a similar catalog, see William Harrison's *Description of England*, edited by Georges Edelen (Ithaca: Cornell University Press, 1968), 146–7. My thanks to Valerie Traub for this reference.

46 Many of these beard styles are also mentioned in Robert Greene's *A Quip for an Upstart Courtier* (London, 1592), 24.

47 Hugh Crompton, *The Glory of Women. . .first written in Latine by Henricus Cornelius Agrippa, Knight* (London, 1652), 14, lines 399–403.

48 One example of this is a pair of portraits of the archbishop Thomas Cranmer painted only a couple of years apart. One of these portrays him entirely beardless,

and the other one portrays him with a large white beard. While it is possible that both are realistic, it is equally possible that the beard was exaggerated in the latter for ideological purposes. Cranmer's biographer Diarmaid MacCulloch notes the religious significance of beards in *Thomas Cranmer, A Life* (New Haven: Yale University Press, 1996), 361.

49 These quotations are from Thomas Hall, who was pastor at King's Norton. See *The Loathsomeness of Longe Hair* (London, 1653), 48.

50 This is Diarmaid MacCulloch's formulation. He is explaining the context of Thomas Cranmer's decision to grow his beard after the death of Henry VIII. See *Thomas Cranmer, A Life*, 361.

51 MacCulloch suggests that this woodcut may have been made for Foxe's *Acts and Monuments*, though it was eventually left out. See *Thomas Cranmer, A Life*, 602.

52 My thanks to Peter Stallybrass for these observations and this formulation.

53 See Giles Constable's discussion of beards in the Middle Ages, where he addresses some of the canonical rules about facial hair. *Apologiae Duae*, 103–4 and 113–14.

54 Valeriano's text was not the only one written on the subject of beards for the clergy. On the continent, Rodolph Hospinien wrote a chapter in his book *De Monachis* that addressed the issue. It was later reprinted on its own under the title *De Rasione Comae & Barbae*, and was published in conjunction with Valeriano's treatise in the 1630s. See Rudolphus Hospinianus, *De Monachis: Hoc est, De Origine et Progressu Monachatus*, Second Edition (Zurich, 1609), Chapter ix, 67v–69v. The text that combines Valeriano and Hospinien was published in Leyden in 1639. Another text on the subject is Ludovicus Tirado de Hinestrosa's *nis de barba et coma necnon clericali habitu diatriba* (Granada, 1643).

55 *Treatise written by Johan Valerian . . . entitled in Latin Pro Sacerdotum barbis* (London, 1533). For more information on Valeriano, see Julia Haig Gaisser's introduction to *Pierio Valeriano: On the Ill Fortune of Learned Men* (Ann Arbor: The University of Michigan Press, 1999).

56 Valeriano, *Pro Sacerdotum Barbis*, 10 and 17–18.

57 The year the text was printed was, of course, the year of Henry's remarriage and excommunication.

58 Daniel Sennert, *The Art of Chirurgery explained in Six Parts* (London, 1663), 2612.

59 Nicholas Culpepper, *Bartholinus Anatomy* (London, 1668), 128. Despite this claim, the text then goes on to mention several instances of "girl[s]" with "long beard[s]."

60 See Thomas Hill, *The contemplation of mankinde, contayning a singular discourse of phisiognomie. In the ende is a little treatise of moles, by Melampus* (London, 1571), 148. The emphasis on sexual difference in this section of the book is even more striking if we consider that most sections are about reading the complexion or the moles on the face in order to determine a person's "character" or "constitution."

61 Helkiah Crooke, *Microcosmographia: Description of the Body of Man* (London, 1615), 70.

62 Marcus Antonius Ulmus' *Physiologia Barbae Humanae* (Bologna, 1603). Most of the other books do not focus only on anatomy, but combine a variety of perspectives: anatomical, historical, philosophical, and theological. Nevertheless, Joannes Barbatius's *Barbae Maiestas, Hoc est de Barbis Elegans, Brevis et*

Accurata descriptio . . . (Frankfurt, 1614), for instance, does repeat the claims found in the more explicitly anatomical texts, such as, "Barba solis viris, non mulieribus est ornamentum" (5). See also Christianus Becmanus and Valentinus Hartungus, *Disceptatio de Barbigenio Hominus mere maris* (Jenae, 1608) and Georg Caspar Kirchmaier, *De Majestate Juribusque Barbae* (Wittenberg, 1698).

63 John Bulwer, *Anthropometamorphosis* (London, 1654), 208.

64 Sir Thomas Browne, *A Letter to a Friend, upon occasion of the Death of his Intimate Friend* (London, 1690), 5. Although this is the first published edition of the work, Geoffrey Keynes argues that it was written much earlier. See his postscript in the 1971 edition published by David R. Godine in Boston.

65 Hugh Crompton, *The Glory of Women . . . first written in Latine by Henricus Cornelius Agrippa, Knight* (London, 1652), 14, lines 399–403.

66 Nicholas Billingsley, *A Treasury of Divine Raptures* (London, 1667), 50.

67 It has been attributed to Barnes. The nineteenth-century editor, F. J. Furnivall, suggests that the text was printed in 1542 or 1543. See *Andrew Boorde's Introduction and Dyetary with Barnes in the Defence of the Berde*, Early English Text Society (London, 1870), 308 and 16.

68 Antoine Hotman, *Pogonias, sive, De barba dialogus* (Antwerp, 1586). Interestingly, Hotman also wrote a book called *Traicté de la dissolution du mariage par l'impuissance & froideur de l'homme ou de la femme* (Paris, 1581).

69 Andrew Boorde, *The Breviary of Healthe* (London, 1552), xLIxr. The chapter on the face is 133.

70 This procedure continues to this day. Perper argues that "secondary" sexual characteristics such as hair growth are still imagined to conform to a strict bipolarity because they are seen as emblematic essences (emblematic of primary sexual characteristics which are now almost always imagined as "naturally" bipolar). Moreover, although we might expect that this ideology would actively work to *produce* a bipolar distribution of facial hair (and it does to some extent, insofar as women still often remove or dye their facial hair), the fact that these differences are not fully materialized in twentieth-century western culture may be taken as an index of the diminishing emphasis placed on facial hair. T. Perper, *Sex Signals: The Biology of Love* (Philadelphia: ISI Press, 1985), 184–6.

71 Crooke, *Microcosmographia*, 70.

72 Culpepper, *Bartholinus Anatomy*, 128.

73 Thomas Laqueur, *Making Sex: Body and Gender From the Greeks to Freud* (Cambridge, MA: Harvard University Press, 1990), 8.

74 Helkiah Crooke, *A description of the body of man. The second edition corrected and enlarged* (London, 1631), 70.

75 Bulwer, *Anthropometamorphosis*, 193.

76 *Haec Vir*, printed in *Half Humankind: Contexts and Texts of the Controversy about Women in England, 1540–1640*, by Katherine Usher Henderson and Barbara F. McManus (Urbana: University of Illinois Press, 1985), 286.

77 This is Bulwer's description of Ulmus' argument. See *Anthropometamorphosis*, 208.

78 Hill, *The Contemplation of Mankinde*, 145–6.

79 Crooke, *A Description of the Body of Man*, 67.

80 In *Francis Bacon: A Selection of his Works*, edited by Sidney Warhaft (New York: The Odyssey Press, 1965), 302–3.

81 *The Plays and Poems of William Cartwright*, edited by G. Blakemore Evans (Madison: University of Wisconsin Press, 1951), 347.

82 Laevinus Lemnius, *The Secret Miracles of Nature* (London, 1658), 282.

83 The fact that Lemnius conceptualizes masculinity both in terms of reproduction and in terms of sexuality resonates powerfully with the argument I made in my chapter on codpieces.

84 Thomas Dekker, *The Shoemaker's Holiday*, edited by Anthony Parr (New York, W.W. Norton, 1990), 11.37–9.

85 Ben Jonson, *Epicoene, or The Silent Woman*, edited by L. A. Beaurline (Lincoln: University of Nebraska Press, 1966), 5.3.171–2.

86 *The Plays and Poems of Phillip Massinger*, edited by Philip Edwards and Colin Gibson (Oxford: Oxford University Press, 1976), 4:119.

87 *The Diary of Montaigne's Journey to Italy in 1580 and 1581*, translated with introduction and notes by E. J. Trechmann (New York: Harcourt, Brace and Company, 1929), 6.

88 Bartholomeus Cocles, *A brief and most pleasau[n]t epitomye of the whole art of phisiognomie* (London, 1556), D2r–D3v.

89 Bulwer, *Anthropometamorphosis*, 198.

90 This may help to explain the seemingly contradictory statements in anatomy books.

91 William Shakespeare, *Macbeth*, 1.3.45–7. See also James Shiffer's "Macbeth and the Bearded Women," *In Another Country: Feminist Perspectives on Renaissance Drama*, edited by Dorothea Kehler and Susan Baker (Metuchen, NJ: The Scarecrow Press, Inc., 1991), 205–18.

92 John Evelyn, *The Diary of John Evelyn*, edited by E. S. de Beer (Oxford: Oxford University Press, 1955), 3:197–8.

93 Samuel Pepys, *The Diary of Samuel Pepys*, edited by Robert Latham and William Matthews (London: G. Bell and Sons, 1976), 9:398.

94 The portrait was painted in 1631.

95 Bulwer, *Anthropometamorphosis*, 215. Tilley mentions a similar, though less violent, proverb ("Greet . . . a bearded woman three miles off") in his collection of sayings from the early modern period. Morris Palmer Tilley, *A Dictionary of Proverbs in England in the Sixteenth and Seventeenth Centuries* (Ann Arbor: University of Michigan Press, 1950).

96 See Lorraine Daston and Katharine Park, *Wonders and the Order of Nature, 1150–1750* (New York: Zone Books, 2001) and Julie Crawford, *Marvelous Protestantism* (Baltimore: Johns Hopkins University Press, 2005).

97 The punishment suggested for the bearded woman in the proverb is likely meant to be a symbolic corollary of her supposed "transgression": the "stones" that the proverb says should be used to "greet her from a distance" could be seen as a figurative displacement of the masculine stones ("testicles") which she supposedly possesses.

98 Sir Philip Sidney, *The Countess of Pembroke's Arcadia*, intro by Carl Dennis (Kent, OH: Kent State University Press, 1970), 36.

99 Lemnius, for one, acknowledges that it is possible for "such as have no beards nor down on chins [to] show themselves men in the marriage-Bed," but he insists that "more frequently for want of heat, their forces fail . . . and they want children so much hoped for." See *The Secret Miracles of Nature*, 282.

100 Benedick, Leonato, and Antonio all use this epithet when challenging Claudio "to trial of a man" (5.1.66). Benedick says "Fare you well, boy, you know my mind" (5.1.176) in the same speech where he calls Claudio "lord Lackbeard." Earlier in the same scene, Leonato says "If thou kill'st me, boy, thou shalt kill a man" (5.1.79) and Antonio likewise says "He shall kill two of us, and men indeed . . . Let him answer me. Come follow me boy, come sir boy, come follow me, Sir boy" (5.1.80–4).

101 Diana Fuss, *Essentially Speaking: Feminism, Nature and Difference* (New York: Routledge, 1989), 6.

102 Nevertheless, it is worth saying that these ideas eventually began to wane. Valerie Traub notes that "Over the course of the seventeenth century, medical writers increasingly denied the possibility of metamorphosis, arguing that such phenomena were attributable either to hermaphroditism or to unusual genital anatomy." Valerie Traub, *The Renaissance of Lesbianism in Early Modern England* (Cambridge: Cambridge University Press, 2002), 45.

103 As I noted in my introduction, Stephen J. Gould has argued that the current debates about the relative importance of nature and nurture as causes of behavioral expression are misguided and that the real discussion ought to be about the malleability or alterability of those behavioral expressions.

104 Bulwer, *Anthropometamorphosis*, 208.

105 Lemnius, *The Secret Miracles of Nature*, 282–3. This might help to explain the origins of the belief (still common today) that shaving increases the growth of facial hair. As this quotation indicates, this folk wisdom could be given a powerful ideological spin.

106 Crompton, *Glory of Women*, 14, line 404–8.

107 Tellingly, Crompton doesn't acknowledge the possibility that women's "face[s]" might "remaine" beardless through shaving. His disavowal of this possibility might help to explain the tortured logic of this passage: why, we might ask, would a woman shave in the first place if "every female beardless doth remaine"?

108 Hall, *The Loathsomeness of Longe Hair*, 8.

109 Bulwer, *Anthropometamorphosis*, 206–7.

110 Crooke, *Microcosmographia*, 82 and 70.

111 All subsequent references to *The Book of Sir Thomas More* are from the Gabrieli and Melchiori edition. Anthony Munday and others; revised by Henry Chettle . . . [et al.], *Sir Thomas More: a play*, edited by Vittorio Gabrieli and Giorgio Melchiori (Manchester, UK: Manchester University Press, 1990).

112 John Harrington, *Metamorphosis of Ajax*, critical and annotated edition by Elizabeth Story Donno (London: Routledge, 1962), 101.

113 John Foxe, *The Ecclesiastical Historie, conteining the Acts and Monuments of Martyrs* (London, 1583), 1069. See also *The Third Volume of Chronicles . . . first compiled by Raphael Holinshed* (London, 1586–7), 938.

114 Doyle claims that it was Francis Bacon who first gave the anecdote this punch-line in his *Apophtegmes New and Old* (1625). See Charles Clay Doyle, "The Hair and Beard of Thomas More," *Moreana* 28 (1981): 5–6.

115 Jeffrey Masten, "*More* or Less: Editing the Collaborative," Paper presented in the "Editing Shakespeare Revisited" panel of the Shakespeare Association of America Annual Meeting, 2000. As will be clear from the following discussion, I am deeply indebted to this article. I thank Jeff for sharing it with me. It was subsequently published in *Shakespeare Studies*, 29 (2001): 109–31.

116 Masten, "*More* or Less," 12.

117 More may also be implicitly contrasting Wit and Wisdom, and suggesting that Wit does not need to wear a beard because it is Wisdom that is traditionally associated with facial hair (as in the figure of the bearded philosopher). In this regard, it is worth saying that Good Counsel, who is the Wisdom figure in the play-within-the-play, is played by the bearded More himself.

118 As the note in the Vittorio and Melchiori edition points out, this is the sixth definition listed in the *OED*.

119 Another possibility, however, would be that a bearded actor wore a mask like the one Flute wears in *A Midsummer Night's Dream* in order to create the illusion of a "smooth court shaving."

120 There has been a lot of fascinating work on some of these issues in recent years. See particularly Elliott Horowitz's analysis of beards and emergent discourses of racial difference in "The New World and the Changing Face of Europe," *Sixteenth Century Journal*, 28:4 (1997): 1181–201. Also see Londa Schiebinger's fascinating book, *Nature's Body*, which contains a chapter on the racialization of facial hair in the eighteenth century. *Nature's Body: Gender in the Making of Modern Science* (Boston: Beacon Press, 1993).

4 "THE ORNAMENT OF THEIR SEXE": HAIR AND GENDER

1 *James Brown, The Godfather of Soul*, by James Brown with Bruce Tucker, foreword by Reverend Al Sharpton with Karen Hunter (New York: Thunder Mouth Press, 2002).

2 Ambroise Paré, *The workes of that famous chirurgion Ambrose Parey translated out of Latine and compared with the French by Th: Johnson* (London, 1634), 973.

3 W. T., *A Godly Profitable Treatise* (London, 1590); William Prynne, *The Unlovelinesse of Love-lockes* (London, 1623); *A Looking-Glasse for Women . . . Shewing the unlawfulness of any outward adorning of any attire of Haire* (London, 1644); *Seasonable Advice . . . to the Professors of this backsliding Age* (London, 1650); Thomas Hall, *The Loathsomenesse of Longe Haire* (London, 1653); Thomas Wall, *Spiritual Armour to Defend the Head from a Superfluity of Naughtiness* (London, 1688) and *God's Holy Order in Nature* (London, 1690). There were also books that concerned themselves with other issues relating to hair. See Synesius, *A Paradoxe, Proving by reason and example, that baldnessse is much better than bushie haire* (London, 1579) and *Coma Berenices, or the hairy comet being a Prognostick of malignant influences from the many blazing stars wandring in our horizon* (London, 1674).

4 See Jean Tardin, *Disquisitio Physiologica de Pilis* (Touron, 1609) and Adrianus Junius, *De coma commentarium* (Basil, 1556). Rodolph Hospinianus's text was originally published as a chapter *De Monachis: Hoc est, De Origine et Progressu Monachatus*, Second Edition (Zurich, 1609), Chapter IX, 67v–69v. It was then reprinted as a separate book under the title *De Rasione Comae & Barbae*. This text was published in Leiden in 1639 in conjunction with Pierio Valeriano's treatise on beards that I discussed at length in the last chapter. The polemical texts include: Claude de Saumaise, *Epistola ad Andream Colvium: super Cap. XI. Primae ad Corinth. Epist. De Casarie Virorum et Mulierum Coma* (Elzevier, 1644); and *De Coma Dialogus, Primus. Caesarius et Curtius interlocutores* (Leiden, 1645); Johannes Polyandrus a Kerckhoven, *Judicium & Consilium de Comae & Vestium Usu & Abusu* (Leiden, 1644); and Jacobus Revius, *Libertas Christiana circa usum capillitii defensa qua Sex ejusdem Disputationes de Coma ab exceptionibus viri cujusdam docti vindicantur* (Leiden, 1647).

There also appears to have been a controversy about hair in the Netherlands during the 1640s paralleling the one in England. See Jacobus Borstius, *Predicatie van't langh hair* [Sermon on long hair] (Utrecht, 1973). This is a reprint of the first edition from 1644. Marcus Zuerius van Boxhorn, *Spiegeltien, vertoonende 't lanck hayr ende hayrlocken, by de oude Hollanders ende Zeelanders gedragen* [A Mirror, showing the long hair and locks of hair, worn by the old (past) Hollanders and Zeelanders] (Middelburg, 1644) and *Spiegeltien, vertoonende 't cort hayr ende hayrlocken, by de oude Hollanders ende Zeelanders gedragen* [A Mirror, showing the short hair and locks of hair, worn by the old (past) Hollanders and Zeelanders] (Middelburg, 1644). Florentius Schuyl, *Raedt voor de scheer-siecke hair-cloovers* [Advice for the shear-sick hair-splitters] ('s-Hertogenbosch, 1644). Michael Spranger, *Hayrige vverelt waer in verthoont wert de heden-daegsche hair-cloovery* [Hairyworld, in which is shown the present-day hair-splitting] (Amsterdam, 1645); Hieronymus Vogellius, *Eernstige klaghte over't openbaer krakkeel der hedendaegsche hayr-draghten* [Serious Complaint about the public wrangling over the current hairstyles] (Enkhuizen, 1645); Irenaeus Poimenander [pseud for Godefridus Udemans] *Absaloms-hayr off Discovrs, daerinne ondersocht wordt, wat daer te houden zy vande wilde vliegende hayr-trossen, [. . .] die in onsen tijdt [. . .] gedragen worden* [Absalom's hair, or a Discourse in which is investigated, what there is to like about the wild, flying hair-tresses . . . which in our time . . . are being worn] (Dordrecht, 1643). I am grateful to Frans de Bruyn for helping me to understand these texts and for translating the Dutch titles.

5 *Seasonable Advice*, 1. The verbal allusion here is to Deuteronomy 22:5.8, where it is written that "A woman shall not wear anything that *pertains* to a man, nor shall a man put on a woman's garment."

6 *A Discovery of Six Women Preachers* (London, 1641), 2. There is some reason to be skeptical about whether this is actually a real sermon, since this description comes from a text which mocks female preachers, but it was apparently a common topic for sermons. My thanks to Julie Schutzman for this reference.

7 Edward Reynolds, *Three Treatises of The Vanity of the Creature, The Sinfulnesse of Sinne, The Life of Christ. Being the substance of severall sermons preached at Lincolns Inne*, Fourth Edition (London, 1652), 125.

8 Hall, *The Loathsomenesse of Longe Hair*, 1.

9 Samuel Rowlands, *Earth's Vanity* (London, 1632).

10 Thomas Dekker, *The Wonderful Year and Selected Writings*, edited by E. D. Pendry (London: Edward Arnold, 1967), 87.

11 *Hic Mulier*, printed in *Half Humankind: Contexts and Texts of the Controversy about Women in England, 1540–1640*, by Katherine Usher Henderson and Barbara F. McManus (Urbana: University of Illinois Press, 1985), 270.

12 John Bulwer, *Anthropometamorphosis* (London, 1654), 58.

13 Prynne, *The Unlovelinesse of Love-locks*, 10.

14 Hall, *The Loathsomenesse of Longe Hair*, 33. On the following page, Hall acknowledges that "some men, by reason of their constitution, if they suffered their haire to grow to its utmost length, would exceed some women's."

15 Helkiah Crooke, *Microcosmographia* (London, 1615), 68.

16 There are two primary factors which determine how long a person's hair will grow if left unchecked. The first is the temporal length of the growth cycle (known as *anagen*), and the second is the speed at which the hair grows. According to Dr. John Gray's *The World of Hair: A Scientific Companion*, anagen differs from person to person, but is usually "between three and seven years." It is "determined genetically, and varies between the sexes" (22) and it is also "influenced by the levels of various hormones in the blood" (24). Taking both genetic and hormonal factors into consideration, the general consensus of hair scientists is that anagen is longer for women than for men. According to Kevin J. McElwee, a scientist who does research on hair and who administers the website keratin.com, "The general view of the hair world is that . . . women have a longer hair growth cycle than men, but there is no hard data to back that up." The studies have simply not been performed. The speed at which hair grows is the other crucial factor. McElwee points out that "There are a few studies to show that the rate of scalp hair growth is faster in women (but slower for body hair) compared to men. Men have a rate of about 0.31mm a day for scalp hair while women have about 0.34mm a day. So even if the cycle time period was the same, it is likely that women [would still] grow longer scalp hair on average compared to men." My sincere thanks to Dr. McElwee for his detailed personal response to my query. See also Dr. John Gray's *The World of Hair: A Scientific Companion*, contributors R. Dawber and C. Gummer (London: Proctor and Gamble Haircare Research Centre, 1997).

17 For instance, all men are thought to have xy chromosomes and all women to have xx chromosomes. Another interesting example is the "sex" hormones testosterone and estrogen. Despite the fact that all people have both of these hormones, males are often imagined to be the only ones who have testosterone and females to be the only ones with estrogen. For further problems with this model, see Alice Domurat Dreger, *Hermaphrodites and the Medical Invention of Sex* (Cambridge, MA: Harvard University Press, 1998).

18 Daniel Sennert, *The Art of Chirurgery: explained in six parts . . . being the whole fifth book of practical physick* (London, 1661), 2611.

19 Bulwer, *Anthropometamorphosis*, 58.

20 Ovid, *Ouids Metamorphosis Englished . . . by G.S.* (London, 1632), 336.

21 Michel de Montaigne, *The Complete Works: Essays, Travel Journals, Letters*, translated by Donald M. Frame (London: Everyman Library, 2003), 83.

22 Ovid, *The xv. Bookes of P. Ouidius Naso, entitled, Metamorphosis* (London, 1584), 129.

23 Ovid, *Ouids Metamorphosis Englished*, 318.

24 Prynne, *The Unlovelinesse of Love-locks*, A3–4.

25 Wall, *A Spiritual Armour*, 21–2.

26 Laqueur makes a similar argument in *Making Sex*, 11.

27 Wall, *God's Holy Order in Nature*, 3.

28 Prynne, *The Unlovelinesse of Love-locks*, 10.

29 *Seasonable Advice*, 4.

30 Phillip Stubbes, *Anatomy of Abuses* (London, 1583), 34.

31 William Whately, *A Bride-Bush, or a Wedding Sermon* (London, 1619), 201.

32 Whately, *A Bride-Bush*, 201. This language was common. See Hall, *The Loathsomenesse of Longe Hair*, 25; Wall, *God's Holy Order*, 7; and Bulwer, *Anthropometamorphosis*, 57.

33 In *A Godly Profitable Treatise*, the author states that hair is an "outward couverture, which is only to keepe and preserve the body from cold" (19v).

34 According to Pearl Hogrefe, "When a woman married in Tudor England (and later and earlier also) her property came immediately under the control of her husband . . . By law, she was under his guardianship, becoming a feme covert." See *Tudor Women: Commoners and Queens* (Ames, IA: Iowa State University Press, 1975), 12.

35 Richard Corson, *Fashions in Hair: The First Five Thousand Years* (New York: Hastings House, Publishers, 1965), 171.

36 Prynne, *The Unlovelinesse of Love-locks*, 10.

37 *Seasonable Advice*, 1.

38 Whately, *A Bride-Bush*, 201.

39 Wall, *God's Holy Order in Nature*, 3.

40 Crooke, *Microcosmographia*, 70.

41 Although nature was often imagined to be an expression of God's will and an indication of the social order that he supposedly created, we need to be careful not to assume that the terms of our modern conceptual binary were simply reversed in the Renaissance, for there are some instances in which nature – and specifically the "natural" difference in men's and women's hair – does seem to provide a foundation for social hierarchy.

42 Wall, *God's Holy Order in Nature*, title page.

43 Almost all of the writers I've been discussing in this chapter cite these verses.

44 As I noted in my introduction, Lorraine Daston and Katharine Parks claim that "In the early modern period, nature was regulated by 'customs' rather than by ironclad laws, encompassed much of the psyche as well as the body, and bristled with moral directives." See Lorraine Daston and Katharine Park, "The Hermaphrodite and the Orders of Nature: Sexual Ambiguity in Early Modern France," in *GLQ: A Journal of Lesbian and Gay Studies*, 1:4 (1995): 432.

45 Hall, *The Loathsomenesse of Longe Hair*, 28.

46 Sennert, *The Art of Chirurgery*, 2611.

47 Crooke, *Microcosmographia*, 68.

48 W. T., *Godly Profitable Treatise*, 10v.

49 Ibid, 20v.

50 C. G., *The Minte of Deformities* (London, 1600), BV.

51 Diana Fuss, *Essentially Speaking: Feminism, Nature and Difference* (New York: Routledge, 1989), 6.

52 Bulwer, *Anthropometamorphosis*, 57–8.

53 Wall, *God's Holy Order in Nature*, 6.

54 Corson, *Fashions in Hair*, 171.

55 Wall, *God's Holy Order in Nature*, 31. While the claim that the fashion for long hair appeared during James' reign corresponds, more or less, with the judgements of historians, the claim that short hair had been worn in England since the reign of Henry I is almost certainly exaggerated.

56 Jacqueline Eales, *Puritans and Roundheads: The Harleys of Brampton Bryan and the Outbreak of the English Civil War* (Cambridge: Cambridge University Press, 1990), 143. The works she refers to are W. Macray, ed, *History of the Rebellion and Civil Wars in England Begun in 1641, by Edward, Earl of Clarendon* (Oxford, 1688), I, 456; and John Rushworth, ed., *Historical Collections of Private Passages of State, IV* (1721), 463–4.

57 *Twenty Lookes over all the round-heads that ever lived in the world* (London, 1643), 6.

58 *An Exact Description of a Roundhead, and A Long-head Shag-poll* (London, 1642).

59 *Compassionate Conformist, Englands Vanity: or the Voice of God Against the Monstrous Sin of Pride, in Dress and Apparel* (London, 1683), 118–19.

60 Tamsyn Williams, "Magnetic Figures: Polemical Prints of the English Revolution," in *Renaissance Bodies: The Human Figure in English Culture, c. 1540–1660*, edited by Lucy Gent and Nigel Llewellyn (London: Reaktion Books, 1990), 93.

61 *A Medicine for Malignancy. . .[a] Dialogue or Discourse between a Royalist & a Loyalist* (London, 1644), 36. Tamsyn Williams also mentions a tract entitled *A Short, Compendious, and True description of the Roundheads, and the Long-Heads* (London, 1642) that "recalls the Apostle's rule that long hair was shameful to men but was a glory to women in providing a covering (I Corinthians 11:14)." The tone of this pamphlet is somewhat more conciliatory than that of *A Medicine for Malignancy*. See Williams, "Polemical Prints," 93.

62 These comments were apparently part of a sermon delivered by "Mr. Nabe. W." and quoted by Hall in *The Loathsomenesse of Longe Hair*, 51.

63 There are a few, however, that appeared either before or after that period: Prynne's *Unlovelinesse of Love-lockes* was published in 1627; Thomas Wall's books were published around the Glorious Revolution in 1688 and 1690.

64 Hall, *The Loathsomenesse of Longe Hair*, 18.

65 Hall also cites Reverend Master Gipps' "sermon before the Honourable House of Commons" where he supposedly said: "when I came to London . . . I had much adoe to believe . . . what Ruffianly haire, what Cavalerian garbe of cloathes, with answerable diet we are falne upon, even in these sad times." See Hall, *The Loathsomenesse of Longe Hair*, 3.

66 Kerckhoven's *Judicium & Consilium de Comae* seems to adopt a stance that is somewhat similar to that of Salmasius. Indeed, one of the copies held by the British Library is bound together with *Epistola*.

67 Although I will focus on Salmasius, it is worth saying that Hall mentions other writers who made similar claims: namely, Revius and Dematius. The former is Jacobus Revius, who wrote *Libertas Christiana*.

68 Salmasius, *Epistola ad Andream Colvium*, 3–6.

69 This is Hall's formulation of Salmasius' argument; the citation he gives is "Salmasius Dialog. de coma. p.16." See *The Loathsomenesse of Longe Hair*, 60.

70 Ibid., 12.

71 *A Looking-Glasse for Women*, 1.

72 There are other texts from the period where the difficulties of materializing any type of identity through hair length are more openly acknowledged. For example, the seventeenth-century Puritan Lucy Hutchinson notes "that the name of round-head became the scornefull terme given to the whole Parliament party," but then explains that even though the New Model Army did indeed "march out" with their "hair cut close around their heads," it is "as if they had only bene sent out till their haire was growne: [for] two or three years after, any stranger that had seen them would have enquir'd the reason of that name." Hutchinson is quoted in Christopher Hibbert, *Cavaliers and Roundheads: the English Civil War, 1642–1649* (New York: C. Scribner's Sons), 49. Also see Christopher Hill's comments on Hutch-inson in *Milton and the English Revolution* (London: Faber and Faber, 1977), 429. Similarly, the pamphlet *An Exact Description of a Roundhead* acknowledges that it is true that "all that weare not long hair are not Roundheads" (8).

73 *The Complete English Poetry of John Milton*, edited by John T. Shawcross (New York: New York University Press, 1963), Book iv, lines 296–311.

74 *Seasonable Advice*, 4.

75 Hall, *The Loathsomenesse of Longe Hair*, 13.

76 Wall, *God's Holy Order in Nature*, 3.

77 My argument here about Milton's representation of Adam's locks incorporating elements of his own hairstyle is substantiated by Roland Frye. He notes that Milton's description of Adam's "parted forelock" is quite unconventional, but that "two men who wore their hair with a parted forelock just like that of Milton's Adam . . . were Oliver Cromwell and John Milton." See Frye, *Milton's Imagery and the Visual Arts: Iconographic Tradition in the Epic Poems* (Princeton: Princeton University Press, 1978), 272.

78 Aubrey is quoted in Leo Miller's *Milton's Portraits; an impartial inquiry into their authentication* (Athens, OH: [NS], 1976), 3.

79 Ibid, 3.

80 William Riley Parker, *Milton: A Biography* (Oxford: Oxford University Press, 1968), 70.

81 Francis Blackburne, *Memoirs of Thomas Hollis* (London, 1780), 620.

82 Palmer, *The Samson Saga and its Place in Comparative Religion* (New York: Arno Press, 1977), 33–4.

83 *The Riverside Milton*, edited by Roy Flannagan (New York: Houghton Mifflin Company, 1998), 785.

84 John Rogers, "The Secret of *Samson Agonistes*," *Milton Studies*, 33 (1997), 111–32.

85 Milton's treatment of hair and gender in *Samson* is anticipated by the allusion to Samson in *Areopagitica*. There, Milton describes England as a "noble and puissant Nation rousing herself like a strong man after a sleep, shaking her invincible locks"

and "purging and unscaling her long abused sight at the fountain itself of heav'nly radiance." In this passage, Milton clearly imagines England as none other than the regenerated Samson – regaining strength and overcoming blindness. But as Milton transfers Samson's locks (and by extension his strength) from his head to England's, he simultaneously shifts those locks from the head of a male figure to that of a female figure: England is described as "rousing *herself*" and "shaking *her* invincible locks." While in gendered terms this shift might appear to be a kind of restitution in which the long locks of Samson are returned to their "proper" place atop the head of a "woman," it soon becomes evident that this is not the case. In Milton's formulation, long hair actually appears to *masculinize* England: with her regenerated locks, England is compared to "a strong *man*." See John Milton, *The Complete Prose Works* (New Haven: Yale University Press, 1953–82), 2:558.

86 Richard Rogers, *A Commentary upon the Whole Booke of Judges* (London, 1615). My thanks to Joe Wittreich for this reference.

87 Hall, *The Loathsomenesse of Longe Hair*, 82.

88 John Guillory, "Dalila's House: *Samson Agonistes* and the Sexual Division of Labor," in *Rewriting the Renaissance*, edited by Margaret W. Ferguson et al. (Chicago: University of Chicago Press, 1986), 114.

89 Stanley Fish, "Spectacle and Evidence in *Samson Agonistes*," *Critical Inquiry* 15 (1989): 584.

90 Rogers, "The Secret of *Samson Agonistes*," 112.

91 Quoted in Elizabeth Baldwin's *Sumptuary Legislation and Personal Regulation in England* (Baltimore: Johns Hopkins University Press, 1926), 253.

92 *A Looking-Glasse for Women*, title page.

93 Frye points out that in describing Eve's tresses in this way, Milton "excludes a frequent, though not predominant feature in representations of her": namely, hair which is "neatly set about her head" or "bound up." See *Milton's Imagery*, 274.

94 Joseph Wittreich, *Interpreting Samson Agonistes* (Princeton: Princeton University Press, 1986), 215.

95 Judith Butler, *The Psychic Life of Power: Theories in Subjection* (Stanford: Stanford University Press, 1997), 2.

96 Milton's decision to wear long locks may be further complicated by issues of status. The Puritan writer Richard Rogers maintains that some men "nourish" long hair "as a supposed ornament of their person, or marke of gentrie; or at least imitation of gentlemen." See Rogers' *A Commentary upon the Whole Booke of Judges*.

CONCLUSION: DETACHABLE PARTS AND THE INDIVIDUAL

1 Jacob Burckhardt, *The Civilization of the Renaissance in Italy*, translated by S. G. C. Middlemore, with a new introduction by Peter Burke and notes by Peter Murray (New York: Penguin, 1990).

2 According to the *OED*, the first use of "individual" as a substantive referring to "A single human being, as opposed to Society, the Family, etc." was in 1626.

3 Throughout much of the early modern period, the indivisible "individual" would have stood in tension with the notion that individuals were what we might call "prosthetic gods."

4 Steven Lukes, *Individualism* (London: Basil Blackwell, 1973). He mentions several of these characteristics.

5 Paul Smith, *Discerning the Subject*, foreword by John Mowitt (Minneapolis: University of Minnesota Press, 1988), xxxiii–xxxiv.

6 Raymond Williams, *Keywords: A Vocabulary of Culture and Society* (New York: Oxford University Press, 1976), 133.

7 "Shakespeare, the Individual, and the Text," in *Cultural Studies*, edited by Lawrence Grossberg et al. (New York: Routledge, 1992), 594. See also Jeffrey Masten's "Playwrighting: Authorship and Collaboration" in *A New History of Early English Drama,* edited by John D. Cox and David Scott Kastan, foreword by Stephen J. Greenblatt (New York: Columbia University Press, 1995), 357–82, especially 358 and the second chapter of *Textual Intercourse: Collaboration, Authorship, and Sexualities in Renaissance Drama* (Cambridge: Cambridge University Press, 1997).

8 As Stallybrass notes, "the uses of 'individual' suggesting indivisibility and those suggesting divisibility emerge *together*." See "Shakespeare, the Individual, and the Text," 595.

9 Andrew G. Van Melsen, *From Atomos to Atom: A History of the Concept of the Atom* (New York: Harper Torchbooks, 1960), 81. Also see Bernard Pullman's *The Atom in the History of Human Thought,* translated by Axel Reisinger (New York: Oxford University Press, 1998). Interestingly, Van Melsen quotes Lasswitz's *Geschichte der Atomistik,* explaining a major shift that took place in the way in which the atom was understood: "The transition from terminus of division to building block is, indeed, of the greatest importance for physical science" (117).

10 John Rogers, *The Matter of Revolution: Science, Poetry, and Politics in the Age of Milton* (Ithaca: Cornell University Press, 1996) and William Kerrigan, "Atoms Again: The Deaths of Individualism," in *Taking Chances: Derrida, Psychoanalysis, and Literature,* edited by Joseph H. Smith and William Kerrigan (Baltimore: Johns Hopkins University Press, 1984), 86–107.

11 Rogers, *The Matter of Revolution*, 36.

12 Bishop Walton, *Considerator Considered* (London, 1659), 75.

13 The term "atom" comes from the Greek *atomos* which also means "undividable."

14 Alan Ryan, "Hobbes and Individualism," in *Perspectives on Thomas Hobbes*, edited by G. A. J. Rogers and Alan Ryan (Oxford: Oxford University Press, 1988), 81.

15 Ryan, "Hobbes and Individualism," 82.

16 Thomas Hobbes, *Leviathan* (London, 1651), 1.

17 Hobbes, *Leviathan*, 62.

18 Quentin Skinner, *Reason and Rhetoric in the Philosophy of Hobbes* (Cambridge: Cambridge University Press, 1996), 313.

19 See Genesis 2:7 in the *King James Version*.

20 Hobbes, *Leviathan*, 1.

21 This is one of the examples included in the *OED*.

22 Thomas Hobbes, *On the Citizen*, translated by Michael Silverthorne and edited by Richard Tuck (Cambridge: Cambridge University Press, 1998), 72.

23 Skinner makes an analogous point in *Reason and Rhetoric in the Philosophy of Hobbes*, 312.

24 Hobbes, *On the Citizen*, 72.
25 Nigel Smith, *Literature and Revolution in England, 1640–1660* (New Haven: Yale University Press, 1994), 158.
26 Descartes, *Meditations on First Philosophy*, "Sixth Meditation: The Existence of Material Things," in *Descartes: Philosophical Writings*, a selection edited and translated by Elizabeth Anscombe and Peter Thomas Geach, introduction by Alexander Koyre (New York: Macmillan Publishing Company, 1971), 121.
27 At another point, Descartes discusses the phenomenon of phantom limbs (which I mentioned in my introduction) as a further means of drawing the distinction between body and mind. See *Descartes: Philosophical Writings*, 113.
28 Jonathan Sawday, *The Body Emblazoned: Dissection and the Human Body in Renaissance Culture* (New York: Routledge, 1995), 145–6.
29 Dalia Judovitz, *Subjectivity and Representation in Descartes: The Origins of Modernity* (Cambridge: Cambridge University Press, 1988).
30 This is Elaine Scarry's formulation from *The Body in Pain: The Making and Unmaking of the World* (New York: Oxford University Press, 1985), 325.
31 In my opinion, it makes more sense to approach this question historically or politically, rather than philosophically. Throughout this book, I have concerned myself with some of the social ramifications of locating this hypothetical line in one place or another.
32 Kerrigan, "Atoms Again," 99.
33 This has not featured prominently in subsequent narratives about "the rise of the individual" since the characteristics usually associated with modern subjectivity are things like autonomy, interiority, and agency. In the end, I believe that all of these traits ultimately work to reinforce one another.
34 Helkiah Crooke, *Microcosmographia* (London, 1615), 82.
35 John Bulwer, *Anthropometamorphosis* (London, 1654), 50.
36 Carolyn Walker Bynum, *Fragmentation and Redemption: Essays on Gender and the Human Body in Medieval Religion* (New York: Zone Books, 1991), 239. See also *The Resurrection of the Body in Western Christianity, 200–1336* (New York: Columbia University Press, 1995).
37 Thomas Goffe, *Deliverance from the Grave* (London, 1627), 36.
38 Sir Kenelm Digby, *Observations upon Religio Medici* (London, 1643), 78–81.
39 Bynum, *Fragmentation and Redemption*, 244.
40 Warr's paper was presented at the conference "Clothing Culture 1300–1600" at the University of Kent, sponsored by The Canterbury Centre for Medieval and Tudor Studies, 2001.
41 Crooke, *Microcosmographia*, 70.

Bibliography

PRIMARY SOURCES

Anon., *Wiley Beguiled* (London, 1606).

Apologiae Duae: Gozechini Epistola Ad Walcherum; Burchardi, Ut Videtur, Abbatis Bellevallis Apologia De Barbis, edited by R. B. C. Huygens and Giles Constable (Turnhout: Brepols, 1985).

R. B., *Apius and Virginia* (London, 1575).

Francis Bacon: A Selection of his Works, edited by Sidney Warhaft (New York: The Odyssey Press, 1965).

Barbatius, Joannes, *Barbae Maiestas, Hoc est de Barbis Elegans, Brevis et Accurata descriptio . . .* (Frankfurt, 1614).

Barry, Lording, *Ram Alley* (London, 1607–8).

Becmanus, Christianus and Valentinus Hartungus, *Disceptatio de Barbigenio Hominus mere maris* (Jenae, 1608).

Billingsley, Nicholas, *A Treasury of Divine Raptures* (London, 1667).

The Book of Common Prayer (London, 1604).

The Book of Sir Thomas More (Oxford: Malone Society Reprints, 1990).

Boorde, Andrew, *The Breviary of Healthe* (London, 1552).

Andrew Boorde's Introduction and Dyetary with Barnes in the Defence of the Berde, Early English Text Society (London, 1870).

Boreman, Thomas, *Curiosities in the Tower of London* (London: Thomas Boreman, 1741).

Borstius, Jacobus, *Predicatie van't langh hair* [Sermon on long hair] (Utrecht, 1973).

Browne, Sir Thomas, *A Letter to a Friend, upon occasion of the Death of his Intimate Friend* (London, 1690).

Bulwer, John, *Anthropometamorphosis* (London, 1654).

Chirologia, or the Natural Language of the Hand (London, 1644).

Burton, Robert, *The Anatomy of Melancholy* (London, 1621).

Carew, Thomas, *The Poems of Thomas Carew*, edited by R. Dunlap (Oxford: Oxford University Press, 1949).

Cartwright, William, *The Plays and Poems of William Cartwright*, edited by G. Blakemore Evans (Madison: University of Wisconsin Press, 1951).

Cavanaugh, M. Jean Carmel, *Technogamia by Barten Holyday, A Critical Edition* (Washington, DC: The Catholic University of America Press, 1942).

Cocles, Bartholomeus, *Contemplation of mankinde, contayning a singuler discourse after the art of phisiognomie*, translated by Thomas Hill (London, 1571).

A brief and most pleasau[n]t epitomye of the whole art of phisiognomie (London, 1556).

Coma Berenices, or the hairy comet being a Prognostick of malignant influences from the many blazing stars wandring in our horizon (London, 1674).

Crompton, Hugh, *The Glory of Women . . . first written in Latine by Henricus Cornelius Agrippa, Knight* (London, 1652).

Crooke, Helkiah, *Microcosmographia: Description of the Body of Man* (London, 1615).

Culpepper, Nicholas, *Bartholinus Anatomy; made from the Precepts of his Father* (London, 1668).

de Hinestrosa, Ludovicus Tirado, *Solemnis de barba et coma necnon clericali habitu diatriba* (Granada, 1643).

Dekker, Thomas, *Blurt Master-Constable* (London, 1602).

The Shoemaker's Holiday, edited by Anthony Parr (New York, W. W. Norton, 1990).

The Wonderful Year and Selected Writings, edited by E. D. Pendry (London: Edward Arnold, 1967).

de Saussure, César, *A Foreign View of England in the Reigns of George I and George II: The Letters of Monsieur César de Saussure to his family*, translated and edited by Madame Van Muyden (London: John Murray, 1902).

Descartes, René, *Descartes: Philosophical Writings*, a selection edited and translated by Elizabeth Anscombe and Peter Thomas Geach, introduction by Alexander Koyre (New York: Macmillan Publishing Company, 1971).

Digby, Sir Kenelme, *Observations upon Religio Medici* (London, 1643).

A Discovery of Six Women Preachers (London, 1641).

Donne, John, *The Complete English Poems*, edited by C. A. Patrides, introduced and updated by Robin Hamilton (North Clarendon, VT: Dent, 1994).

Dunton, John, *Voyage Round the World* (London 1691).

Englands Vanity: Or the Voice of God Against the Monstrous Sin of Pride, in Dress and Apparel (London, 1683).

Evelyn, John, *The Diary of John Evelyn*, edited by E. S. de Beer (Oxford: Oxford University Press, 1955).

An Exact Description of a Roundhead, and A Long-head Shag-poll (London, 1642).

Foxe, John, *The Ecclesiastical Historie, conteining the Acts and Monuments of Martyrs* (London, 1583).

C. G., *The Minte of Deformities* (London, 1600).

Gamage, William, *Linsi-Woolsi* (London, 1613).

Gibson, Thomas, *The Anatomy of Humane Bodies Epitomized* (London, 1688).

Goffe, Thomas, *Deliverance from the Grave* (London, 1627).

Greene, Robert, *A Quip for an Upstart Courtier* (London, 1592).

Guazzo, Francesco Maria, *Compendium Maleficarum: The Montague Summers Edition*, translated by E. A. Ashwin (New York: Dover Publications, 1988).

Haec Vir: or, The Womanish-Man (London, 1620).

Half Humankind: Contexts and Texts of the Controversy about Women in England, 1540–1640, by Katherine Usher Henderson and Barbara F. McManus (Urbana: University of Illinois Press, 1985).

Hall, Thomas, *The Loathsomenesse of Longe Hair* (London, 1653).

Harrington, John, *Metamorphosis of Ajax*, critical and annotated edition by Elizabeth Story Donno (London: Routledge, 1962).

Harrison, William, *Description of England*, edited by Georges Edelen (Ithaca: Cornell University Press, 1968).

Hayman, Robert, *Quodlibets, Lately Come over from New Britaniola* (London, 1628).

Hic Mulier, or The Man-Woman (London, 1620).

Hill, Thomas, *A Pleasant History: Declaring the whole Art of Physiognomy* (London, 1613).

History of the Rebellion and Civil Wars in England Begun in 1641, by Edward, Earl of Clarendon, edited by W. Macray (Oxford, 1688).

Hobbes, Thomas, *Leviathan* (London, 1651).

   On the Citizen, translated by Michael Silverthorne and edited by Richard Tuck (Cambridge: Cambridge University Press, 1998).

Holinshed, *The Third Volume of Chronicles . . . first compiled by Raphael Holinshed* (London, 1586–7).

Holme, Randall, *The Academy of Armory* (Chester, 1688).

Hospinianus, Rudolphus, *De Monachis: Hoc est, De Origine et Progressu Monachatus*, Second Edition (Zurich, 1609).

Hotman, Antoine, *Pogonias, sive, De barba dialogus* (Antwerp, 1586).

   Traicté de la dissolution du mariage par l'impuissance et froideur de l'homme ou de la femme (Paris, 1581).

Huarte, Juan, *The Examination of Men's Wits*, facsimile reproduction with an introduction by Carmen Rogers (Gainesville: Scholars' Facsimiles and Reprints: 1959).

Jonson, Ben, *Epicoene, or The Silent Woman*, edited by L. A. Beaurline (Lincoln: University of Nebraska Press, 1966).

Junius, Adrianus, *De coma commentarium* (Basel, 1556).

Kerckhoven, Johannes Polyander a, *Judicium et Consilium de Comae et Vestium Usu & Abusu* (Leiden, 1644).

Kirchmaier, Georg Caspar, *De Majestate Juribusque Barbae* (Wittenberg, 1698).

Lemnius, Laevinus, *The Secret Miracles of Nature* (London, 1658).

A Looking-Glasse for Women . . . Shewing the unlawfulness of any outward adorning of any attire of Haire (London, 1644).

Marston, John, *The Metamorphosis of Pigmalions Image and Certaine Satyres* (London, 1598).

   Antonio's Revenge (London, 1602).

A Medicine for Malignancy. . .[a] Dialogue or Discourse between a Royalist and a Loyalist (London, 1644).

Medwall, Henry, *The Plays of Henry Medwall*, edited by Alan H. Nelson (Totowa, NJ: Rowman and Littlefield Inc, 1980).

Mexía, Pedro, *The Treasurie of auncient and moderne Times* (London, 1613).

Middleton, Thomas, *The Works of Thomas Middleton*, edited by A. H. Bullen (London: John C. Nimmo, 1885).

   Your Five Gallants (London, 1608).

Middleton, Thomas and Thomas Dekker, *The Roaring Girl*, edited by Paul A. Mulholland (Manchester: Manchester University Press, 1987).

   The Honest Whore, Part I (London, 1604).

Milton, John, *The Complete English Poetry of John Milton*, edited by John T. Shawcross (New York: New York University Press, 1963).

The Complete Prose Works (New Haven: Yale University Press, 1953–82).

The Riverside Milton, edited by Roy Flannagan (New York: Houghton Mifflin Company, 1998).

Montaigne, Michel de, *The Complete Works: Essays, Travel Journals, Letters*, translated by Donald M. Frame (London: Everyman Library, 2003).

The Diary of Montaigne's Journey to Italy in 1580 and 1581, translated with introduction and notes by E. J. Trechmann (New York: Harcourt, Brace and Company, 1929).

Munday, Anthony and others, revised by Henry Chettle, *Sir Thomas More: A Play*, edited by Vittorio Gabrieli and Giorgio Melchiori (Manchester, UK: Manchester University Press, 1990).

Musculus, Andreas, *Hosen Teuffel* (Frankfurt, 1555).

Nash, Thomas, *The Unfortunate Traveller*, edited by Philip Henderson, illustrated by Haydn Mackey (London: The Verona Society, 1930).

Niccols, Richard, *The Furies with Vertues Encomium* (London, 1614).

Ovid, *Ouids Metamorphosis Englished . . . by G. S.* (London, 1632).

The xv. Bookes of P. Ouidius Naso, entitled, Metamorphosis (London, 1584).

Paré, Ambroise, *On Monsters and Marvels*, translated with an introduction and notes by Janis L. Pallister (Chicago: University of Chicago Press, 1982).

The workes of that famous chirurgion Ambrose Parey translated out of Latine and compared with the French by Th. Johnson (London, 1634).

Pepys, Samuel, *The Diary of Samuel Pepys*, edited by Robert Latham and William Matthews (London: G. Bell and Sons, 1976).

Poimenander, Irenaeus [pseud for Godefridus Udemans] *Absaloms-hayr off Discovrs, daerinne ondersocht wordt, wat daer te houden zy vande wilde vliegende hayr-trossen, [. . .] die in onsen tijdt [. . .] gedragen worden* [Absalom's hair, or a Discourse in which is investigated, what there is to like about the wild, flying hair-tresses . . . which in our time . . . are being worn] (Dordrecht, 1643).

Prynne, William, *The Unlovelinesse of Love-lockes* (London, 1623).

Rabelais, François, *Gargantua and Pantagruel, Book 1 English* (London, 1653).

Revius, Jacobus, *Libertas Christiana circa usum capillitii defensa qua Sex ejusdem Disputationes de Coma ab exceptionibus viri cujusdam docti vindicantur* (Leiden, 1647).

Reynolds, Edward, *Three Treatises of The Vanity of the Creature, The Sinfulnesse of Sinne, The Life of Christ. Being the substance of severall sermons preached at Lincolns Inne*, Fourth Edition (London, 1652).

Rogers, Richard, *A Commentary upon the Whole Booke of Judges* (London, 1615).

Rowlands, Samuel, *Earth's Vanity* (London, 1632).

Saumaise, Claude de, *Epistola ad Andream Colvium: super Cap. XI. Primae ad Corinth. Epist. De Caesarie Virorum et Mulierum Coma* (Elzevier, 1644).

De Coma Dialogus, Primus. Caesarius et Curtius interlocutores (Leiden, 1645).

Saunders, Richard, *Palmistry, The Secrets thereof Disclosed* (London, 1664).

Schuyl, Florentius, *Raedt voor de scheer-siecke hair-cloovers*. [Advice for the shear-sick hair-splitters] ('s-Hertogenbosch, 1644).

Seasonable Advice . . . to the Professors of this backsliding Age (London, 1650).

Sennert, Daniel, *The Art of Chirurgery: Explained in six parts. . .being the whole fifth book of practical physick* (London, 1661).

Shakespeare, William. *The Norton Shakespeare*, edited by Stephen Greenblatt (New York: W. W. Norton and Co., 1997).

A Short, Compendious, and True description of the Roundheads, and the Long-Heads (London, 1642).

Sidney, Sir Philip, *The Countess of Pembroke's Arcadia*, intro by Carl Dennis (Kent, OH: Kent State University Press, 1970).

Spranger, Michael, *Hayrige vverelt waer in verthoont wert de heden-daegsche hair-cloovery* [Hairyworld, in which is shown the present-day hair-splitting] (Amsterdam, 1645).

Stubbes, Phillip, *Anatomy of Abuses* (London, 1583).

Synesius, *A Paradoxe, Proving by reason and example, that baldnessse is much better than bushie haire* (London, 1579).

W. T., *A Godly Profitable Treatise* (London, 1590).

Tardin, Jean, *Disquisitio Physiologica de Pilis* (Touron, 1609).

Taylor, John, *All the Works of John Taylor, the Water-Poet* (London, 1630).
    The Praise of Cleane Linnen (London, 1624).
    Superbiae Flagellum, or, the Whip of Pride (London, 1621).

The Treatyse answerynge the boke of berdes (London, 1541).

Twenty Lookes over all the Round-heads that ever Lived in the World (London, 1643).

Udall, Nicholas, *Thersites* (London, 1537).

Valeriano, Pierio, *Treatise written by Johan Valerian . . . entitled in Latin Pro Sacerdotum barbis* (London, 1533).

van Boxhorn, Marcus Zuerius, *Spiegeltien, vertoonende 't lanck hayr ende hayrlocken, by de oude Hollanders ende Zeelanders gedragen* [A mirror, showing the long hair and locks of hair, worn by the old (past) Hollanders and Zeelanders] (Middelburg, 1644).
    Spiegeltien, vertoonende 't cort hayr ende hayrlocken, by de oude Hollanders ende Zeelanders gedragen [A mirror, showing the short hair and locks of hair, worn by the old (past) Hollanders and Zeelanders] (Middelburg, 1644).

Vicary, Thomas, *The Englishemans Treasure, or Treasor for Englishmen* (London, 1586).

Vogellius, Hieronymus, *Eernstige klaghte over't openbaer krakkeel der heden-daegsche hayr-draghten* [Serious Complaint about the public wrangling over the current hairstyles] (Enkhuizen, 1645).

Wall, Thomas, *Spiritual Armour to Defend the Head from a Superfluity of Naughtiness* (London, 1688).
    God's Holy Order in Nature (London, 1690).

Walton, Bishop, *Considerator Considered* (London, 1659).

Wanley, Nathaniel, *Wonders of the Little World* (London, 1678).

Ward, Ned, *The London Spy Compleat in Eighteen Parts*, with an introduction by Ralph Straus (London: Casanova Society, 1924).

Webster, John, *The White Devil* (London, 1622).

Whately, William, *A Bride-Bush, or a Wedding Sermon* (London, 1619).

Wild, Robert, *The Benefice* (London, 1689).

Wilson, Robert, *The Three Lordes and Three Ladies of London* (London, 1590).

SECONDARY SOURCES

Althusser, Louis, "Ideology and Ideological State Apparatuses," in *Lenin and Philosophy and Other Essays*, translated by Ben Brewer (New York: Monthly Review, 1971).

Artificial Parts, Practical Lives: Modern Histories of Prosthetics, edited by Katherine Ott, David Serlin, and Stephen Mihm (New York: New York University Press, 2002).

Bach, Rebecca Anne, "Tennis Balls: *Henry V* and Testicular Masculinity; or, According to the *OED*, Shakespeare doesn't have any balls," *Renaissance Drama* 30 (1999–2001): 3–23.

Baldwin, Elizabeth, *Sumptuary Legislation and Personal Regulation in England* (Baltimore: Johns Hopkins Press, 1926).

Barish, Jonas, *The Antitheatrical Prejudice* (Berkeley: University of California Press, 1981).

Batterberry, Michael and Ariane Batterberry, *Mirror, Mirror: A Social History of Fashion* (New York: Holt, Rinehart and Winston, 1977).

Berger, Harry, "Second-World Prosthetics: Supplying Deficiencies of Nature in Renaissance Italy," in *Early Modern Visual Culture: Representation, Race, and Empire in Renaissance England*, edited by Peter Erickson and Clark Hulse (Philadelphia: University of Pennsylvania Press, 2000), 98–147.

"Impertinent Trifling: Desdemona's Handkerchief," *Shakespeare Quarterly*, 47:3 (1996): 235–50.

Beyond the Cultural Turn: New Directions in the Study of Society and Culture, edited by Victoria E. Bonnell and Lynn Hunt (Berkeley: University of California Press, 1999).

Binder, Pearl, *The Peacock's Tail* (London: Harrap, 1954).

Blackburne, Francis, *Memoirs of Thomas Hollis* (London, 1780).

Blending Genders: Social Aspects of Cross-Dressing and Sex-Changing, edited by Richard Ekins and David King (New York: Routledge, 1996).

The Body and Physical Difference: Discourses of Disability, edited by David T. Mitchell and Sharon L. Snyder (Ann Arbor: University of Michigan Press, 1997).

Boose, Lynda, "Scolding Brides and Bridling Scolds," *Shakespeare Quarterly*, 42:2 (1991): 179–213.

"Othello's Handkerchief: 'The Recognizance and Pledge of Love'," *English Literary Renaissance*, 5 (1975): 360–74.

Bornstein, Kate, *Gender Outlaw: On Men, Women and the Rest of us* (Routledge, 1994).

My Gender Workbook: How to Become Real Man, a Real Woman, the Real You, or Something Else Entirely (New York: Routledge, 1998).

Boucher, François, *20,000 Years of Fashion: The History of Costume and Personal Adornment*, 2nd edn. (New York: Harry N. Abrams, 1987).

Bourdieu, Pierre, *Outline for a Theory of Practice*, translated by Richard Nice (Cambridge: Cambridge University Press, 1977).

Braudel, Fernand, *Afterthoughts on Material Civilization and Capitalism*, translated by Patricia M. Ranum (Baltimore: Johns Hopkins University Press, 1977).

The Structures of Everyday Life: The Limits of the Possible, translated by Siân Reynolds (Berkeley: University of California Press, 1992).

Braun-Ronsdorf, M., *The History of the Handkerchief* (London: F. Lewis Publishers, Ltd., 1967).

Brown, James with Bruce Tucker, *James Brown, The Godfather of Soul*, foreword by Reverend Al Sharpton with Karen Hunter (New York: Thunder Mouth Press, 2002).

Brown, Kathleen, "'Changed . . . into the fashion of a man': The Politics of Sexual Difference in a Seventeenth-Century Anglo-American Settlement," *Journal of the History of Sexuality*, 6:2 (1995): 171–93.

Bruster, Douglas, *Drama and the Market in the Age of Shakespeare* (New York: Cambridge University Press, 1992).

Burckhardt, Jacob, *The Civilization of the Renaissance in Italy*, translated by S. G. C. Middlemore, with a new introduction by Peter Burke and notes by Peter Murray (New York: Penguin, 1990).

Butler, Judith, *Bodies that Matter: On the Discursive Limits of "Sex"* (New York: Routledge, 1993).

"Doing Justice to Someone: Sex Reassignment and Allegories of Transsexuality," *GLQ*, 7:4 (2001): 621–36.

The Psychic Life of Power: Theories in Subjection (Stanford: Stanford University Press, 1997).

Bynum, Carolyn Walker, *Fragmentation and Redemption: Essays on Gender and the Human Body in Medieval Religion* (New York: Zone Books, 1991).

The Resurrection of the Body in Western Christianity, 200–1336 (New York: Columbia University Press, 1995).

Cadden, Joan, *Meanings of Sex Difference in the Middle Ages: Medicine, Science, Culture* (Cambridge: Cambridge University Press, 1993).

Callaghan, Dympna, "'And all is semblative a woman's part': Body Politics and *Twelfth Night*," *Textual Practice*, 7 (1993): 428–52.

Colapinto, John, *As Nature Made Him: The Boy who was Raised as a Girl* (New York: Harper Collins, 2000).

A Collection of Ballads Originally Formed by John Selden (London, c.1575–1703).

Collections (Malone Society), general editor W. W. Greg (Oxford: The Malone Society, 1909).

Colman, Ernest Adrian Mackenzie, *The Dramatic Use of Bawdy in Shakespeare* (London: Longman, 1974).

Corson, Richard, *Fashions in Hair: The First Five Thousand Years* (New York: Hastings House, Publishers, 1965).

Couser, Thomas G., *Recovering Bodies: Illness, Disability, and Lifewriting* (Madison: University of Wisconsin Press, 1997).

Crane, Diana, *Fashion and its Social Agendas: Class, Gender, and Identity in Clothing* (Chicago: University of Chicago Press, 2000).

Crawford, Julie, *Marvelous Protestantism* (Baltimore: Johns Hopkins University Press, 2005).

Culler, Jonathan, *On Deconstruction: Theory and Criticism after Structuralism* (Ithaca: Cornell University Press, 1982).

Cunnington, C. W., P. Cunnington, and C. Beard, *A Dictionary of English Costume* (Philadelphia: Doufour, 1960).

Daston, Lorraine and Katharine Park, *Wonders and the Order of Nature, 1150–1750* (New York: Zone Books, 2001).

"The Hermaphrodite and the Orders of Nature: Sexual Ambiguity in Early Modern France," *GLQ: A Journal of Lesbian and Gay Studies*, 1:4 (1995): 419–38.

Davenport, Milla, *The Book of Costume* (New York: Crown, 1976).

de Certeau, Michel, *The Practice of Everyday Life*, translated by Steven Rendall (Berkeley: University of California Press, 1984).

de Grazia, Margreta, "The Ideology of Superfluous Things: *King Lear* as Period Piece," in *Subject and Object in Early Modern Culture*, edited by Margreta de Grazia, Maureen Quilligan, and Peter Stallybrass (Cambridge: Cambridge University Press, 1996).

Derrida, Jacques, *Of Grammatology*, translated by Gayatri Chakravorty Spivak (Baltimore: Johns Hopkins University Press, 1998).

The Truth in Painting, translated by Geoff Bennington and Ian McLeod (Chicago: University of Chicago Press, 1987).

Desire in the Renaissance: Psychoanalysis and Literature, edited by Valeria Finucci and Regina Schwartz (Princeton: Princeton University Press, 1994).

Dickey, Stephanie S., "Women Holding Handkerchiefs in Seventeenth-Century Dutch Portraits," in *Beeld en zelfbeeld in de Nederlandse kunst, 1550–1750 = Image and Self-Image in Netherlandish Art, 1550–1750*, edited by Reindert Falkenburg, Jan de Jong, Herman Roodenburg, and Frits Scholten, *Kunsthistorisch Jaarboek*, 45 (Zwolle: Waanders Uitgevers, 1995).

The Disability Studies Reader, edited by Lennard J. Davis (New York: Routledge, 1997).

Disability Studies: Definitions and Diversity, edited by Gary Kiger, Stephen C. Hey and J. Gary Linn (Salem, OR: Society for Disability Studies and Willamette University, 1994).

Documents relating to the Office of the Revels in the Time of Queen Elizabeth, edited by Albert Feuillerat (Louvain: A. Uystpruyst, 1908).

Doyle, Charles Clay, "The Hair and Beard of Thomas More," *Moreana* 28 (1981): 5–14.

Dreger, Alice Domurat, *Hermaphrodites and the Medical Invention of Sex* (Cambridge, MA: Harvard University Press, 1998).

Dulaure, Jacques Antoine, *Pogonologia, or a Philosophical and Historical Essay on Beards* (Exeter: R. Thorn, 1786).

Dynasties: Painting in Tudor and Jacobean England 1530–1630, edited by Karen Hearn (London: Tate Publishing, 1995).

Eales, Jacqueline, *Puritans and Roundheads: The Harleys of Brampton Bryan and the Outbreak of the English Civil War* (Cambridge: Cambridge University Press, 1990).

Elias, Norbert, *The Civilizing Process, The History of Manners*, translated by Edmund Jephcott (New York: Urizen Books, 1978).

Epstein, Julia, "Either/Or – Neither/Both: Sexual Ambiguity and the Ideology of Gender," *Genders*, 7 (1990): 99–142.

Fangé, Augustin, *Mémoires pour servir a l'histoire de la barbe de l'homme* (Liège: Jean-François Broncart, 1774).

Fausto-Sterling, Anne, *Sexing the Body: Gender Politics and the Construction of Sexuality* (New York: Basic Books, 2000).

Feinberg, Leslie, *Trans Liberation: Beyond Pink or Blue* (Boston: Beacon Press, 1998).

Fish, Stanley, "Spectacle and Evidence in *Samson Agonistes*," *Critical Inquiry*, 15 (1989): 556–86.

Fisher, Will, "The Renaissance Beard: Masculinity in Early Modern England and Europe," *Renaissance Quarterly*, 54:1 (2001): 155–87.

"'His Majesty the Beard': Facial Hair and Masculinity on the Early Modern Stage," in *Staged Properties: Props and Property in Early Modern England*, edited by Natasha Korda and Jonathan Gil Harris (Cambridge: Cambridge University Press, 2002), 230–57.

Fletcher, Anthony, *Gender, Sex, and Subordination in England 1500–1800* (New Haven: Yale University Press, 1995).

Forse, James, *Art Imitates Business: Commercial and Political Influences on the Elizabethan Theater* (Bowling Green, OH: Bowling Green State University Press, 1993).

Foucault, Michel, *Discipline and Punish: The Birth of the Prison* (New York: Penguin, 1977).

Freud, Sigmund, *Civilization and its Discontents* in *The Standard Edition of the Complete Psychological Works of Sigmund Freud*, translated under the general editorship of James Strachey (London: Hogarth Press, 1961).

Jokes and their Relation to the Unconscious, translated by James Strachey (NY: Norton, 1963).

On Dreams. The Freud Reader, edited by Peter Gay (New York: W. W. Norton and Company Inc., 1995).

Frye, Roland, *Milton's Imagery and the Visual Arts: Iconographic Tradition in the Epic Poems* (Princeton: Princeton University Press, 1978).

Fumerton, Patricia, *Cultural Aesthetics: Renaissance Literature and the Practice of Social Ornament* (Chicago: University of Chicago Press, 1991).

Fuss, Diana, *Essentially Speaking: Feminism, Nature and Difference* (New York: Routledge, 1989).

Gair, W. Reavley, *The Children of Paul's: The Story of a Theatre Company, 1553–1608* (Cambridge: Cambridge University Press, 1982).

Gaisser, Julia Haig, *Pierio Valeriano: On the Ill Fortune of Learned Men* (Ann Arbor: The University of Michigan Press, 1999).

Garber, Marjorie, *Vested Interest: Cross-Dressing and Cultural Anxiety* (New York: Routledge, 1992).

Gilbert, Ruth, *Early Modern Hermaphrodites: Sex and Other Stories* (New York: Palgrave, 2002).

Goldberg, Jonathan, *Writing Matter: From the Hands of the English Renaissance* (Stanford: Stanford University Press, 1990).

Gould, Stephen J., *The Mismeasure of Man*, revised and expanded edition (New York: W. W. Norton, 1996).

Gowing, Laura, *Common Bodies: Women, Touch and Power in Seventeenth-Century England* (New Haven: Yale University Press, 2003).

Gray, John, *The World of Hair: A Scientific Companion*, contributors R. Dawber and
    C. Gummer (London: Proctor and Gamble Haircare Research Centre, 1997).
Green, Juana, "The Semster's Wares: Merchandising and Marrying in *The Fair Maid
    of the Exchange* (1607)," *Renaissance Quarterly*, 53:4 (2000): 1084–118.
Greenblatt, Stephen, *Shakespearean Negotiations* (Berkeley: University of California
    Press, 1988).
Griggs, Claudine, *S/he: Changing Sex, Changing Clothes* (New York: Berg, 1998).
Guillory, John, "Dalila's House: *Samson Agonistes* and the Sexual Division of Labor,"
    in *Rewriting the Renaissance*, edited by Margaret W. Ferguson et al. (Chicago:
    University of Chicago Press, 1986), 106–22.
Haraway, Donna J., *Simians, Cyborgs, and Women: The Reinvention of Nature* (New
    York: Routledge, 1991).
Harré, Rom, "Sex and Gender, Man and Woman," in *Body and Flesh: A Philosophical
    Reader*, edited by Donn Welton (London: Blackwell, 1998), 11–27.
Heroic Armor of the Italian Renaissance: Filippo Negroli and his Contemporaries,
    catalog by Stuart W. Pyhrr and José-A. Godoy (New York: Metropolitan Museum
    of Art, 1998).
Hibbert, Christopher, *Cavaliers and Roundheads: The English Civil War, 1642–1649*
    (New York: C. Scribner's Sons).
Hill, Christopher, *Milton and the English Revolution* (London: Faber and Faber, 1977).
Historical Collections of Private Passages of State, IV, edited by John Rushworth
    (London, 1721).
A History of Private Life, edited by Philippe Ariès and Georges Duby (Cambridge,
    MA: Belknap Press of Harvard University Press, 1987).
Hogrefe, Pearl, *Tudor Women: Commoners and Queens* (Ames, IA: Iowa State
    University Press, 1975)
Hollander, Anne, *Seeing through Clothes* (New York: Viking Press, 1978).
    Sex and Suits: The Evolution of Modern Dress (New York: Knopf, 1994).
Horowitz, Elliott, "The New World and the Changing Face of Europe," *Sixteenth
    Century Journal*, 28.4 (1997): 1181–201.
Howard, Jean, *The Stage and Social Struggle in Early Modern England* (New York:
    Routledge, 1994).
Howard, Jean and Phyllis Rackin, *Engendering a Nation: A Feminist Account of
    Shakespeare's English Histories* (New York: Routledge, 1997).
Hutson, Lorna, *The Usurer's Daughter: Male Friendship and Fictions of Women in
    Sixteenth-Century England* (New York: Routledge, 1994).
Ingram, Martin, *Church Courts, Sex, and Marriage in England, 1570–1640*
    (Cambridge: Cambridge University Press, 1987).
James, William, "The Consciousness of Lost Limbs," in *Essays on Psychology*
    (Cambridge: Harvard University Press, 1983).
Jardine, Lisa, "Twins and Travesties: Gender, Dependency, and Sexual Availability in
    Twelfth Night," in *Erotic Politics: Desire on the Renaissance Stage*, edited by
    Susan Zimmerman (New York: Routledge, 1992), 27–38.
    "Boy Actors, Female Roles, Elizabethan Eroticism," in *Staging the Renaissance:
    Reinterpretations of Elizabethan and Jacobean Drama*, edited by David Scott
    Kastan and Peter Stallybrass (New York: Routledge, 1991), 57–67.
Jenkins, Elizabeth, *Elizabeth and Leicester* (New York: Coward-McCann, Inc., 1961).

Jones, Ann Rosalind and Peter Stallybrass, *Renaissance Clothing and the Materials of Memory* (Cambridge: Cambridge University Press, 2000).

Jordan, Neil, *The Crying Game*, in *A Neil Jordan Reader* (New York: Vintage International, 1993).

Judovitz, Dalia, *Subjectivity and Representation in Descartes: The Origins of Modernity* (Cambridge: Cambridge University Press, 1988).

Kerrigan, William, "Atoms Again: The Deaths of Individualism," in *Taking Chances: Derrida, Psychoanalysis, and Literature*, edited by Joseph H. Smith and William Kerrigan (Baltimore: Johns Hopkins University Press, 1984), 86–107.

King, T. J., *Casting in Shakespeare's Plays: London Actors and their Roles, 1590–1642* (Cambridge: Cambridge University Press, 1992).

Knott, Jan, "Bottom and the Boys," *New Theater Quarterly*, 9:36 (1993): 307–15.

Korda, Natasha, *Shakespeare's Domestic Economies: Gender and Property in Early Modern England* (Philadelphia: University of Pennsylvania Press, 2002).

Laqueur, Thomas, *Making Sex: Body and Gender From the Greeks to Freud* (Cambridge, MA: Harvard University Press, 1990).

Laver, James, *The Concise History of Costume and Fashion* (New York: Scribners, 1969).

Lefebvre, Henri, *Everyday Life in the Modern World*, translated by Sacha Rabinovitch, with a new introduction by Philip Walker (New Brunswick, NJ: Transaction, 1999).

Lester, Katherine Morris and Bess Viola Ierke, *Accessories of Dress* (Peoria, IL.: Manual Arts Press, 1940)

Lukes, Steven, *Individualism* (London: Basil Blackwell, 1973).

McAtee, W. L., *On Codpieces* (Chapel Hill, 1954).

MacCulloch, Diarmaid, *Thomas Cranmer, A Life* (New Haven: Yale University Press, 1996).

MacIntyre, Jean, *Costumes and Scripts in the Elizabethan Theaters* (Edmonton: University of Alberta Press, 1992).

McLuhan, Marshall, *Understanding Media: The Extensions of Man* (New York: McGraw-Hill, 1964).

McMillin, Scott, *The Elizabethan Theater and the Book of Sir Thomas More* (Ithaca: Cornell University Press, 1987).

Marks, A. A., *A Treatise on Artificial Limbs with Rubber Hands and Feet* (New York: A. A. Marks, 1903).

Masten, Jeffrey, *Textual Intercourse: Collaboration, Authorship, and Sexualities in Renaissance Drama* (Cambridge: Cambridge University Press, 1997).

"*More* or Less: Editing the Collaborative," *Shakespeare Studies*, 29 (2001): 109–31.

"Playwrighting: Authorship and Collaboration," in *A New History of Early English Drama*, edited by John D. Cox and David Scott Kastan, foreword by Stephen J. Greenblatt (New York: Columbia University Press, 1995), 357–82.

Miller, Leo, *Milton's Portraits: An Impartial Inquiry into their Authentication*, (Athens, OH: [N. S.], 1976).

Montrose, Louis, "The Elizabethan Subject and the Spenserian Text," in *Literary Theory/Renaissance Texts*, edited by Patricia Parker and David Quint (Baltimore: Johns Hopkins University Press, 1986).

Neill, Michael, "'Ampitheatres of the Body': Playing with Hands on the Shakespearean Stage," *Shakespeare Survey 48* (Cambridge: Cambridge University Press, 1995), 23–50.

The New Cultural History, edited by Lynn Hunt (Berkeley: University of California Press, 1989).

Newman, Karen, *Fashioning Femininity and English Renaissance Drama*, foreword by Catharine R. Stimpson (Chicago: University of Chicago Press, 1991).

Nichols, John, *The Progresses and Public Processions of Queen Elizabeth, among which are interspersed other solemnities, public expenditures, and remarkable events during the reign of the illustrious Princess* (London: John Nichols and Son, 1823).

Norton, Mary Beth, *Founding Mothers and Fathers: Gendered Power and the Forming of American Society* (New York: Knopf, 1996).

O'Connor, Erin, *Raw Material: Producing Pathology in Victorian Culture* (Durham, NC: Duke University Press, 2000).

O'Hara, Diana, "The Language of Tokens and the Making of Marriage," *Rural History* (1992): 1–40.

Orgel, Stephen, *Impersonations: The Performance of Gender in Shakespeare's England* (Cambridge: Cambridge University Press, 1996).

Palmer, Andrew Smyth, *The Samson Saga and its Place in Comparative Religion* (New York: Arno Press, 1977).

Parker, William Riley, *Milton: A Biography* (Oxford: Oxford University Press, 1968).

Paster, Gail Kern, *The Body Embarrassed: Drama and the Disciplines of Shame in Early Modern England* (Ithaca: Cornell University Press, 1993).

Percy Society, *Poetry, Ballads, and Popular Literature of the Middle Ages* (London, 1849).

Perper, T., *Sex Signals: The Biology of Love* (Philadelphia: ISI Press, 1985).

Persel, Jeffrey C., "Bragueta Humanística, or Humanism's Codpiece," *Sixteenth Century Journal*, 28 (1997): 79–99.

Peterkin, Allan, *One Thousand Beards: A Cultural History of Facial Hair* (Vancouver: Arsenal Pulp Press, 2001).

Poe, Edgar Allen, "The Man that Was All Used Up," in *Collected Works of Edgar Allan Poe, Tales and Sketches, 1831–1842*, edited by Thomas Ollive Mabbott (Cambridge, MA: The Belknap Press, 1978).

Poovey, Mary, *Uneven Developments: The Ideological Work of Gender in mid-Victorian England* (Chicago: University of Chicago Press, 1988).

Pullman, Bernard, *The Atom in the History of Human Thought*, translated by Axel Reisinger (New York: Oxford University Press, 1998).

Rambuss, Richard, "Machinehead," *Camera Obscura: A Journal of Feminism, Culture, and Media Studies*, 42 (1999): 97–122.

Randall, Dale B. J., "The Rank and Earthy Background of Certain Physical Symbols in *The Duchess of Malfi*," *Renaissance Drama*, 18 (1987): 171–203.

Records of Early English Drama, Cambridge, Volume 1: The Records, edited by Alan H. Nelson (Toronto: University of Toronto Press, 1989).

Renaissance Culture and the Everyday, edited by Patricia Fumerton and Simon Hunt (Philadelphia: University of Pennsylvania Press, 1999).

Reynolds, Reginald, *Beards: Their Social Standing, Religious Involvements, Decorative Possibilities and Value in Offence and Defence through the Ages* (London: Allen and Unwin Ltd., 1950).

Rhymer, Thomas, "A Short View of Tragedy" in *The Critical Works of Thomas Rhymer*, edited by Curt A. Zimansky (New Haven: Yale University Press, 1956).

Ribeiro, Aileen, *Dress and Morality* (New York: Holmes and Meier Publishers, Inc., 1986).

Rich, Adrienne, *Blood, Bread and Poetry: Selected Prose 1979–85* (New York: W. W. Norton, 1986).

Roche, Daniel, *A History of Everyday Things: The Birth of Consumption in France, 1600–1800*, translated by Brian Pearce (Cambridge: Cambridge University Press, 2000).

Rogers, John, *The Matter of Revolution: Science, Poetry, and Politics in the Age of Milton* (Ithaca: Cornell University Press, 1996).

"The Secret of *Samson Agonistes*," *Milton Studies*, 33 (1997): 111–32.

Roper, Lyndal, *Oedipus and the Devil: Witchcraft, Sexuality and Religion in Early Modern Europe* (London: Routledge, 1994).

Rowe, Katherine, *Dead Hands: Fictions of Agency, Renaissance to Modern* (Stanford: Stanford University Press, 2000).

"God's Handy Worke," in *The Body in Parts: Fantasies of Corporeality in Early Modern Europe*, edited by David Hillman and Carla Mazzio (New York: Routledge, 1997), 285–313.

Ryan, Alan, "Hobbes and Individualism," in *Perspectives on Thomas Hobbes*, edited by G. A. J. Rogers and Alan Ryan (Oxford: Oxford University Press, 1988).

Sacks, Oliver, *The Man who Mistook his Wife for a Hat, and other Clinical Tales* (New York: Harper and Row, 1970).

Sawday, Jonathan, *The Body Emblazoned: Dissection and the Human Body in Renaissance Culture* (New York: Routledge, 1995).

Scarry, Elaine, *The Body in Pain: The Making and Unmaking of the World* (New York: Oxford University Press, 1985).

Schiebinger, Londa, *Nature's Body: Gender in the Making of Modern Science* (Boston: Beacon Press, 1993).

Schiffer, James, "Macbeth and the Bearded Women," in *In Another Country: Feminist Perspectives on Renaissance Drama*, edited by Dorothea Kehler and Susan Baker (Metuchen, NJ: The Scarecrow Press, Inc., 1991), 205–18.

Schoenfeldt, Michael C., *Bodies and Selves in Early Modern England: Physiology and Inwardness in Spenser, Shakespeare, Herbert, and Milton* (Cambridge: Cambridge University Press, 1999).

Schor, Naomi, *Reading in Detail: Aesthetics and the Feminine* (New York: Routledge, 1987).

Severn, Bill, *The Long and the Short of It: Five Thousand Years of Fun and Fury over Hair* (New York: David McKay Company, Inc, 1972).

Shapiro, Michael, *Children of the Revels: The Boy Companies of Shakespeare's Time and their Plays* (New York: Columbia University Press, 1977).

Siraisi, Nancy G., *Medieval and Early Renaissance Medicine: An Introduction to Knowledge and Practice* (Chicago: University of Chicago Press, 1990).

Skinner, Quentin, *Reason and Rhetoric in the Philosophy of Hobbes* (Cambridge: Cambridge University Press, 1996).

Smith, Bruce, *Shakespeare and Masculinity* (Oxford: Oxford University Press, 2000).

Smith, Nigel, *Literature and Revolution in England, 1640–1660* (New Haven: Yale University Press, 1994).

Smith, Paul, *Discerning the Subject*, foreword by John Mowitt (Minneapolis: University of Minnesota Press, 1988).

Snow, Edward A., "Sexual Anxiety and the Male Order of Things in *Othello*," *English Literary Renaissance*, 10 (1980): 384–412.

Sofer, Andrew, *The Stage Life of Props* (Ann Arbor: University of Michigan Press, 2003).

Stallybrass, Peter, "Patriarchal Territories: The Body Enclosed," in *Rewriting the Renaissance*, edited by Margaret W. Ferguson et al. (Chicago: University of Chicago Press, 1986), 123–42.

"Shakespeare, the Individual, and the Text," in *Cultural Studies*, edited by Lawrence Grossberg et al. (New York: Routledge, 1992), 593–612.

"Worn Worlds: Clothing, Mourning and the Life of Things," *Yale Review*, 81 (1993): 35–50.

Steele, Valerie, *Fetish: Fashion, Sex, and Power* (Oxford: Oxford University Press, 1996).

Steinberg, Leo, *The Sexuality of Christ in Renaissance Art and Modern Oblivion* (New York: Pantheon/October, 1983).

Strong, Roy C., *Tudor and Jacobean Portraits* (London: HMSO, 1969).

Sutton, John, *Philosophy and Memory Traces: Descartes to Connectionism* (Cambridge: Cambridge University Press, 1998).

Tanner, Lawrence E., *Westminster School: A History* (London: Country Life Ltd., 1934).

Taylor, Gary, *Castration: An Abbreviated History of Western Manhood* (New York: Routledge, 2000).

Thirsk, Joan, *Economic Policy and Projects: The Development of a Consumer Society in Early Modern England* (Oxford: Oxford University Press, 1978).

Thompson, Rosemarie Garland, *Extraordinary Bodies: Figuring Physical Disability in American Culture and Literature* (New York: Columbia University Press, 1997).

Tilley, Morris Palmer, *A Dictionary of Proverbs in England in the Sixteenth and Seventeenth Centuries* (Ann Arbor: University of Michigan Press, 1950).

Traub, Valerie, *The Renaissance of Lesbianism in Early Modern England* (Cambridge: Cambridge University Press, 2002).

Desire and Anxiety: Circulations of Sexuality (New York: Routledge, 1992).

Unseen Genders: Beyond the Binaries, edited by Felicity Haynes and Tarquam McKenna (New York: Peter Lang, 2001).

Van Melsen, Andrew G., *From Atomos to Atom: A History of the Concept of the Atom* (New York: Harper Torchbooks, 1960).

Vicary, Grace Q., "Visual Art as Social Data: The Renaissance Codpiece," *Cultural Anthropology* (1989): 3–25.

Von Boehn, Max, *Modes and Manners: Sixteenth Century*, translated by J. Joshua (London: Harrap, 1932).

White, Allon, *Carnival, Hysteria, and Writing: Collected Essays and Autobiography* (Oxford: Oxford University Press, 1993).

Wilchins, Riki Anne, *Read My Lips: Sexual Subversion and the End of Gender* (Ithaca: Firebrand, 1997).

Williams, Gordon, *A Dictionary of Sexual Language and Imagery in Shakespearean and Stuart Literature* (London: The Athlone Press, 1994).

Williams, Neville, *All the Queen's Men: Elizabeth I and her Courtiers* (New York: Macmillan, 1972).

Williams, Raymond, *Keywords: A Vocabulary of Culture and Society* (New York: Oxford University Press, 1976).

Williams, Tamsyn, "Magnetic Figures: Polemical Prints of the English Revolution," in *Renaissance Bodies: The Human Figure in English Culture, c. 1540–1660*, edited by Lucy Gent and Nigel Llewellyn (London: Reaktion Books, 1990), 86–110.

Wills, David, *Prosthesis* (Stanford: Stanford University Press, 1995).

Wittreich, Joseph, *Interpreting Samson Agonistes* (Princeton: Princeton University Press, 1986).

Index

Althusser, Louis 26
Andreadis, Harriette 174
Ariès, Philippe 25
Arnold, John 84
Artificial Parts, Practical Lives 31
Arundel, Countess of 40
As Nature Made Him (see Colapinto)
Aubrey, John 149
Saint Augustine 130

Bach, Rebecca Anne 69
Bacon, Francis 15, 109
Bakhtin, Mikhail 42
The Ballad of the Beard 95
Barbatius, Joannes 102, 191
Barish, Jonas 11
Barry, Lording
  Ram Alley 78, 88, 107
beard
  and eunuchs 111
  and gender in 1970s 3
  and marriage discourses 109–11
  and social roles of men 106–8
  bearded women 112–17, 122
  books about 102, 191
  constituting masculinity 87–93, 94
  different styles of 94
  in plays performed by boys'
    companies 86–90
  in plays performed by adult companies 3,
    10, 42, 159, 167, 170
  in portraiture 94
  men without beards 117–19
  prosthetic nature of 87, 90, 91–3, 99,
    119–28
  use of false beards on stage 83–93
Beatles, The 3
Beckmann, Christian and Valentius
    Hartungus 102
Berger, Harry 45, 54, 177
Billingsley, Nicholas 102

body, concept of 27–9
body parts (see also beard; hair
    of the head; testicles; penis)
  body hair 1, 2, 4, 65
  breasts 1, 2, 4, 20
  chromosomes 1, 2, 4, 9, 10
  face 1, 2, 4
  fundament 2
  thighs 4
  voice 1, 2, 9, 10, 88, 113
Bonnell, Victoria and Lynn Hunt 177
The Book of Sir Thomas More 85,
    89, 124–8
Boorde, Andrew 103
Boose, Lynda 45, 53
Bornstein, Kate 108.9
Bourdieu, Pierre 25, 40
boy actors
  "in drag" when playing men 89
  use of false beards 83–90
boys
  characteristics of 88, 109
  gendered difference between boys
    and men, 87–93, 108–11
Braudel, Fernand 25
Braun-Ronsdorf, M. 38, 55
Breitenberg, Mark 13
Brown, James 129, 131
Brown, Thomas 102
Bruster, Douglas 41, 45
Bulwer, John 46, 48, 59, 66, 102,
    111, 116, 118, 120, 123,
    167, 170
Burckhardt, Jacob 159, 160
Butler, Judith 18–24, 62, 104, 157
Bynum, Caroline Walker 11, 122,
    168, 169, 178

Callaghan, Dympna 11, 122, 168,
    169, 178
Carew, Thomas 182

Cartwright, William
  The Ordinary 109
Charles I 94
Chase, Cheryl 172
Chaucer, Geoffrey 92
Clarke, Deborah 149
clothing (see also codpiece; handkerchiefs)
  and gender identity 4, 10–17, 19–24,
    32, 64, 65, 86, 115
  and sexual transformation see sexual
    transformation
Cocles, Bartholomeus 111
codpiece
  and competing models of masculinity,
    69–70, 73–4, 81
  as phallic 59, 67
  as testicular/scrotal 59, 68, 74
  as fertility symbol 73
  condemnations of 66, 76–8
  conflated with male genitalia 66–7, 77
  constituting masculinity 12, 20, 64–8, 77
  different types of 20, 59
Colapinto, John 172
Coleman, E. A. M. 50
Constable, Giles 190, 191
Corson, Richard 102, 142, 190
coverture
  legal concept of 137
  related to discourses on hair 137
  related to headdresses 137
Cranmer, Thomas 100
Crawford, Julie 193
Crompton, Hugh 102, 121
Crooke, Helkiah 8, 15, 70, 102, 105,
    106, 108, 122, 123, 167, 170
The Crying Game (see Neil Jordan)
Culpepper, Nicholas 70, 102, 105, 106, 122
cultural history 177

Daston, Lorraine
  on the power of the imagination 14, 15
Daston, Lorraine and Katharine Park 2,
    4, 50, 193, 198
de Bruyn, Frans 196
de Certeau, Michel 20–2, 23, 24, 26, 41, 56
de Grazia, Margreta 178
Dekker, Thomas
  Blurt Master-Constable 50
  Gulls Hornbook 130
  Shoemaker's Holiday 109, 182
Democritus 160
Derrida, Jacques 26, 93
Descartes, René 165, 482.6, 499.5
Dickey, Stephanie 40, 50
Digby, Kenelm 168

disability studies 179
Donne, John 183
Doyle, Charles Clay 195
Dreger, Alice 2, 197
Dudley, Robert (1st Earl of Leicester)
    36–8, 42, 44
Dunton, John 72

Edward VI 74
Elias, Norbert 25, 33, 40
Elizabeth I 36–8, 42–4
essentialism/constructivism debate
    (see also sex/gender) 28.31
Evelyn, John 84, 112, 113, 118
everyday life, history of 25–6, 177

Fausto-Sterling, Anne 172
femininity (see gender; coverture;
    handkerchiefs; hair of the head;
    headdresses and wimples)
  and adornment 145–6, 152, 155–6
  and beard 112–17
  and coverture 137–8
  and the hair of the head 129–58
  and handkerchief 36–58
  and women's work 74
  resistance to ideology of 33, 57
  social roles of women 112, 113
  violence used to regulate 116–17, 118
Fish, Stanley 153
Flannagan, Roy 150
Fletcher, Anthony 173, 175
Forse, James 188
Foucault, Michel 25
Foxe, John 99, 124
Freud 72, 78, 123, 126
  on "auxiliary organs" 1, 27, 30–1
Fumerton, Patricia 171
Fuss, Diana 6, 17, 19, 120, 172

Gair, W. Reavley 86
Galen 6, 70
Gamage, William 80
Garber, Marjorie 68, 188
gender (see also boys; femininity; masculinity;
    sex/gender distinction; sexual
    transformation)
  and Galenic medicine 6, 10, 13, 17, 41, 50
  and prosthetic parts 3, 13, 17
  religious framework for 15, 106, 141,
    327.6, 332.9
  genitocentric 7, 173, 174
  how constituted 2–3, 17; agency and social
    control in this process 2–3, 17
  feminist reconceptualization of 4, 17–19, 22

rooted in fixed "nature" 5, 6, 7, 64
and sex/gender schema 4, 6
viewed as developmental process 4
viewed as dimorphic 7
gestures of courtesy 46–9
Gilbert, Ruth 2
Giles, Thomas 84
Goffe, Thomas 168
Goldberg, Jonathan 45, 49
Gould, Stephen J.
critique of nature/culture binary 5, 194
Gowing, Laura 175
Green, Juana 40, 58
Greenblatt, Stephen 8, 11, 32
Guazzo, Francesco Maria 8, 12, 14
Guillory, John 152, 153

Haec Vir 64, 107
Hair 3
hair of the head (see also coverture;
headdresses and wimples; Milton;
Roundheads and Cavaliers)
and civil war politics 142–7
books about 129
bound vs. unbound 145–6; and Protestant
condemnation of adornment 146, 440.6
compared with beard growth 133
constituting gender 1, 2, 4, 65; modern vs.
early modern notions of 378.16–405.5
definitions of "long" and "short" hair 206
humoral explanations of hair growth 132
in 1960s 3, 131; compared with
seventeenth century 131
in satirical literature 130
in sermons 130, 145
in stories of sexual transformation 9
malleability of 134, 140–2
religious framework for 139–41
women's hair naturally longer
than men's 18
Hall, Thomas 123
Hall, Thomas(ine) 10–11
handkerchiefs
and gender formation 12, 22, 40–55
as gifts 36–8
as prosthesis 53–5, 57
as tokens of love 38
in Othello 44–58
"new" cultural artifact 38
hands (see also gestures of courtesy)
and erotic agency 51
hand kissing 46
hand wringing 48
in Othello 45–58
palm reading 50

Haraway, Donna 17, 24, 30
Harrington, John 124
Harris, Jonathan Gil and Natasha
Korda 187
Hayman, Robert 75
headdresses and wimples
and coverture 137
disappearance of 137, 138, 142
related to the Reformation 142
Hearn, Karen 74
Hempstall, Anne 130
Henry I 142
Henry VIII 71–4, 103
Hic Mulier 12–13, 16–17, 131
Hill, Thomas, 102, 107
Hobbes, Thomas 162–5
Holbein 74
Hollander, Anne 19–20, 23, 26, 53, 77
Holme, Randall 88, 110, 175
Holyday, Barten 66, 77
Horowitz, Elliott 171, 195
Hospinien, Rodolph 191
Hotman, Antoine 8, 103
Howard, Jean 11, BN–86, 180, 182
Howard, Jean and Phyllis Rackin 69, 82
Howard, Thomas (4th Duke of Norfolk)
36–8, 42, 44
Huarte, Juan 9–10
Hunt, Lynn (see Victoria Bonnell)
Hutson, Lorna 181

imagination, power of 14, 15
Iphis and Ianthe 14, 174

James I 83, 94
James, William 32
Jardine, Lisa 88
Jones, Ann Rosalind and Peter
Stallybrass 11, 32
Jonson, Ben
Epicoene 109
Jordan, Neil 1, 7
Judovitz, Dalia 203
Junius, Adrianus 130

Kendall, Thomas 83–5
Kerckhoven, Johannes Polyander a 83–5
Kerrigan, William 166
King, T. J. 189
Kirchmaier, Georg Caspar 102
Kirkham, Edward 83–5, 160
Knox, John 94
Korda, Natasha (see also Jonathan
Gil Harris) 45, 171
Kynaston, Francis 78

Laqueur, Thomas 8, 23, 87, 105, 176
Lefebvre, Henri 25
Leicester (see Dudley, Robert)
Lemnius, Laevinus 121
Lester, Katherine Morris 38
Leucippus 160
A Looking-Glasse for Women 129, 146, 156
Lukes, Stephen 200

MacCulloch, Diarmaid 191
McElwee, Kevin J. 197
McLuhan, Marshall 24
McMillin, Scott 189
Marston, John 65, 66, 76, 77, 82
masculinity (see also beard; boys; codpiece;
    gender; testicles)
  and beard 83–128
  and castration 69
  and eunuchs 111
  and hair 130–42, 144–6, 147–57
  and indivisibility 152–5
  and martial ability 12, 117–18
  and rape 69, 72
  and reproduction 69, 73, 107–10, 112
  and sexual penetration 69, 72, 73
  social roles of men 106–8
Massinger, Philip
  The Guardian 109
Masten, Jeffrey 125
The Matrix 89.11
Medwall, Henry 64, 66
Middleton, Thomas
  Your Five Gallants 78
  A Mad World My Masters 89–90,
    91, 93, 119, 120
  and Thomas Dekker
  The Roaring Girl 78
  The Honest Whore 79, 82
Miller, Leo 149
Milton, John
  and Royalist writers on hair 151–6
  Defense of the English People 145
  Milton's hair 149
  hair in Paradise Lost 147–9, 156, 157
  hair in Samson Agonistes 147, 148
Montaigne, Michel de
  story about Marie/Germain 8–9, 10,
    14–15, 111
Montrose, Louis 74
Munroe, Lucy 188
Musculus, Andreas 67

Nashe, Thomas 74
nature, meanings of in early modern period 5

Neill, Michael 45, 52
Newman, Karen 45, 171
Niccols, Richard 64, 65
Norfolk (see Howard, Thomas)

O'Connor, Erin 30, 85
Ogel, John 30, 85
O'Hara, Diana 38
Orgel, Stephen 11, 88
Ovid 8, 14

Palmer, Andrew Smyth 150
Paré, Ambroise 1–2, 3, 8, 13
Park, Katharine (see Lorraine Daston)
Parker, William Riley 149, 151
Paster, Gail Kern 41, 172, 173, 174
penis (see also codpiece)
  and masculinity 1, 3, 69
  opposed to testicles 69
Pepys, Samuel 73, 113, 115
Percels, Jeffrey C. 184
Peterkin, Allan 172
Petrarch 42
Poe, Edgar Allan 29
Poovey, Mary 186
prosthesis
  coded as superfluous 26, 27, 31–2, 54
  liminality of 26, 27, 31–2, 54
  and concept of "the body" 27–9
  and identity formation 44
  modern fantasies of 27, 29–31
  detachability of 44
Prynne, William 16

Rabelais, François 77
Rackin, Phyllis (see Jean Howard and
    Phyllis Rackin)
Rambuss, Richard 179
Randall, Dale B. J. 183
Reimer, David 172
Renaissance Culture and the Everyday 25
Revius, Jacobus 130, 145
Reynolds, Edward 130
Reynolds, Reginald 190
Rhymer, Thomas 45, 190
Ribeiro, Aileen 59
Ribera, José de
  The Bearded Woman 113–16
Roche, Daniel 25
Rogers, John 161
Rogers, Richard 151
Roper, Lyndal 67
Roundheads and Cavaliers, derivation
    of terms 396

Rowe, Katherine 45, 52
Rowlands, Samuel 130
Ryan, Alan 202

Sacks, Oliver 31
Sandys, George 8
Saumaise, Claude de (Salmasius)
    antagonist of Milton 145
    books on hair 130, 145–6, 151, 155
    Defensio Regia 145
Sawday, Jonathan 166
Scarry, Elaine 203
Schiebinger, Londa 171, 195
Schoenfeldt, Michel C. 173
Schutzman, Julie 196
Seasonable advice 129, 130, 136, 137, 149
Sennert, Daniel 102, 122
sex/gender distinction (see essentialism/
        constructivism)
    in the early modern period 4, 5, 7, 172
    related to primary, secondary, tertiary
        sexual characteristics 4, 5, 17,
        64, 111, 120
    in contemporary society 17–242
sexual transformation
    in the early modern period 6, 8–15
    and "peripheral" body parts 8–10, 111–12
    in contemporary society 7, 173
Shakespeare, William (see handkerchiefs;
        hands; gestures of courtesy)
    As You Like It 88, 91, 107
    Coriolanus 91, 117
    Hamlet 46
    Henry IV, Part 1 118
    Macbeth 112
    Measure for Measure 51
    A Midsummer Night's Dream 91–3, 119
    Much Ado about Nothing 52, 110, 119
    Othello 44–58
    Romeo and Juliet 47–8
    Taming of the Shrew 53
    Troilus and Cressida 108
    Twelfth Night 11, 51
    Two Gentlemen of Verona 65, 75
    Venus and Adonis 50
    The Winter's Tale 47, 52
Shiffer, James 193
Sidney, Philip
    Arcadia 117
The Six Million Dollar Man 30
Skinner, Quentin 162
Smith, Bruce 189
Smith, Nigel 165
Smith, Paul 159

Snow, Edward A. 45
Sofer, Andrew 45
The Somerset Treaty Portrait 94
Stallybrass, Peter (see also Ann Jones and
        Peter Stallybrass) 45, 159, 165, 177, 191
Star Trek 29
Steinberg, Leo 67, 94
Stowe's *Chronicle* 38
Strong, Roy 94
Stubbes, Phillip 16
Sutton, John 15

Tardin, Jean 129
Taylor, Gary 69, 82
Taylor, John 56, 94
testicles (see also codpiece)
    and masculinity 69–70, 74
    opposed to phallus 69–70
    as the principal part of the body 69–70
Traub, Valerie 183, 190, 194
Treatyse Answerying the Boke of Berdes
        (Barnes) 103, 106
Twiggy 131

Udall, Nicholas
    Thersites 88, 90, 91, 95, 107
Ulmus, Marcus Antonius
    Physiologia Barbae Humana 102, 107

Valeriano, Pierio
    Pro Sacerdotum Barbis 100, 116
Van Melsen, Andrew G. 160
Vicary, Grace Q. 184
Vicary, Thomas 70
Von Boehn, Max 78
Voorthuis, Jacob 36

Wall, Thomas 15
Walton, Bishop 161, 167
Wanley, Nathaniel 12, 14
Ward, John 11
Ward, Ned 72
Warr, Cordelia 169
Whately, William 136, 138
White, Allon 26
Wild, Robert 87
Wiley Beguiled 64, 66
Wilkinson, Robert 155
Williams, Raymond 23, 159, 165
Williams, Tamsyn 144
Wills, David 178
Wilson, Robert 90
Wittreich, Joseph 157
Woolf, Virginia 25

Cambridge Studies in Renaissance Literature and Culture

General Editor
STEPHEN ORGEL
Jackson Eli Reynolds Professor of Humanities, Stanford University

1. Douglas Bruster, *Drama and the Market in the Age of Shakespeare*
2. Virginia Cox, *The Renaissance Dialogue: Literary Dialogue in its Social and Political Contexts, Castiglione to Galileo*
3. Richard Rambuss, *Spenser's Secret Career*
4. John Gillies, *Shakespeare and the Geography of Difference*
5. Laura Levine, *Men in Women's Clothing: Anti-Theatricality and Effeminization, 1579–1642*
6. Linda Gregerson, *The Reformation of the Subject: Spenser, Milton, and the English Protestant Epic*
7. Mary C. Fuller, *Voyages in Print: English Travel to America, 1576–1624*
8. Margreta de Grazia, Maureen Quilligan, Peter Stallybrass (eds.), *Subject and Object in Renaissance Culture*
9. T. G. Bishop, *Shakespeare and the Theatre of Wonder*
10. Mark Breitenberg, *Anxious Masculinity in Early Modern England*
11. Frank Whigham, *Seizures of the Will in Early Modern English Drama*
12. Kevin Pask, *The Emergence of the English Author: Scripting the Life of the Poet in Early Modern England*
13. Claire McEachern, *The Poetics of English Nationhood, 1590–1612*
14. Jeffrey Masten, *Textual Intercourse: Collaboration, Authorship, and Sexualities in Renaissance Drama*
15. Timothy J. Reiss, *Knowledge, Discovery and Imagination in Early Modern Europe: The Rise of Aesthetic Rationalism*
16. Elizabeth Fowler and Roland Greene (eds.), *The Project of Prose in Early Modern Europe and the New World*
17. Alexandra Halasz, *The Marketplace of Print: Pamphlets and the Public Sphere in Early Modern England*
18. Seth Lerer, *Courtly Letters in the Age of Henry VIII: Literary Culture and the Arts of Deceit*
19. M. Lindsay Kaplan, *The Culture of Slander in Early Modern England*
20. Howard Marchitello, *Narrative and Meaning in Early Modern England: Browne's Skull and Other Histories*
21. Mario DiGangi, *The Homoerotics of Early Modern Drama*
22. Heather James, *Shakespeare's Troy: Drama, Politics, and the Translation of Empire*
23. Christopher Highley, *Shakespeare, Spenser, and the Crisis in Ireland*
24. Elizabeth Hanson, *Discovering the Subject in Renaissance England*
25. Jonathan Gil Harris, *Foreign Bodies and the Body Politic: Discourses of Social Pathology in Early Modern England*

26. Megan Matchinske, *Writing, Gender and State in Early Modern England: Identity Formation and the Female Subject*

27. Joan Pong Linton, *The Romance of the New World: Gender and the Literary Foundations of English Colonialism*

28. Eve Rachele Sanders, *Gender and Literacy on Stage in Early Modern England*

29. Dorothy Stephens, *The Limits of Eroticism in Post-Petrarchan Narrative: Conditional Pleasure from Spenser to Marvell*

30. Celia R. Daileader, *Eroticism on the Renaissance Stage: Transcendence, Desire, and the Limits of the Visible*

31. Theodore B. Leinwand, *Theatre, Finance, and Society in Early Modern England*

32. Heather Dubrow, *Shakespeare and Domestic loss: Forms of Deprivation, Mourning, and Recuperation*

33. David Posner, *The Performance of Nobility in Early Modern European Literature*

34. Michael C. Schoenfeldt, *Bodies and Selves in Early Modern England: Physiology and Inwardness in Spenser, Shakespeare, Herbert, and Milton*

35. Lynn Enterline, *Rhetoric of the Body from Ovid to Shakespeare*

36. Douglas A. Brooks, *From Playhouse to Printing House: Drama and Authorship in Early Modern England*

37. Robert Matz, *Defending Literature in Early Modern England: Renaissance Literary Theory in Social Context*

38. Ann Jones and Peter Stallybrass, *Renaissance Clothing and the Materials of Memory*

39. Robert Weimann, *Author's Pen and Actor's Voice: Playing and Writing in Shakespeare's Theatre*

40. Barbara Fuchs, *Mimesis and Empire: The New World, Islam, and European Identities*

41. Wendy Wall, *Staging Domesticity: Household Works and English Identity in Early Modern Drama*

42. Valerie Traub, *The Renaissance of Lesbianism in Early Modern England*

43. Joe Loewenstein, *Ben Jonson and Possessive Authorship*

44. William N. West, *Theatres and Encyclopedias in Early Modern Europe*

45. Richmond Barbour, *Before Orientalism: London's Theatre of the East, 1576–1626*

46. Elizabeth Spiller, *Science, Reading, and Renaissance Literature: The Art of Making Knowledge, 1580–1670*

47. Deanne Williams, *The French Fetish from Chaucer to Shakespeare*

48. Douglas Trevor, *The Poetics of Melancholy in Early Modern England*

49. Christopher Warley, *Sonnet Sequences and Social Distinction in Renaissance England*

50. Garrett A. Sullivan, Jr., *Memory and Forgetting in English Renaissance Drama: Shakespeare, Marlowe, Webster*

51. Michael Wyatt, *The Italian Encounter with Tudor England: A Cultural Politics of Translation*

52. Will Fisher, *Materializing Gender in Early Modern English Literature and Culture*

BRESCIA UNIVERSITY
COLLEGE LIBRARY